SELF-INCRIMINATION IN JEWISH LAW

by Aaron Kirschenbaum

Introduction by
The Honorable Arthur J. Goldberg

THE BURNING BUSH PRESS
NEW YORK

395300

The publication of this volume has been assisted by a grant from The
Aaron Rabinowitz–Simon H. Rifkind Foundation in Ethics and Law of
The Jewish Theological Seminary of America.

Standard Book Number: 8381-3111-5
Library of Congress Catalogue Card Number: 70-82311

MANUFACTURED IN THE UNITED STATES OF AMERICA
BY AMERICAN BOOK–STRATFORD PRESS, INC.

To
My Parents

Introduction

This volume is not of merely parochial interest. It is a comprehensive and timely study of the Jewish law which rejects criminal confessions, pleas of guilty and self-incriminatory statements of the accused.

Considering the antiquity of the Jewish legal system, the reader cannot help but be impressed with its rejection of a suspect's confession as an item of evidence and with its insistence that no man may incriminate himself in court. Indeed, in the eyes of a modern lawyer, this principle is maintained to a remarkably wide extent. Even pleas of guilty and voluntary confessions cannot serve as the basis of conviction of a criminal offense.

It is not that the talmudic jurists viewed the accused as a passive pawn unworthy of being heard in the courtroom, for he *is* allowed to speak in his own behalf. Moreover, one cannot assert that the Talmud did not recognize the probative value of a man's own admission of guilt; on the contrary, it uses rather vivid language to describe an admission of fault or liability in a civil case as having "the power of one hundred witnesses." This power, however, was consistently limited to civil cases exclusively. Rather, despite the permission Jewish law gives the accused to play an active role in his own defense and in the face of its recognition of the probative value of a man's acknowledgment of monetary liability, talmudic law insists that a defendant may in no wise contribute to his own conviction. The accusatorial principle of criminal jurisprudence whereby, in the words of Justice Frankfurter, "Society carries the burden of proving its charge against the accused not out of his own mouth," is carried to its ultimate conclusion.

We have something to learn from this ancient tradition, particularly now, when our constitutional privilege against self-incrimination, embodied in the Fifth Amendment, is under attack. Jewish law serves as a reminder that the Fifth Amendment is no luxury. It is more than a manifestation of an exaggerated sense of fair play; it is our vital means of protecting our privacy against the all too inquisitive state. Privacy does not exist as an absolute concept, but as a relationship with other entities. One may maintain physical privacy against "the world" with a wall, even though a mailman, milkman, and salesman regularly come through your gate. Passersby may peer through the chinks, and children may scale your wall in search of errant balls. Still there is privacy in the enclosure in the sense that one can act reasonably assured that he is not in fact being observed. Privacy against the government is similarly incomplete, sometimes erratic. But it must have the quality that allows the feeling that one is unnoticed, at least some of the time. The government naturally requires information of various types, but that does not require invasion of other areas of secrecy. And there will be occasions when almost a total account of one's life may be required. But to preserve the feeling of autonomy, those occasions must be rare, like the breaches of a solid wall. The individual must know that in the usual case, his life is his own, not his government's. This is the teaching of our Constitution; it is likewise the teaching of Jewish tradition, both being sensitive to human values.

We are greatly indebted to the author for making alive the Judaic tradition of safeguarding individual rights. This is indeed a significant contribution to the legal and political thinking of our day. Congratulations and gratitude are also in order for The Aaron Rabinowitz–Simon H. Rifkind Foundation in Ethics and Law of the Jewish Theological Seminary of America, where the research for this book was done, and for the United Synagogue of America, which made the sponsorship of this excellent study one of its projects.

ARTHUR J. GOLDBERG

July 1969
New York City

Acknowledgments

The initial research out of which the present volume developed was made under a Research Fellowship of the Fund for the Republic. This grant was secured for me by Dr. Bernard Segal, Executive Director of the United Synagogue of America. It is to him that I express my gratitude for his confidence in me and for his constant encouragement. I am also grateful to Mr. Henry N. Rapaport, President of the United Synagogue, and to Rabbi Harry Halpern, Chairman of the Joint Commission on Social Action of the Jewish Theological Seminary of America, the Rabbinical Assembly of America and the United Synagogue, for their financial assistance.

I wish to express my appreciation to the Honorable Arthur J. Goldberg for writing the Introduction to this book.

The following graciously agreed to read my work in manuscript and were most helpful in their suggestions for improvement: Mr. Morris Laub, Director of the Joint Commission on Social Action; Dr. Menahem Schmelzer, Librarian of the Jewish Theological Seminary, and Stuart

Marks, Esq., of New York City. Thanks are especially due to Rabbi Marvin S. Wiener, Editor of The Burning Bush Press, for his expert assistance and devoted care.

The work was read by Professor Saul Lieberman and the late Professor Boaz Cohen and accepted as a dissertation for the degree of Doctor of Hebrew Literature by the Seminary. Professor A. Arthur Schiller of Columbia Law School was kind enough to read those parts relating to Roman law. I thank my teachers for the benefit of their scholarship and wisdom. To Doctor Louis Finkelstein, Chancellor of the Seminary, I wish to express my gratitude for creating a climate most conducive to sustained research and creative scholarship.

I also wish to thank Mrs. Gertrude Serata, Mrs. Gabriel Gilead, Miss Dorothy Sachs and Miss Isabel Moser for their many kind acts of assistance. Rabbi Eleazar Katzman was helpful to me with a number of valuable bibliographical suggestions.

Finally, I thank the Lord, God of Israel, who has seen fit to grant me the privilege of being among those who sit in the House of Study *lehagdil toratho uleha'adirah.*

AARON KIRSCHENBAUM

Ḥeshvan 5730
October 1969
Jerusalem

Contents

Introduction by the Honorable
  Arthur J. Goldberg   vii
Acknowledgments   xi

PART ONE: A COMPARATIVE TREATMENT

I. The Jewish Law of Confession in the Light of
   General Legal History   3

PART TWO: AN HISTORICAL STUDY

II. The Biblical Period   25
III. Tannaitic Times   34
IV. Amoraic Development   50
V. Post-Talmudic Exegesis, Commentary and
   Expansion   59
VI. Medieval Rabbinic Criminal Procedure   82

PART THREE: A JURIDICAL PRESENTATION

VII. Range of Applicability   95
VIII. Confession Accompanied by Corroborating
        Factors   113

A CONCLUDING WORD CONCERNING SOME
        PRACTICAL CONSIDERATIONS   133

Appendices   138
Abbreviations   150
Notes   151
Bibliography   192
Index   205

PART ONE
A COMPARATIVE TREATMENT

CHAPTER I

The Jewish Law of Confession in the Light of General Legal History

ACCUSATORIAL VS. INQUISITORIAL SYSTEMS

Students of comparative law and legal history have discerned two divergent systems of court procedure in the prosecution of crimes: the accusatorial system and the inquisitorial system. Without attempting a precise definition and an exhaustive description of these two systems, it will nevertheless serve us well to summarize the salient features which characterize them.[1]

In an accusatorial trial, accuser and judge are distinct and separate one from the other. The accuser must level a specific charge against the accused, and, with the burden of proof upon him, he must proceed to present all the evidence he has uncovered in an attempt to convince the judge of the truth of his accusation. The judge is neutral; he remains a spectator observing the attempts of the accuser to prove the truth of his allegation, occasionally interceding in his role as umpire to assure fairness and regu-

3

larity in the conduct of the trial. The courtroom resembles an arena in which a battle is taking place, a contest (hence the term, "adversary system") between the prosecutor and the defendant and/or their respective representatives for the (heart and) mind of the judge.

In addition to the above-mentioned essential characteristics, in European and American history the accusatorial system has usually been associated with the following: The proceedings are open, and the accused is presumed innocent until proven guilty. Torture of the accused as well as other methods of coercion applied to him are excluded, not merely because they create an imbalance in the contest by providing one side with additional weapons such as new information or self-incriminating evidence elicited from the side he is opposing, but more significantly, because they illogically presuppose the very conclusion the accuser has set out to establish. The proceedings will usually be oral, for in a contest seeking the truth, questioning and cross-examination, debate and refutation, argument and counter-argument are essential. Moreover, the clarity and specific nature of the charges and the firmness of the grounds on which they must be based in order to justify the very institution of the trial render any attempt at cloaking the proceedings in secrecy logically indefensible and morally inexcusable.

In an inquisitorial trial, on the other hand, the line between judge and prosecutor is blurred and often erased, the judge frequently becoming chief interrogator. The trial is investigative rather than deliberative; and the court is a board of active inquiry rather than of passive observation and judicious decision-making. The accused is the center of this inquiry, the focal point of the questioning.

But the word, "inquisitorial," although descriptive of procedure, carries with it certain connotations which are historically, not essentially, associated with it. There are usually no specific charges, no clear allegations; on the contrary, the very purpose of the proceedings is to achieve clarity and specificity of accusation, to define and delineate the charges. Thus, the proceedings are a kind of "fishing expedition," searching to find a crime which can be attributed to the suspect; or, more usually, seeking to implicate the suspect in a specific crime. He is considered guilty until proven innocent. Whereas an accusatorial trial is limited in duration by the amount of evidence the accuser can present, the inquisitorial hunt is endless. The questioning of the suspect is interminably repeated in different words and in varied forms so that the answers may be minutely scrutinized for inconsistencies and contradictions. "Evidence" sometimes takes the form of hearsay and rumors, of written depositions that cannot be subjected to critical analysis and cross-examination, and of secret testimony. Inasmuch as accusers, rumormongers, or those harboring suspicions need not be certain and specific in their accusations, and suspicions may be vague and statements by witnesses indirect, direct confrontation between accuser and accused is usually not feasible. Moreover, since such confrontation rarely takes place, the accuser does not have to speak with the same scrupulous care, caution and accuracy he would of necessity have to exercise were the accused present and able to defend himself on the spot.

In describing these two opposing systems, distortion and caricature must be avoided. It is true that in the inquisitorial system the judge wields great power. But it is equally true that jurisdictions following the accusatorial procedure vary greatly in the powers granted to the judicial magistrate. Some codes of criminal procedure grant overriding power to the individual judge or to the judicial panel; other codes have extremely strict rules of evidence and strict scales of consequences therefrom, leaving little to the discretion of the judicial authority; and many others represent gradations between these extremes.[2]

Similarly, there are not always clear lines of demarcation between the two systems with regard to the attitude to, and the evaluation of, criminal confessions. A comparative survey will illustrate this point.

CLASSICAL ANTIQUITY

Greek Law

In ancient Greece, the confession of a defendant was excellent evidence. When Andocides confessed his guilt in the mutilation of the Hermae, he was sentenced to suffer the disgrace of exclusion from the *agora* and from the holy places. Admission of guilt was sufficient basis for the prosecution of the offender.[3] Similarly, all sorts of malefactors (*kakourgai*), when summarily arrested, could be executed by the magisterial Eleven at once, without a regular trial, if they confessed.[4] Scholars are of the belief, however, that the confession itself was carefully scrutinized and subject to critical investigation before it was acted upon.[5]

But confession was not merely the verbal admission of guilt. A number of acts were construed as confessional in nature, and the consequences thereof were equal to those of an acknowledgment of culpability. Thus, a homicide might, at the end of the first speech of the prosecutor, withdraw from the case and go into exile. This acceptance of exile was tantamount to an actual confession of guilt; and, in the event that he returned illegally from exile, he was subject to the death penalty—he could be killed with impunity, or taken for execution to the *thesmothetai*, or informed against.[6] In a public prosecution, if the accused fled the country, his flight, too, was looked upon as a confession of guilt, and he was condemned *in absentia*.[7] A letter to a friend, relating how one committed a crime, could, if proven genuine, be conclusive evidence.[8]

Torture as a judicial tool was mainly applied to slaves to elicit from them reliable evidence. The orators speak of it as an infallible means of ascertaining the truth; Demosthenes asserts that it has never been known to fail. Although it was indispensable for the admissibility of the testimony of slaves, we find that in cases of particularly horrifying crimes, cries to apply it to suspects themselves were occasionally heard. Thus, there was the proposal to torture forty-two free citizens accused of mutilating the Hermae and violating the mysteries. We do not know if the proposal was accepted.[9]

In sum, Greek legal procedure, with its mob-like juries and demogogic orator-advocates, from a modern point of view, leaves much to be desired. Indeed, as one observer has put it, "it would be difficult to devise a judicial system less adapted to the due administration of justice."[10] It is to Rome that we look for an orderly and well worked-out system of criminal procedure.

Classical Roman Law

The criminal procedure of the classical Roman law, *i.e.*, that of the Late Republic and the Early Empire (*ca.* 150 B.C.E.–235 C.E.), was accusatorial. It was not the business of the court to actively inquire and find out the truth, but only to listen as an impartial arbiter to the facts and arguments brought before it. By means of the *interrogatio ex lege* the accuser would put questions to the accused and, on the basis of the answers, would then have the exact foundation necessary for his complaint. Beyond that there was no regular examination of the defendant.

A confession on the part of the accused, however, had top priority in the considerations of the judge.

habes . . . quod est accusatori maxime optandum confitentem reum.	You have . . . that which is of optimum value to an accuser, a confessing defendant (Cicero, *Pro Ligario,* 1. 2) .

Nevertheless, there was no attempt to extort a confession from the accused.

Under the Later Empire, the power of the state was more developed, and the conception of punishment changed; as a result, more inquisitorial elements were introduced into criminal procedure. The accused was regularly subject to torture, and the aim of the usual examination on the part of the magistrate was to procure a confession. Indeed, confession of the accused is on a par with, if not superior to, the testimony of all witnesses to the matter.

> If any person is about to pronounce sentence, he shall maintain such moderation that he shall not pronounce a capital sentence or a severe sentence against any person unless such person has been convicted of the crime of adultery, homicide, or magic, either by his own confession, or at any rate by the testimony of all witnesses who have been subjected to torture or to questioning when such testimony is concordant and in agreement, pointing to the same end of the matter (Constantine, *Codex Theodosianus,* 9.40.1 = *Codex Iustinianus,* 9.47.16) .[11]

This holds true not only in pronouncing sentence. In laying down the rules with regard to those whose appeals are not to be accepted, the same Emperor Constantine again declared the confession of the accused as removing all doubts concerning the case.

Hence, when his own confession or a clear and well sub-stantiated investigation of the truth has shown by proof and evidence that a man is a homicide, an adulterer, a magician, or a sorcerer, all most atrocious criminals, appeals must not be accepted which appear to hold no hope of disproving what has been established but rather are an attempt to delay the sentence (*C. Th.*, 11.36.1) .[11]

And even though the Roman jurists in no wise overlooked the possibility of confessions contrary to the truth, namely those made on the rack, nevertheless as a rule confessions resulted in condemnation and served as the basis for exe-cution.[12]

Non-Classical Roman Law

Contemporaneous with the law of the City of Rome de-veloped by the classical Roman jurists, there existed nu-merous legal systems governing the city-states and their respective surrounding territories throughout the Empire. Generally speaking, the personality principle prevailed, and when a member of a city moved elsewhere in the Empire, he continued to be governed by the law of his home city. Thus, in the province of Egypt, Egyptian law prevailed for the Egyptian people whereas the Greek popu-lation was subject to Greek law. The influence of these systems on each other and the resolution of conflicts be-tween them do not concern us. It is however significant that in criminal cases in Egypt, where members of various nationalities were involved, it was the Greek law that was applied exclusively.

But superimposed upon the indigenous legal system of an individual city-state (*Volksrecht*) , yet different, some-times in a marked degree, from the classical and post-classical Roman law of the City (*Reichsrecht*) , was a third,

contemporaneous system, the Roman law for the provinces (*Provinzialrecht*). This comprised the aggregate of legal principles contained in the imperial decrees, edicts and constitutions for the Roman citizenry residing throughout the Empire, the law for the provinces emanating from the administrative center at Rome. This, too, is Roman law, albeit non-classical.[13]

Two manifestations of the Roman law of the provinces are of particular interest to us:

(1) The criminal law of Greco-Roman Egypt (332 B. C.E.–640 C.E.). Police procedure invariably included the summoning of the alleged culprit for questioning. The investigation attempted to force the defendant to confess his guilt (and restore the stolen property, if any). This police procedure was common to the earlier Ptolemaic, subsequent Roman, and later Byzantine periods.[14]

There is little information on the course of proceedings before the courts. There are, however, indications of the use of a purgation oath administered to the accused in order to pressure him, if guilty, into confessing to the alleged crime.[15]

(2) The Roman criminal law in Palestine (during the first centuries C.E.). The Palestinian Talmud and Midrashim as well as the *Acta Martyrum* vividly portray the utilization of judicial torture as the standard tool by which confessions were elicited from the accused. (This should not be confused with the use of torture which was regularly required in the Greek and Roman legal systems when a slave was called upon to testify.) [16]

Coupled with anonymous denunciations and the absence of any confrontation with the accusers is the assumption on the part of the judge that the allegations are true. This assumption serves as the basis of the judge's incriminating questioning of the accused.[17] We have here all the ingredients which served as forerunners of the medieval method of inquisitorial questioning.

CANON LAW

In the Canon Law of the Medieval Church the inquisitorial system of court procedure was developed to its classical fullness. If rumors and suspicions as to the commission of a crime focused on a particular person so that a judge could establish *mala fama* or *infamia,* this was sufficient to create a certain right of action against the *infamatus.* According to the customary law of the barbarian (*i.e.,* non-Roman) codes, the accused was obliged to exculpate himself from the crime imputed to him by undergoing a trial by ordeal—by fire, water, battle, or compurgation.* In the ninth century, the Church introduced more rational modes of proof, and trials by ordeal were gradually abolished. By the thirteenth century, the inquisitorial system was the established practice in the Church, and it was characterized by the following basic features: Suspicion and rumor served as the basis for the judicial establishment of *infamia;* the *infamatus* was presumed guilty and had to actively exculpate himself from the charges imputed to him. Judge and accuser were one party; interrogation—prolonged and thoroughgoing—of the accused was regular procedure. The accused, under oath, was compelled to reply; the use of torture to extract a confession from the reluctant lips of the suspect is, of course, very well known.[18]

---

* Compurgation was the practice of invoking the oaths of friends or neighbors of the accused who appeared in court and who swore that they believed him on his oath.

EUROPEAN CONTINENTAL LAW

The inquisitorial method has been completely repudiated by all modern legal systems,* so much so that even totalitarian and despotic regimes that still adhere to it are careful to arrange a public trial conducted on the basis of accusatorial principles after the secret inquisition has taken place. Modern legal systems have not, however, found it necessary to reject the criminal confession. With regard to the criminal confession, the main differences between the inquisitorial and the accusatorial procedures have been two: (1) The central goal of the former has generally been the confession; and the confession alone, unsubstantiated by auxiliary proof, has usually sufficed to satisfy the tribunal's standards necessary for conviction. The latter, however, has almost invariably demanded additional evidence corroborating the admissions of the accused. (2) There has been a general repugnance on the part of the practitioners of the accusatorial system to forced self-incrimination.

Thus, the right of the accused to remain silent has been incorporated or is implied in Continental criminal procedures, though it has not been raised to the level of a constitutional principle. The French Code of Penal Procedure, for example, declares plainly, "The accused is free not to make any declaration"; and the present Polish code says, "The accused may not answer the questions he is

---

* "The Fifth Amendment is an old friend, and a good friend. It is one of the great landmarks in man's struggle to be free of tyranny, to be decent and civilized. It is our way of escape from the use of torture. It protects man against any form of Inquisition. It is part of our respect for the dignity of man. It reflects our ideas of the worth of rugged individualism" (W. O. Douglas, *An Almanac of Liberty*, p. 238) .

asked." The Austrian and German rules of criminal procedure also clearly imply the freedom of the suspect to refuse to answer any questions of substance.[18a]

Dr. Aleksander Witold Rudzinski of the Columbia University Research Institute on Communist Affairs has pointed out as follows:

> This right is, however, seldom used by the accused because he is free to lie in his defense with legal impunity. Whatever he is saying during the inquiry or trial is legally not considered to represent "testimony" but an "explanation" or "declaration," and is therefore not subject to punishment for perjury or false testimony.
>
> In other words, a suspect or an accused cannot take the stand to testify even if he so desires. His plea of guilty must be corroborated by the totality of other evidence to be sufficient for sentencing.[18b]

Thus, modern Continental criminal procedures, in denying statements by the accused the status of testimony, resemble talmudic criminal procedure as described in the fourth chapter below (pp. 56–58). By this simple legalistic device, the Europeans have overcome the cruel inquisitorial trilemma which forced a suspect to tell the truth and thus to accuse himself, or to lie and be punished for perjury, or, if silent, to be punished for contempt of court.

Self-incriminating statements and voluntary confessions may certainly be considered as evidence against the defendant if and when the court becomes convinced that they are true, for the court is free to ponder and evaluate according to its inner conviction the probative value of evidence it itself has seen and heard. Thus, for example, although a simple plea of guilty is not enough to bring about the conviction of the accused, Polish penal procedure does allow the court to refrain from taking further evidence if it and the prosecution agree that the confession of the accused is convincing and raises no doubts as to its veracity.[18c]

ANGLO-AMERICAN TRADITION

The extreme distaste for torture and coerced confessions received its classical Anglo-American formulation as part of the Fifth Amendment to the Constitution of the United States:

> No person . . . shall be compelled in any criminal case to be a witness against himself,

a provision which has been steadfastly maintained, protected, and expanded throughout American history by subsequent decisions of the United States Supreme Court, especially during the past few years from the ill-famed era of Senator Joseph R. McCarthy to the very present.[19]

But the most enlightened adherents of the accusatorial system have been generally agreed that the voluntary confession on the part of a criminal is a prime item of evidence and a choice source of conviction. Indeed, if the accused enters a plea of guilty, the need for a trial is obviated altogether.*

The Anglo-American tradition of law, for example, is replete with detailed rules against detention without indictment, against forced confessions, against the accused's taking the witness stand involuntarily; rules concerning the desirability of corroborating evidence, the duty of the prosecutor to establish the reliability of the confession, the requirement of caution on the part of judge and jury in evaluating the criminal's words; the solemn duty of the

---

* "The admissions or confessions of the prisoner, when voluntarily and freely made, have always ranked high in the scale of incriminating evidence" (*Brown v. Walker*, 161 U.S. 591, 596).

court to assure the accused his right to silence, to convince him that the exercise of this right will not be held against him, to impress upon him the serious consequences of his act of confession.[20]

The principle is clear: Only statements given freely and voluntarily without coercion and without duress may be admitted in evidence.[21] The recent cases of *Gideon*,[22] *Escobedo*,[23] and *Miranda*[24] represent the dramatic strengthening of this principle. The first insisted almost absolutely on the right to counsel. The second ruled that police denial to a suspect of his right to silence, is a denial of his constitutional right to assistance of counsel. And the third firmly made the constitutional privilege against self-incrimination and right of counsel to advise the accused how to cope with his interrogators operative at every stage of the criminal process—including the critical points of interrogation, apprehension and arraignment. Thus, the principle has been brought liberally and humanely to its logical conclusion.*

In the last analysis, however, the total downgrading of the reliability and worth of all (voluntary) confessions would be lacking constitutional warrant and openly contrary to the Anglo-American legal tradition. Indeed, if a defendant wishes to stand up, with his lawyer beside him, and plead guilty, no one true to the Common Law would reject his plea. Further, such an attitude of total downgrading and rejection of confession of guilt would strike modern lawyers and jurists of all legal traditions as extreme and unreasonable. If the proper precautions for freedom from coercion and intimidation in any form are rigorously provided for and honestly enforced, the confession

---

* Cf. Appendix III for a graphic illustration of how, until these court decisions, inquisitional police practices were part and parcel of a supposedly modern and enlightened accusatorial system of justice.

of the accused emerges as the obviously best and most convincing basis for his conviction.*

This position has gone virtually unchallenged in the annals of legal theory. There is but one hint of some hesitation on this point in modern times.

RUSSIAN LAW IN THE NINETEENTH CENTURY

The Russian rules of criminal procedure as promulgated by Czar Alexander II in the nineteenth century were looked upon at the time (and for many decades thereafter) as one of the most liberal and most humane pieces of legislation in the world. Under that system, confession to the accusation—however voluntarily made—did not end the case and the jury could still maintain an open mind. Mindful of the possibility that the admission of guilt might be contrary to the actual truth of the matter, the presiding judge insisted on a full, detailed statement by the criminal so that his account could be subjected to a critical examination. On the other hand, however, if the account was consistent, sensible and credible, containing no glaring inconsistencies, nothing incoherent nor any unreasonable statement, then, generally speaking, investigation was dispensed with, witnesses and experts were dismissed, and documents and depositions were left unread. The need for further investigation was decided upon by the judges, not

* Indeed, a prominent American jurist did not view the law against compulsory self-incrimination as indispensable to justice and liberty: "Few would be so narrow or provincial as to maintain that a fair and enlightened system of justice would be impossible without [trial by jury and without the immunity from prosecution except as the result of an indictment]. What is true of jury trials and indictments is true also, as the cases show, of the immunity from compulsory self-incrimination. This too might be lost, and justice still be done. . . . No doubt there would remain the need to give protection against torture, physical or mental. Justice, however, would not perish if the accused were subject to a duty to respond to orderly inquiry" (Mr. Justice Cardozo, *Palko v. Connecticut,* 302 U.S. 325–326). See further S. Hook, *Common Sense and the Fifth Amendment,* Ch. I.

by the members of the jury. Nevertheless, despite the judges' decision that no further investigation or examination was warranted, the law provided that the jury could still validly absolve the confessed criminal, *e.g.,* on grounds of extenuating circumstances that rendered the perpetrator of the act devoid of moral responsibility. This provision seems to contradict a second rule that if the jury found that the accused had indeed committed the criminal act, and then proceeded to acquit him, it could be (and invariably was) overruled by a higher authority. The explanation has been offered that the promulgators of the law felt subconsciously an uneasiness about criminal confessions and were plagued by the suspicion that perhaps they were not true. In the last analysis, however, they could not resist the prevalent acceptance of confessions, hence the practice of overruling acquittals in the face of such confessions.[25]

JEWISH LAW

What may have been a subconscious groping and inchoate feeling in a classic expression of nineteenth century legal liberalism, is precisely the open, conscious and deliberate position of Jewish talmudic law: Not only may a man not be compelled to be a witness against himself, but even were he voluntarily to testify against himself and confess wholly or partially to a crime, his testimony is rejected completely and has no status in court. The accusatorial principle whereby, in the words of Mr. Justice Frankfurter:[26]

> . . . society carries the burden of proving its charge against the accused not out of his own mouth. It must establish its case, not by interrogation of the accused even under judicial safeguards, but by evidence independently secured through skillful investigation,

is carried to its ultimate, extreme conclusion. Not only is the judge separated from the prosecutory process,[26a] but the accused, also, is totally divorced from the process and may in no way contribute to its success. Accusation must be corroborated by objective evidence, evidence independent of the accused and obtained from sources independent of the accused. This principle holds true in criminal cases (capital or otherwise), ritual or ethico-moral infractions, and cases punishable by fines. Moreover, although a criminal is disqualified from acting as a witness in cases involving others, this is true only if one is adjudged criminal by due process, *i.e.,* not through his own admission of criminality. The only area of jurisprudence in which a man's testimony to his own disadvantage is accepted is that of civil cases, *i.e.,* those involving private torts in which only monetary compensation is involved.

But whereas the difference between Anglo-American and Talmudic law represents an interesting variation on the accusatorial theme, the contrast between Canon and Talmudic law is both breathtaking and sobering. I say "sobering," for we live at a time when it has become fashionable for jurists and lawyers to invoke the Judaeo-Christian tradition as the root of Western law and tradition; and rightfully so, for this tradition has impressed itself upon the Anglo-American system of law whereby "righteous ends by just means as a unitary concept"[27] has become the rationale of its existence and the style of its implementation. In the interest of truth and the advancement of religio-ethnic individuality, however, it is important to point out occasionally that there are some areas of the law where the Jewish and Christian components of this Anglo-American legal tradition are at variance with each other. One of the areas where this variance is at its greatest is in that of self-incrimination and criminal confession.

As a result of this study, we shall see that, according to rabbinic law, not only can a man not be forced to testify against himself, but even voluntary self-incrimination is rejected. Needless to say, in a system of law where this is a principle fundamental to the rules of evidence, no distinctions need be drawn between confessions made before the trial (to the police or to the arraigning magistrate) and those made at the trial; no subtle gradations of coercion or of voluntariness need be delineated; no problems of undue pressure or of unfair inducement ever arise. In addition, there is no occasion which gives rise to an anomalous situation in which there is a "natural" presumption of guilt[28] attached to a person who has availed himself of a privilege granted to him by the law of the land (and thereby ruined his reputation though he saved his neck[29]). Police brutality is unheard of because the police authorities gain nothing from a confession, and the accused loses nothing by such a confession. Torture as a method of investigation is virtually[30] unheard of in Jewish history.[31] Indeed, who knows—perhaps the obviation of torture as a judicial tool was the very intention of the biblical Lawgiver and of the rabbinic interpreter.[32] The repugnance and horror one experiences as one contemplates the barbarism of the judicial torture practiced in ancient and medieval times are accompanied by the realization of the absurdity of "rating a man's virtue by the hardiness of his constitution and his guilt by the sensitiveness of his nerves."[33]

Indeed, there was an attempt in the last decade to trace the Anglo-American law on self-incrimination to the Hebrew law as formulated in talmudic literature, with the sixteenth and seventeenth century Hebraists of England —particularly John Selden[34]—as the bridge.[35]

The author of this thesis is Mr. George Horowitz of the New York Bar who rejects the tendency of historians of

English Law to ascribe the origin of the law to Lord Coke's maxim, *Nemo tenetur seipsum prodere*, "No one is compelled to accuse himself." Although by enunciating these words Coke was distorting the meaning they had had within the context of the Canon Law, the case to which he applied them indicates that he never thought that persons duly charged and indicted by the Crown should not be compelled to testify against themselves.

In place of this maxim, the author presents the following passage from John Selden's *De Synedriis Veterum Ebraeorum* ("Concerning the Courts of the Ancient Hebrews") as the first formulation of the doctrine against self-incrimination that was brought to the knowledge and attention of Englishmen:

Ex constitutione autem veteri inolevit ut nemo aut neci (qua de re ante monitum) traderetur aut poenae verberum ex Confessione sua, sed tantum ex aliorum Testimonio. Ne scilicet ipse ex animi impotentia et malitioso accusatorum impetu praesumto temere persuasus, ad id, cujus reus non omnino esset, agnoscendum, aerumnosi contestationis incommodi evitandi gratia, perperan adigeretur. Adjicit Maimonides, וכללו של דבר גזירה *של מלך היא Atque hoc totum ex decreto regio evenit.*

By an old law, moreover, it became established that no person (having been previously warned concerning the matter) should be delivered up to be executed or for punishment [by lashes] by his own confession, but only by the testimony of others. Undoubtedly so that, out of feelings of powerlessness and because of the malicious and bold attack of his accusers, he, having been persuaded unwittingly, should not be pressured falsely into confessing altogether to the charge of which he was accused—for the sake of avoiding a wretched and troublesome trial. Maimonides adds: וכללו של דבר גזירה של מלך היא, "And this entire matter arises out of a Royal Decree."[36]

The thesis is a fascinating one, but one of its main pitfalls is its tendency to glide over the most significant difference between the two systems of law. Anglo-American law prohibits involuntary confession whereas Jewish law prohibits *all* criminal confession. Moreover, the former's rejection of torture has been generally justified on grounds of "repugnance," almost with an esthetic connotation, whereas the Jewish rejection of torture has been generally rationalized as motivated by psychological and/or philosophical considerations.[36a] Nevertheless, it may serve as a salutary antidote to claims made by eminent American jurists that the Common Law principle that no person could be compelled to be a witness against himself distinguished it from all other systems of jurisprudence[37] and to their allegations that "the privilege against self-incrimination is not to be found in ancient systems of law and that it is unique to Anglo-American law."[38]

In the interests of historical accuracy, we pray that this study will serve as an effective refutation of such statements.

PART TWO
AN HISTORICAL STUDY

CHAPTER II

The Biblical Period

There are four episodes in the Bible which contain instances of confession to criminal acts; we present an exposition of each case in accordance with a strictly literal interpretation of the biblical passages:

(1) In the book of Joshua, chapters 6 and 7, it is related that, after the conquest of Jericho, Joshua declared the city, its inhabitants and all the possessions therein *herem,* devoted to the Lord with a special degree of sanctity dooming them to destruction—forever removed from the possibility of secular use (Leviticus 27:28–29). When Akhan ben Karmi secretly took from the *herem,* the Israelites were punished by an unexpected defeat in battle. The Lord thereupon declared that there is the curse of the *herem* in their midst: They must solemnly prepare themselves, be brought before the Lord, and be tested until the culprit is found and executed.

So Joshua rose up early in the morning, and brought Israel near by their tribes; and the tribe of Judah was taken. And he brought near the family of Judah; and he took the family of the Zeraḥites. And he brought near the family of the Zeraḥites man by man; and Zabdi was taken. And he brought near his household man by man; and Akhan, the son of Karmi, the son of Zabdi, the son of Zeraḥ, of the tribe of Judah, was taken (6:16–18).

Commentators, ancient and modern,[1] are agreed that the culprit was identified by means of some kind of lot cast before the Holy Ark of the Lord as each unit, and then sub-unit, was brought near.

> And Joshua said unto Akhan: "My son, give, I pray thee, glory to the Lord, God of Israel, and make confession unto Him (ותן לו תודה); and tell me now what thou hast done; hide nothing from me." And Akhan answered Joshua, and said: "Of a truth I have sinned against the Lord, the God of Israel, and thus and thus have I done: When I saw among the spoil a goodly Babylonian mantle, and two hundred shekels of silver, and a wedge of gold of fifty shekels weight, then I coveted them, and took them; and behold, they are hid in the earth in the midst of my tent, and the silver under it." So Joshua sent messengers, and they ran unto the tent; and behold, it was hid in his tent, and the silver under it (7:19-21).

The punishment was a grim one: Akhan and all that belonged to him were stoned to death and burned to destruction and buried under a great heap of stones. "And the Lord turned from the fierceness of His anger" (7:26).

(2) In the first chapter of Second Samuel, the story is told of how a man came from the camp of the defeated Israelites and informed David of the deaths of Saul and Jonathan. In reply to David's question, "How knowest thou that Saul and Jonathan his son are dead?" the young man answered that, at the request of the wounded king,

I stood beside him, and slew him, because I was sure that he could not live after he was fallen; and I took the crown that was upon his head, and the bracelet that was on his arm, and have brought them hither unto my lord [David] (1:10).

After mourning the deaths of King Saul and of his beloved friend, Jonathan, David puts the young man on trial:

And David said unto the young man that told him: "Whence art thou?" And he answered: "I am the son of an Amalekite stranger." And David said unto him: "How wast thou not afraid to put forth thy hand to destroy the Lord's anointed?" And David called one of the young men, and said: "Go near, and fall upon him." And he smote him that he died. And David said unto him: "Thy blood be upon thy head (דמך על ראשך); for thy mouth hath testified against thee (פיך ענה בך) saying: 'I have slain the Lord's anointed' " (1:13-16).

(3) Second Samuel, chapter 4, relates that Rekhab and Ba'anah, the sons of Rimmon the Beerothite, assassinated Ish-bosheth, the son of Saul, who was the only obstacle standing between David and the throne of all of Israel.

And they brought the head of Ish-bosheth unto David to Hebron, and said to the king: "Behold the head of Ish-bosheth the son of Saul thine enemy, who sought thy life; and the Lord hath avenged my lord the king (David) this day of Saul, and of his seed." And David answered . . . and said unto them: "As the Lord liveth, who hath redeemed my soul out of all adversity, when one told me, saying: 'Behold, Saul is dead,' and he was in his own eyes as though he brought good tidings, I took hold of him, and slew him in Ziklag, instead of giving a reward for his tidings. How much more, when wicked men have slain a righteous person in his own house upon his bed shall I not now require his blood of your hand, and take you away from the earth?"[2] And

David commanded his young men, and they slew them . . .
(4:8–12).

On the basis of these three accounts,[3] some scholars
have concluded that according to the Bible's code of criminal procedure, a confession of guilt in itself was sufficient
to bring about conviction and execution.[4] This conclusion
is patently unwarranted. Any lawyer would be quick to
perceive that each of the confessions is accompanied by
significant corroborating evidence: In the case of Akhan,
the *corpus delicti* was subsequently recovered; in that of
the Amalekite stranger, the royal insignia were simultaneously produced; and in the case of Rekhab and Ba'anah,
the head of their victim was in their hands as they told of
their deed.[5]

The finding, however, that these stories point to a biblical rule that a criminal confession *supported by corroborating circumstantial evidence* suffices to bring about conviction and execution[6] is a more reasonable one, at least
for cases 2 and 3, and deserves our critical attention.

As for case 1, the Akhan episode, it is clear that the crucial source of conviction was the Lot. An examination of
the exact procedure of casting the Lot by Joshua would
take us too far afield. Suffice it to say that biblical Israel
had a number of instruments whereby the Will of God
was divined: the *Urim WeThumim, the Ḥoshen HaMishpat* (the Breastplate of the High Priest), and the Ark of
the Covenant. The mode of operation of each one of these
instruments as well as the relationship of one to the other
are somewhat obscure.[7] It is clear, however, that the ancient Israelite looked upon them with the utmost awe,
as nothing less than a communication from Above. Although civil cases and criminal trials were entrusted to the
human courts and the procedure was carefully prescribed,

nevertheless in those areas where *iudicium Dei* was invoked, its decision was accepted unquestioningly.[8] Joshua 7:15 (God is speaking: "And it shall be that he that is taken with the devoted thing shall be burnt with fire, he and all that he hath; because he hath wrought a wanton deed in Israel") *precedes* Joshua's request for a confession and proves that Akhan's conviction was independent of any confession he might make. Thus, it is the Lot that plays the role crucial for conviction. The function of the confession is to vindicate the *iudicium Dei;* this vindication, however, is not necessarily indispensable for conviction and execution.[9]

Nor need Joshua's call to Akhan for this vindication of the Lot be construed as evidence of any scepticism concerning its authenticity or validity. Don Isaac Abravanel (fl. 1500) suggests that Joshua pleaded for a confession so that the *ḥerem,* the possessions of Jericho that had been devoted to God, be found, restored to its proper place, and thus no longer contaminate the camp.[10] Although this suggestion is undoubtedly true, it seems to me that it does not go far enough; and that the plea שים נא כבוד לה׳ אלהי ישראל, "Give, I pray thee, glory to the Lord, God of Israel," indicates considerations that are beyond the immediate and practical.

The key to an understanding of Joshua's desire that Akhan confess is the biblical word for confession, תודה, *todah.*

Various forms of biblical worship reveal the influence of legal procedure. The ancient Hebrew conceived of the relationship between God and man as being subsumed under the rule of law.[11] For example, the word for prayer, תפלה, *tephillah,* is derived from the root פלל which is associated with legal judgment.[12] Similarly, the word *todah* means both a confession and a doxology (a formulaic glorification of God) .[13] And the well-known communion-offering קרבן תודה was a sacrifice, the central purpose of which was doxological praise.[14] Biblical law asked the criminal who had been condemned to death to make a public confession of his sin and to praise God.[15] Although not necessary for conviction, it was necessary for atonement, for the penitential confession transformed the execution from mere punishment to expiation.[16] Of course, it carried with it the additional role of assuring the judges the correctness of their decision;[17] but this was a psychological advantage, not a legal requirement. The importance of confession in the ritual of atonement is well-known.[18]

It is thus clear that the true basis for Akhan's conviction was the testimony of the Lot. Akhan's confession, although corroborating the decision taken on the basis of the Lot, served principally an expiatory function. It proves little concerning biblical criminal procedure.

On the other hand, indications of the admissibility of criminal confessions in the Bible are to be found in cases 2 and 3, where David condemns criminals to death on the basis of their self-incriminating statements, albeit accompanied by corroborative evidence. The exclamation of David to the Amalekite stranger, פיך ענה בך, "Thy mouth hath testified against thee," using the technical expression, ענה ב-, "to testify against,"[19] would indicate that a trial of some sort was being conducted;[20] and David's declaration דמך על ראשך, "Thy blood be upon thy head," seems to be the formula constituting the sentence of death.

The suggestion that the intention of the biblical narrator was to condemn the procedure—for the reader knows that the confession was not true (I Samuel 31:4) [21]—is untenable. Not only does the narrative contain no hint of disapproval, but in addition (in case 3) David subsequently cites this trial as precedent, again with no hint of condemnation on the part of the biblical narrator.

Of an entirely different nature is the fourth biblical episode, which deals with an act of theft:

(4) Judges 17:1-4 narrates the following:

> Now there was a man of the hill-country of Ephraim, whose name was Micah. And he said unto his mother: "The eleven hundred pieces of silver that were taken from thee, about which thou didst utter a curse (ואת אלית), and didst also speak it in mine ears, behold, the silver is with me; I took it." And his mother said: "Blessed be my son of the Lord." And he restored the eleven hundred pieces of silver to his mother, and his mother said: "I verily dedicate the silver unto the Lord from my hand for my son, to make a graven image and a molten image; now therefore I will restore it unto thee." And when he restored the money unto his mother, his mother took two hundred pieces of silver, and gave them to the silversmith who made thereof a graven image and a molten image; and it was in the house of Micah.

The son says to his mother, *we-at alith,* "thou didst utter a curse." We have here a somewhat unusual use of the *alah*. Ordinarily, the maledictory *alah* was the regular means of inducing reluctant *witnesses* to come forth and to testify.[22] In the passage from the book of Judges, the woman, a victim of theft, pronounces the *alah* in an attempt to recover her money. This *alah*-curse is essentially a conditional imprecation: a prayer to God asking for the punishment of the unknown thief. (It should be noted that the mother's response to her son's confession was an invocation of blessing to counteract her preceding curse.)[23] Thus, in this passage, the purpose of pronouncing this *alah* in public was to induce the unknown *offender* to confess and make restitution.[24] Be that as it may, such a confession, having been made in monetary matters, was clearly valid and effective in creating the obligation to make restitution.

Thus, disregarding for the time being any teachings of the Jewish Oral Tradition and examining the four scriptural episodes which describe cases of confessions to forbidden acts according to their literal interpretation, we have found that the first one, that of Akhan, is totally inconclusive as far as the admissibility of confessions in evidence is concerned because of the crucial role played by the Lot as the instrument of a *iudicium Dei*. The fourth episode, from the book of Judges, may be in a class by itself because the confession therein is, strictly speaking, related not to a criminal case which would give rise to criminal penalties (*i.e.*, usually, punishments inflicted upon the person of the offender), but to a civil case, a monetary matter, which would be amenable to monetary restitution. I say, *may* be in a class by itself, for the critical reader may wish to challenge the distinction between criminal and civil cases as an inappropriate one for ancient Israel.

Cases 2 and 3, however, over which David sat in judgment, would appear to furnish us with incontrovertible proof of the acceptability of criminal confessions in biblical law. David's position, first as chieftain and later as king, as well as the language used in the narratives, leaves little doubt that the proceedings were judicial in nature.

This extreme paucity of scriptural passages, however, makes one hesitate in expounding on the legal acceptability of the confession in the criminal law of the Bible with any degree of scientific certainty.

The legal *corpora* of the Pentateuch are silent on the role of the criminal confession. The basic rule of evidence, as laid down in Deuteronomy 17:6 and 19:15, is that "a matter be established" on the basis of the testimony of at least two eyewitnesses. But whether this pentateuchal requirement of two witnesses, adopted as standard Israelite criminal procedure (I Kings 21:10, 13), was construed loosely, as an alternative or supplement to confession— as would appear from David's judicial decisions—or whether it was interpreted strictly, as excluding confession—as taught by the Oral Tradition (to be presented in the next section) —must remain an open question to the critical scholar.

CHAPTER **III**

Tannaitic Times*

THE TANNAITIC SOURCES

Let us examine the four tannaitic passages which are of significance for the law against self-incrimination.

(1) The earliest tannaitic source that I have been able to discover dealing with the law of criminal confession is a passage which forms part of a *midrash* to Leviticus emanating from the School of R. Ishmael,[1] which has been preserved in the Tosephta, Shebuoth (3:8);[2] it is cited in the name of Rabbi Aqiba.

Leviticus 24:17–22, according to the Rabbis, implies that the requirement of *derishah wa-ḥaqirah,* court investigation and examination, applies equally to capital and to monetary cases.

או מה דיני נפשות לשהודה 　　Or perhaps I may say that
מפי עצמו אף דיני ממונות כן?　the equality implied in Levit-
ת״ל רגל ישלם.　　　icus 24:17–22 also teaches us
　　　　　　　　　that just as in capital cases a
man may not be convicted on the basis of his own confes-

---

*"Tannaitic times" is dated variously from (1) Simeon the Just, apparently the high priest Simeon I, ca. 300 B.C.E.; (2) the Maccabees, ca. 165 B.C.E.; or (3) Hillel, Shammai, and their respective schools, the latter half of the 1st century, B.C.E. Its end is identified with the generation of R. Judah HaNasi, ca. 200 C.E.

sion, so in monetary cases a man may not be rendered liable on the basis of his own admission? No! For inasmuch as Scripture (Exodus 21:24) states, "a foot for a foot," which in view of Leviticus 24:19 is superfluous, its intention is to teach us that if someone admits that he maimed his fellow's foot, he is thereby rendered liable to pay.[3]

The passage thus makes three points: (a) In capital cases, a man may not be convicted on the basis of his own confession. (b) In monetary matters, a man may be rendered liable on the basis of his own admission. (c) The distinction between capital and monetary cases is a conscious and deliberate one.

(2) The second passage is an equally unequivocal rejection of criminal confession and is found, with some variations, in two places.[4]

Siphrei, Shophtim (on Deuteronomy 19:15)[5]	Tosephta, Shebuoth 5:4[6]
א"ר יוסי ק"ו ומה במקום שאין פיו מצטרף עם עד אחד למיתה הרי זה נשבע ע"פ עצמו מקום שפיו מצטרף עם פי עד אחד לממון אינו דין שיהא נשבע על פי (עצמו) [עד אחד][7] לאו מה לנשבע מפי עצמו שכן משלם ע"פ עצמו ישבע ע"פ עד אחד שכן [אין] משלם ע"פ עד א' ת"ל לכל עון לעון אינו קם אבל קם הוא לשבועה.	אמ' ר' יוסי וקל וחומ' ומה אם במקום שאין פיו מצטרף עם פי אחד למיתה הרי הוא נשבע על פי עצמו מקום שפיו מצטרף עם אחד לממון אינו דין שישבע על פי עצמו לאו מה לי נשבע על פי עצמו שכן המשלם על פי עצמו ישבע על פי עד אחד שכן המשלם על פי עד אחד תל' לומ' לכל עון לעון אינו קם קם הוא לשבועה.

Translation—Interpretive Paraphrase
R. Jose said: We have a deduction *a fortiori*: Whereas a defendant cannot join a single witness to convict himself of a capital crime, yet this same defendant could render himself liable to an oath (*i.e.*, where he acknowledges liability to part of his creditor's claim on him) ; then if a single witness[8] can join another witness to condemn a defendant to pay

money,[9] doesn't it stand to reason *a fortiori* that this same single witness should be able to render the defendant liable to an oath (*i.e.*, where he testifies on behalf of the creditor) ?[10] No! This reasoning *a fortiori* may be rejected: A man may render himself liable to an oath, for he can also render himself liable to payment (for, "A man's acknowledgment of his own liability is as one hundred witnesses"); shall he then be rendered liable to an oath on the basis of the testimony of one witness, inasmuch as the testimony of one witness cannot render him liable to payment?! Now, since reasoning *a fortiori* could not have established the ability of one witness to render a defendant liable to an oath, Scripture (Deuteronomy 19:15) declares, "One witness shall not rise up against a man for any iniquity or for any sin"—he shall not rise up for *any iniquity* or for *any sin*,[11] but he may rise up to render liability to an oath.

The point of the passage is to investigate the source of the rule that although one witness is insufficient for conviction he does have the power to render the defending litigant liable to an oath. Of the utmost significance to us, however, is the fact that the major premise in the reasoning is the rule against self-incrimination ("Whereas a defendant cannot join a single witness to convict himself of a crime . . .").

That R. Aqiba (fl. first third of the second century C.E.) and R. Jose (ben Halaphta, a disciple of R. Aqiba, fl. middle of the second century C.E.) take this rule for granted, use it as the projected basis of an analogy and a *qal wa-ḥomer* (*a fortiori* deduction), and encounter no opposition, indicates that the rule was well-established in their own day, indeed that it was much older than they.[12]

(3) Tosephta Sanhedrin 9:4. "If the accused should say 'I am able to speak in my own defense,' he is to be heard;

'. . . against myself,' he is to be silenced with a reprimand בנזיפה, ."

It seems that the force of the last word of the passage, (בנזיפה) is to distinguish between an accused's words on behalf of conviction and the words favoring a conviction coming from anyone else who is not a member of the judicial panel. It comes to reject any derogatory statements of the accused concerning himself on two grounds: (a) on the basis of the general rule that (in contrast to the acceptability of statements *favoring* acquittal made by judges, witnesses, or law students in attendance) only a judge may speak *against* acquittal once the examination of the witnesses has been terminated,[13] and (b) on the basis of the rule against criminal confessions.

Incidentally, from the first half of the passage, parallel to the Mishnah (Sanhedrin 5:4), we learn that the law against criminal confession did *not* stem from the concept of an accused as a passive, pawn-like object of inquiry and examination who was not to be consulted and not to be allowed to participate; it was only when the accused desired to make self-incriminating statements that he was reduced to silence.

(4) The fourth tannaitic statement constitutes but indirect proof of the existence of a law against criminal confession.

Tosephta Sanhedrin 11:1. "All other people accused of a capital crime* may be convicted only on the testimony of two witnesses and only if they were forewarned."[14]

In order to complete the presentation of the tannaitic law with regard to confessions, we cite two passages, each concerning a different type of monetary liability:

---

* *I.e.,* except a מסית, one who entices people to idolatry (Deuteronomy 13:7-12) ; he is in a special category.

(5) Tosephta Baba Meẓia 1:10. הודאת בעל דין כמאה עדים, "A man's acknowledgment of his own liability has the power of one hundred witnesses."

(6) Mishnah Kethuboth 3:9. זה הכלל, כל המשלם יתר על מה שהזיק אינו משלם על פי עצמו, "This is the rule: Anyone who commits an act which renders him liable to pay more than the amount of damage he inflicted does not have to pay if he himself confessed to having committed the act."

Thus, pecuniary cases are divided into two types: (a) ממון, mammon, regular civil cases involving monetary restitution, and (b) קנס, qenas, cases in which fines are involved. In the former, (a), the theory is that the losing litigant must pay to restore that which rightfully belongs to his opponent, or, if he was the plaintiff, he may not receive that which he sued for because it was not rightfully coming to him. Accordingly, the trial is merely a method of determining to whom the contested money belongs. With regard to such monies, the Tosephta in Baba Meẓia declares that the testimony of a litigant to his own detriment (confession of guilt, admission of fault, acknowledgment of liability) has the same power as the deposition of one hundred witnesses.[15] In the latter, (b), however, there is no question of the rightful allocation or determination of any contested monies, but of the levying of fines. In contradistinction to adjudication of claims, which in theory is simply the finding of what is the objective truth in the matter, the infliction of penalties is a manifestation of judicial power. In other words, whereas in simple monetary matters it was the original act of the (losing) litigant which created his (presently adjudged) liability, in cases involving penalties it is the court that creates his obligation to pay the fine.[16] Such *judicial* power must be exercised in accordance with the rule controlling court procedure as laid down in the Mishnah of Kethuboth. The talmudic formulation of this rule is מודה בקנס פטור, which may be translated either as, "He who confesses to an act the commission of which makes one liable to a fine is exempted from paying the penalty," or, "He who admits that he is guilty of a crime which is normally punishable by a fine is exempt from that fine."[17]

In sum, the role of confession in legal procedure emerges clearly from the tannaitic sources as follows:

In capital cases, a confession of guilt on the part of the accused is inadmissible in evidence. (The sources are silent as to the admissibility of confession in non-capital criminal cases, *i.e.*, those crimes that are punishable by lashes.) [18]

In simple monetary cases, the admission of a litigant has the power of one hundred witnesses.

In cases involving fines, the admission of a litigant does not render him liable to the fine.

What is not at all clear from the tannaitic sources is the scriptural authority for the above-listed rules of confession. It is in the statements of later authorities that we find formulated the bases in Scripture for these rules.

Taking the rules in reverse order, we find the following:

For the inability of admission of guilt to bring about liability to monetary fines, the Talmud adduces scriptural support from Exodus 22:8, ". . . he whom the judges shall condemn shall pay double," which implies that only he whom the *judges* condemned was to be penalized; he who condemns himself, however, cannot be so penalized.[19]

As for the scriptural basis for the rule that in cases involving simple monetary restitution a man's own admission of guilt has the power of one hundred witnesses, the Talmud is silent. Rashi (1040–1105) on Qiddushin 65b adduces it from Exodus 22:8. A modern scholar[20] takes

Leviticus 5:20–26 in conjunction with Numbers 5:6–7 as indications of the power of a litigant's admission of liability. All of these biblical citations, however, give no indication of the *relative* value of the litigant's confession vis-à-vis witnesses, *i.e.*, that it is *more* powerful than the deposition of one hundred witnesses.[21]

As for the scriptural basis of the rule which rejects confessions of the accused in criminal-capital cases, the Talmud does not address itself directly to the problem. On the basis of its treatment of a related question (to be presented in the following section) we may state with certainty that the Talmud looked upon the law with regard to criminal confessions as based upon two dogmatic principles derived from Sacred Scripture:

(a) No man may be convicted of any crime unless it be attested to by at least two witnesses, for Scripture states: "One witness shall not rise up against a man for any iniquity (עָוֹן) or for any sin (חטאת) in any sin that he sinneth: at the mouth of two witnesses or at the mouth of three witnesses shall a matter be established."[22] In this context, the distinction between עָוֹן (iniquity) and חטאת (sin) would be that the former involves capital or corporal punishment whereas the latter involves pecuniary compensation.[23]

(b) No *qarob*, relative or close kinsman, of a litigant or of a person accused of a crime may act as a witness in the case,[24] neither in his behalf nor against him.[25] The non-rational nature of this rule is pointed out by the Talmud itself which emphasizes that it is *not* based upon suspicion that the relative would give false testimony, for it applies even to Moses and Aaron, the classic exemplars of impeccable honesty.[26] Now, no kinsman is closer to a man than the man himself. If, then, a kinsman is disqualified from acting as a witness, certainly the defendant himself is disqualified.[27]

Scriptural verse (a) was interpreted strictly, *i.e.,* as delineating the sole type of evidence that is acceptable in court, hence as excluding confession: The *only* evidence that may be admitted is the testimony of two eyewitnesses. Moreover, the dogmatic principle (b), itself derived from Scripture through rabbinic exegesis, rendered impossible the acceptance of a man's confession as equal to the testimony of *one* eyewitness which otherwise could have been combined with the testimony of a *second* eyewitness in order to fulfill the pentateuchal requirement of two.[28]

In concluding our presentation of the law of criminal confession as found in the tannaitic literature, it remains to be pointed out that nowhere do the *Tannaim* attempt to reconcile the contradiction between that law and the judicial practice of King David as related in Second Samuel.

THE THEORY OF A CHANGE IN THE TANNAITIC LAW

There have been some modern scholars[29] who maintained that the rabbinic law against self-incrimination is a relatively new one, a product of rather late tannaitic times, and not well-established until the time of the *Amoraim,* Raba and Abbayei (first half of the fourth century C.E.). They have set forth a number of reasons for this allegation. We now propose to present a summary of each one of their arguments as well as a critique thereof.

(1) Biblical law makes no mention of any law against self-incrimination; on the contrary, specific biblical narratives, such as those of Joshua-and-Akhan and David-and-the-Amalekite-stranger (as well as the language used

in those narratives), give proof positive that criminal confessions were accepted by the authorities. I have already dealt with the scientific inconclusiveness of these narratives.

(2) Two aggadic passages preserve the "older" (biblical and early tannaitic) acceptance of criminal confessions.

(a) An aggadic elaboration of the biblical dialogue between Joshua and Akhan found in Joshua 7:19–21 describes the background to the latter's confession.

The Rabbis, aware of the decisive role of the Lot, and attempting to explain the apparently inappropriate plea of Joshua for a confession ("My son, give, I pray thee, glory to the Lord"), relate:

> So Joshua rose up early in the morning, and brought Israel near by their tribes . . . and Akhan, the son of Karmi, the son of Zabdi, the son of Zeraḥ, of the tribe of Judah, was taken. Said Akhan to Joshua: "What! With a Lot do you make search after me?! Let us see: There is none in this generation as righteous as you and as Phineas. Cast lots between you; it will surely fall upon one of you! Moreover, thirty or forty days have not passed since Moses, your Master, died. Did not Moses, our Master, teach us 'At the mouth of two witnesses shall he that is to die be put to death' (Deuteronomy 17:6)? You have already begun to err in judgment!" At that moment Joshua foresaw through Divine Inspiration (רוח הקדש) that he was to apportion the Promised Land by means of the Lot, as it is written, "And Joshua cast lots for them" (Joshua 18:10), and he mused: "Does this mean that we are going to cast aspersions on the Lot? Moreover, if the decision of the Lot is valid in capital cases, then certainly it is valid in monetary matters (such as the apportioning of land). If the Lot, however, fails now, all of Israel will say, 'It failed in capital cases, surely it is to fail in civil matters.' " At that moment, Joshua began to appease

Akhan and adjure him in the name of God of Israel, saying:
"My son, give, I pray thee, glory to the Lord, the God of
Israel, and make confession unto Him. . . ."[30]

The point of the *aggadah* is Joshua's concern that the
Lot's validity not be challenged on the rational grounds of
normal Jewish judicial procedure so that its usefulness as
an instrument for the subsequent division of the Promised
Land among the Israelites should not be impaired.

To invoke this passage as proof of an older *acceptance*
of criminal confessions is a plain misreading; the *aggadah*
patently assumes that the guilt of Akhan was adequately
established by the Lot.

(b) An invidious comparison between an earthly king
and the Heavenly King, found in the Midrash, shows that
criminal confessions were indeed accepted by the earthly
king.

> When a human king sitting in judgment says to the accused,
> "What do you say? Did you commit the murder or not?" If
> he declares, "I am guilty," the judge sentences him to death;
> but if he does not confess the judge does not sentence him
> to death. But the Holy One, blessed be He, does not act this
> way, but He has mercy on the one who confesses before
> Him.[31]

It must be pointed out, however, that at most such confessions were accepted by the extra-halakhic procedure
that constituted part of the royal prerogative (to be explained below). More probably, the *aggadah* was not referring to any Jewish king at all, but rather to the earthly
king at the time, the reigning monarch of the Greco-Roman empire.

(3) Negative proof is adduced from the classic rabbinic
text which rejects circumstantial evidence in criminal
cases:

It has been taught: Rabbi Simeon ben Shetaḥ said: "I swear that I once saw a man pursuing his fellow into a shack. I ran after him and saw him, sword in hand with blood dripping from it—and the murdered man writhing. I exclaimed to him, 'Wicked man, who slew this man? It is either you or I! But what can I do since thy blood does not rest in my hands, for it is written in the Torah, "At the mouth of two witnesses . . . shall he that is to die be put to death" (Deuteronomy 17:6)? May He who knows the thoughts of men exact vengeance from him who slew his fellow!' "

(P.S.) It is related that before they could leave that spot, a serpent came and bit the murderer so that he died.[32]

The scholar,[33] after having cited this passage, asks by implication "Who knows? Would R. Simeon b. Shetaḥ have been powerless had the murderer confessed?" As a matter of fact, if it is true that criminal confessions could bring about a conviction, it is surprising that R. Simeon b. Shetaḥ did not put the culprit on trial and subject him to rigorous interrogation in an intensive effort to extract a confession from him.[34]

(4) (a) The Mishnah states:[35]

When a convicted criminal is about ten cubits away from the place of stoning, the authorities say to him: "Confess,* for such is the practice of all who are executed, that they first confess; for he who confesses has a share in the world to come."*

(b) In connection with this Mishnah, the Gemara[36] quotes the following event recorded by the *Tannaim*:[37]

Our Rabbis taught: It happened once that a man who was being taken to be executed said: "If I am guilty of this sin, may my death *not* atone for any of my sins; but if I am

---

. . . These words may be a quotation of the authorities, as our quotation marks indicate. They may, however, be the comment of the Mishnah, and the authorities may have only urged the prisoner, "Confess."

innocent thereof, may my death expiate all my sins. The
court and Israel are indeed guiltless, but may the witnesses
never be forgiven." Now, when the Sages heard of the matter
they said: "It is impossible to reverse the decision since
sentence has been passed (שכבר נגזרה גזירה). He must therefore be executed; may the chain of responsibility (והקולר),
however, always hang on the neck of the witnesses whose
testimony brought about his conviction."

It is generally agreed by all interpreters, traditional and
modern, that the sense of this *baraitha** is that the authorities, the Sages of Israel, were shaken by the prisoner's extraordinary declaration, for it was a totally unexpected
response to their routine request for a confession from
the mouth of the condemned.

As to the reason for their dismay, opinions vary. Some
moderns, consistent with their interpretation of the Joshua-
Akhan episode, assume that in ancient Israel confession
was a necessary condition for execution—necessary (1) in
order to assure the community of the correctness of the
verdict; (2) in order to ease the conscience of the judges
(which may be identical with the first necessity in a society
in which the whole community constitutes the jury); and/
or (3) in order to remain faithful to the traditions of their
ancestors which originated within the framework of a
simple society where criminal confession was not required
as evidence, as much as a kind of ratification on the part
of the accused of the community's decision. In return for
his confession, the prisoner was assured of his share in the
world to come. This surprising declaration upset the con-
ventional pattern. The court's decision to proceed with
the execution without the normal confession marks a turn-

---

* A *baraitha* is a statement made by *Tannaim* but not found in the
Mishnah itself.

ing point in Jewish legal history: Henceforth confessions were no longer felt to be necessary as a condition for execution but were relegated to the category of private religious acts in the pursuit of expiation and atonement. According to this theory, this turning point took place in the Greek period—as is evidenced by the use of the word קולר, which is the Greek word *kollarion* (Latin *collarium*), an iron collar, a neck fetter, symbolically a "chain of responsibility"[38]—although the exact date cannot be determined.

At first glance the theory would appear to be plausible. An examination of the context of the above-quoted passages, however, forces us to reject the interpretations upon which it is based. Thus:

(a) The Mishnah in Sanhedrin continues:

> And if he knows not how to confess (להתוודות), the authorities tell him, "Say: 'May my death serve as expiation for all my sins.'" R. Judah says: "If he knows that he was the victim of a frame-up, he should say: 'May my death serve as expiation for all my sins except this one.'" The Rabbis said to him: "If so everyone will say this to cleanse himself (and undermine public confidence in the courts)."[39]

What, pray, does the Mishnah mean by stating, "And if he *knows* not how to confess"? Surely a man knows how to confess! I submit that the Mishnah is not referring to a confession of the crime; the verb להתוודות, to confess, must be understood in the same manner as the noun תודה used in Joshua 7:19, *i.e.,* a public confession whose main theme was doxological praise of God and whose main purpose was the expiational cleansing of a man before his death so that his share in the world to come would not be endangered.[40] This is borne out by:

(b) The Tosephta's introductory remarks to the pas-

sage, parallel to the *baraitha* which describes the extraordinary confession of a man who insisted that he was the
victim of an unholy conspiracy:

> Those executed by the courts have a share in the world to
> come שהן מתוודין, because they recite the confessional, על כל
> עוונותיהם, over all their sins.

The point of these introductory remarks is that once the
condemned man has paid his debt to society, his share in
the world to come is no longer at stake as long as he has
also fulfilled the spiritual requirement of repentance—
as manifested in a confession, at least in a plea for atonement before the Lord.[41] To construe the texts as dealing
with problems of the corroboration of the evidence or of
the necessary validation of the court's verdict is to miss this
point.[42] Thus, to see in this incident a turning point in
criminal procedure is to suspend mountains by a non-
existent strand of hair.

The Talmud[43] explains that the reason for the dismay
of the authorities was the irrevocability of the verdict
despite their personal conviction that the accused was
innocent. The examination and cross-examination of the
witnesses had uncovered no discrepancies; the rules of
procedure are strict and do not allow subsequent alteration
of testimony by the witnesses; the exceptional declaration
of the convicted man carried with it great psychological
and emotional weight but no legal significance. (In lieu
of the words of the *baraitha* שכבר נגזרה גזירה, "since sentence has been passed," the Tosephta reads ואין לדבר סוף,
"the matter is endless," *i.e.*, it is impossible to distinguish
an authentic from a simulated protestation of innocence.)

(5) The formulaic הודאת בעל דין כמאה עדים, "A man's
own admission of guilt has the power of one hundred
witnesses," with its stylistic pithiness gives the impression

of great antiquity. Inasmuch as this ancient maxim does not differentiate between criminal and civil cases, it is a faithful continuation of the biblical law which accepted self-incriminating statements. When later jurisprudence rejected criminal confessions, this ancient maxim was limited to money matters.

But בעל דין is never used to refer to the defendant in a criminal trial! The term itself is limited to either litigant in a *civil* case, the plaintiff or the defendant. Indeed, in tannaitic literature, if the term is ever used to refer to one party in a trial, it invariably refers to the plaintiff.[44]

There does not appear to be any word for the accused in a criminal trial other than נדון, when it is occasionally used as a noun.[45]

Strictly speaking, the maxim should be translated: "The acknowledgment (of liability)[46] of a litigant is as one hundred witnesses"; from its inception it never contemplated criminal confessions.

(6) Another argument adduced in support of the possibility that the confession of an accused is accepted is as follows:

The Talmud,[47] citing Deuteronomy 19:15, "One witness shall not rise up against a man for any iniquity or for any sin," makes the following deduction: He shall not rise up for *any iniquity* or for *any sin,* but he may rise up to render liability to an oath. In other words, although one witness cannot bring about the conviction of the accused against whom he is testifying, he can render the person liable to an oath; and if the latter refuses to take the oath, he will lose his case.

Now, runs the argument, since the effectiveness of the single witness to create the liability to an oath is obviously in a case where the defendant is denying the allegations against him, the Talmud may be legitimately construed as viewing the verse in Deuteronomy as concerned exclusively with such cases, namely, where the defendant is denying the charges brought against him. Thus, the rule of evidence requiring two witnesses may *not* apply to cases where the defendant admits that the accusation against him is true.[48]

The argument collapses, however, when it is pointed out that the earliest source of the talmudic deduction is the Siphrei-Tosephta passage, quoted at the beginning of this chapter (*supra,* pp. 34–35), in which the criminal confession is expressly rejected! Thus, it is clear that the context within which the Talmud is interpreting the scriptural requirement of two eyewitnesses for conviction is one which distinguishes between criminal and monetary cases![49]

It is our belief that the thesis of an older tannaitic law which allowed criminal confessions and a later tannaitic development which rejected self-incrimination has no scientific basis whatsoever.

CHAPTER **IV**

Amoraic Development

The Talmud[1] records the following controversy among the *Amoraim:*

> Rabbi Joseph said: "If a man says that so-and-so committed sodomy[2] with him forcibly, he himself with another witness can combine[3] to testify to the crime. If, however, he admits that he acceded to the act, he is a *rasha,* a wicked man disqualified from acting as a witness, since the Torah says: 'Put not thy hand with the wicked to be an unrighteous witness.' "[4]
>
> Raba, however, said: "Every man is considered a kinsman unto himself, ואין אדם משים עצמו רשע and no one can render himself a *rasha.*" (Consequently his evidence is valid only with regard to the criminal but not to himself, on the principle that we consider only half of his testimony as evidence.)[5]

In the previous section, we examined the tannaitic passages which declare that a man's criminal confession is inadmissible in a Jewish court. Raba's dictum represents an extension of this doctrine, for in our passage there is no question of prosecuting the confessant; the sole problem is whether, by having confessed to a crime, a person may render himself a *rasha,* an outlaw or a lawbreaker, who may not act as a witness in a trial. Thus not conviction but, rather, disqualification is at stake.

The dictum אין אדם משים עצמו רשע is usually translated, "No man may incriminate himself." I have carefully avoided this translation in the text, for such a translation would mislead the reader into a total unawareness of the point of the dictum. By rendering Raba's words literally, "No man may render himself a *rasha,*" I mean to emphasize the particular nuance that the *Amoraim* felt when they used the term. When R. Joseph brands the confessed homosexual a *rasha* and cites the verse, Exodus 23:1, "Put not thy hand with the *rasha,* wicked man, to be an unrighteous witness," he is using *rasha* technically, as the term for one whose criminal, sinful or immoral act has disqualified him from acting as a witness in a Jewish court. It is to this *rasha* that Raba is alluding when he declares, "No man may render himself a *rasha*"; hence, the point he is making is that no man can render himself disqualified to act as a witness in court on the basis of his own confession to any criminal, sinful or immoral act that would so disqualify him.[6]

Raba's rule created certain practical advantages. A citizen might seek to evade the burdensome duty of testifying. Inconvenience, fear of one of the litigants, the necessity to perjure himself, might be some of the reasons motivating a man to shun the witness chair. In capital cases, moreover, witnesses were expected to initiate the execution of the defendant who was found guilty on the basis of their testimony (Deuteronomy 17:7). Thus, acting as a witness was a heavy, nay frightening, responsibility. Such responsibility could be avoided by confessing to some violation of the law which would disqualify the confessant by branding him a *rasha*. Raba's dictum thwarted this attempt. By rejecting his voluntary statement of self-incrimination, it became a means of compelling reluctant persons to perform their duty as witnesses.

But whether Raba's dictum represents an amoraic extension of the tannaitic law against self-incrimination or merely formulates a pre-existing tannaitic doctrine was itself a question to which the *Amoraim* addressed themselves, and it evoked a controversy among them.

Thus, we read in B. Yebamoth 25a and b:

> Mishnah: A man who brings a letter of divorce from a country beyond the sea and states, "It was written in my presence and it was signed in my presence," may not marry the divorcer's wife.* Similarly, if he states, "He died," "I killed him" or "We killed him," he may not marry the woman. R. Judah said: If the statement is, "I killed him," the woman may not marry anyone.

It is the second half of the Mishnah ("Similarly. . . .") which is of interest to us; the following is the talmudic discussion thereon:

> Gemara: . . . Only he, then, may not marry the woman; she, however, may be married to another man? But surely R. Joseph has taught: "If a man declares, 'So-and-so committed sodomy with me against my will,' he and any other witness may be combined to procure his execution; if, however, he declares, '. . . with my consent,' he is a *rasha*, a wicked man, concerning whom the Torah said, 'Put not thy hand with the wicked to be an unrighteous witness' (Exodus

---

* Since the validity of the divorce is entirely dependent on his word, he is suspected of giving false evidence with a view to marrying the woman himself. As, however, a woman is permitted to marry even if only a single witness had testified to the death of her husband (an exceptional relaxation of the rules of evidence to save her from a living widowhood), she is allowed to marry any other man.

23:1), which shows that a man who admitted a criminal offence may not act as a witness at all!"

Now were you to reply that matrimonial evidence, *i.e.,* allowing a woman to remarry on evidence of the death of her husband, is different because the Rabbis have relaxed the rules in its case, surely R. Manasseh has stated: "One who according to biblical law is regarded as a law-abiding citizen and only by the standards of rabbinic law is considered a criminal is yet eligible to be a witness in matrimonial matters.* One, however, who according to scriptural law is regarded as a criminal (such as a murderer) is ineligible to act as a witness in matrimonial matters."

R. Manasseh can answer you:† "My statement may be reconciled with the majority view in the Mishnah which accepts the evidence of the admitted murderer: the reasoning here is the same as that of Raba, for Raba has said, 'Every man is a kinsman unto himself, and no man can render himself a *rasha,* wicked.' "

Must it then be assumed that R. Joseph, who disagrees with Raba's dictum and does not admit the evidence of a man who declared himself a criminal, is of the same opinion as the minority in the Mishnah (R. Judah)? R. Joseph can answer you: "My statement may be in agreement with the majority view in the Mishnah, but matrimonial evidence is different, since the Rabbis relaxed the law in its case even to the extent of admitting the evidence of a self-declared murderer; and it is R. Manasseh who adopted the minority view as expressed by R. Judah."

---

* A gambler, for instance, who is biblically not disqualified to act as a witness. Biblical law consists of precepts and standards stated explicitly in the Torah and of others which the Rabbis interpreted and understood as being biblical in origin. Their own rabbinic enactments they themselves looked upon as being of a lesser sanctity. Thus, for example, when it came to relaxing the rules of evidence on behalf of women whose husbands had disappeared, rabbinic standards could be waived more easily and more readily than biblical ones.

† R. Manasseh and R. Joseph, *Amoraim,* desire to have their opinion in line with the majority view in the Mishnah which is binding.

The following conclusions are clear:

The question of law involved is whether the woman may remarry and to whom. No mention is made of prosecuting the confessed murderer.

According to R. Manasseh, the prevailing opinion in the Mishnah (which is in opposition to that of R. Judah) is in line with the dictum of Raba expressed many years later, namely, that a criminal's confession carries no weight in a rabbinic court. Conviction of a crime as well as disqualification as a witness are brought about only by the eyewitness testimony of two unbiased and non-related law-abiding adult citizens. We must therefore split his testimony in two. Our visitor from abroad is believed only to the extent that the husband is dead; his statement as to the identity of the murderer is thrown out of court, even were he to have another, corroborating witness with him.[7]

According to Maimonides,[8] the *point* of contention between the majority and R. Judah in the Mishnah is not so much whether we may split a man's testimony,[9] but whether a man can incriminate himself, whether he can render himself a *rasha*. We have already seen that the *Tannaim* took for granted that a man's confession to a crime could not bring about his conviction. According to Maimonidean exegesis of this Mishnah in Yebamoth, there were *Amoraim* (*i.e.*, R. Manasseh) who held the opinion that the rule that a man could also not render himself a *rasha* was a tannaitic one, antedating Raba by several hundred years.

It remains for us to examine R. Joseph's position and Raba's reasoning more thoroughly. We shall have occasion to point out[10] that inasmuch as R. Joseph did not recognize the possibility of splitting a man's testimony, ordinarily a witness who in the course of his testimony makes a self-incriminating statement thereby brings about

the total rejection of his testimony. In the case set forth
by our Mishnah, however, though our visitor from abroad
will be incriminating himself, we will accept his testimony
and allow the woman to remarry; for the Rabbis relaxed
the law and allowed the testimony of a criminal in matters
affecting matrimonial evidence.[11] According to Raba, who
consistently refuses to allow a man to render himself a
rasha, the Rabbis' reason for allowing her to remarry was
that they were resorting to "splitting the testimony."
Thus, should a *kohen* (priest) declare, "This son of mine
was born of a divorcee whom I deliberately and knowingly married (*contra* Leviticus 21:7) ," thereby rendering
himself a sinner and disqualifying his son from the priestly
office—according to Raba,[12] the entire testimony is rejected;
according to R. Joseph, it is accepted *in toto.*[13]

The Talmud, however, is careful to point out that
wherever possible the court is duty-bound to interpret
such statements in a way that would render them free
from any self-incriminating impact. Thus, on Rabbi Judah's distinction between the statement "I killed him,"
and the statement "We killed him," whereby in the former
case the woman may not remarry but in the latter she may,
the Talmud asks:

> What is the practical difference between "I killed him" and
> "We killed him"? In either case, the witness admits mur-
> der!

and answers:

> Rab Judah said: "We interpret his words as if to say[14] 'I
> was present with the murderers but did not myself partici-
> pate in the crime.' "

Of greater interest and in need of a more extended analysis is Raba's formulation of the juridic reason that a man

may not render himself a *rasha*. The reason given, "A man is a *qarob*, kinsman, unto himself; hence no man may incriminate himself" is surprising, for it runs counter to what we would expect logically. Were we presented with the fact that the law disqualifies a defendant and his *qerobim*, kinsmen, from acting as witnesses at the trial and then informed that these two disqualifications are interrelated, it would have been reasonable for us to assume that the disqualification of the defendant himself was axiomatic and the disqualification of the relatives was a logical extension of this axiom. The talmudic formulation, on the other hand, starts from the dogmatic disqualification of the kinsmen and derives the disqualification of the defendant himself by identifying him as one of those relatives!

I propose to show that the Rabbis of the Talmud did not regard a person as a "kinsman" to himself in the literal and narrow sense of the term; the word *qarob*, "kinsman," is to them nothing more than a convenient metaphor.

In order to arrive at a more accurate understanding of this talmudic formulation, we must present the rabbinic interpretation of the juridic nature of these disqualifications.

On the verse from Deuteronomy (19:15) which lays down the requirement that judicial trials be decided on the basis of the testimony of two or three witnesses (which the Rabbis understood to mean eyewitnesses) the Mishnah[15] asks, "If the matter can be established by means of two, why does Scripture also specify three?"

The various answers given by the *Tannaim* of the Mishnah to this question may be viewed as varied manifestations of one underlying principle in the Jewish law of testimony: All witnesses testifying to the same fact at the same trial constitute what the Romans called a *univer-*

sitas,[16] a unitary (indivisible and inseparable) and irreducible team of "testimony"—a team that, regardless of its quantitative composition, is qualitatively maximal in its evidentiary value. The reasoning appears to be that if two witnesses suffice to bring about one's condemnation to death, their operational effectiveness is unsurpassable,[17] and they are qualitatively equal to a hundred witnesses. Indeed, תרי כמאה, "Two are equal to a hundred," is a jurisprudential maxim of rabbinic court procedure.[18]

If we bear in mind this underlying principle of the *universitas* character of a group of witnesses, we will understand Rabbi Aqiba's answer to the question posed by the Mishnah: The Torah desires thereby to teach us that if, in a group of witnesses testifying in a particular case, one of them is found to be a *qarob,* a kinsman of the accused (or of one of the litigants in a civil suit, or of one of the judges[19]) or is disqualified for some other reason,[20] the entire group is rejected.[21]

In the light of the above, it would appear that every criminal could go scot-free by the simple stratagem of joining the very group of witnesses who have come to testify against him; he would thus become a member of the group, and, by being found to be a *qarob,* a "kinsman," unto himself, he could have the *universitas,* the entire group of witnesses, rejected! Such a possibility, which is obviously absurd, is obviated by a significant addendum to the interpretation of our verse in Deuteronomy:

> Mishnah: If one of the witnesses was found to be related or otherwise disqualified, the evidence of the whole group of witnesses is void.
>
> Gemara: Let the presence of the accused himself in any group of witnesses be made a pretext for disqualifying their evidence?

Raba replied: "Holy Writ prescribes, 'At the mouth of two *witnesses* or at the mouth of three *witnesses* shall the matter be *established*'—the text invalidating the evidence of a whole group through the presence among them of one disqualified person thus refers only to those who have to *establish* the matter, not to a litigant or a defendant who is involved *in* the matter."[22]

Hence, though a man is said to be a "kinsman" to himself, there is a basic difference between him and his "other" relatives. Should any of his kinsmen be discovered among the witnesses who had testified, such an individual's statements in court—having achieved the legal status of "testimony"—bring about the rejection of the *universitas,* the entire group which accompanied him and which comprised his group of witnesses.[23] On the other hand, the defendant's own statements in court never attain the legal status of "testimony" to begin with[24] and thus could never bring about the rejection of any group of witnesses.[25]

Thus the rabbinic dictum אדם קרוב אצל עצמו ואין אדם משים עצמו רשע, "A man is a *qarob,* a kinsman, unto himself, hence no man may incriminate himself," should not be taken literally; and the "kinsman" aspect should not be belabored,[26] for the qualitative distinction between the accused himself and his kinsmen makes it clear that the Rabbis utilized "kinsman" metaphorically, as a convenient legal rubric. In the rules of evidence the disqualification of *qerobim,* kinsmen, of varying degrees of consanguinity was worked out thoroughly, and in the general category, "kinsmen," the talmudic jurists found a ready-made label for the defendant himself whose disqualification was undisputed.[27]

CHAPTER V

Post-Talmudic Exegesis, Commentary and Expansion

INTRODUCTION

(1) The Talmud, its tannaitic and amoraic components combined, applied the rule against the admissibility of confessions in evidence explicitly to two areas: capital offences and cases involving the imposition of monetary fines. It was left to the medieval authorities to extend this rule explicitly to other areas. We propose to trace the main lines of this expansion.

(2) As for the distinction between criminal and simple monetary matters, the Talmud is clear. In the former, a man cannot incriminate himself; in the latter, a man's admission of liability is as potent as the testimony of one hundred witnesses to such liability.[1] This distinction is taken for granted; it is not explained.

But why should there be such a distinction? If a man's own admission of guilt has the power of one hundred witnesses as far as money is concerned, should it not follow logically that it has the power of one hundred witnesses in all cases?

Among the Romans, for example, the rule of private law was *Confessus pro iudicato est,* "A defendant who has acknowledged his liability to a claim is like one who has been adjudged liable by a judge."[2] The rule is followed by an explanation of the reasoning behind it: *qui (a) quodam modo sua sententia damnatur,* "since he is condemned, as it were, by his own judgment." This equation of *confessus* and *iudicatus* is already found in the Twelve Tables (3.1) .[3]

Interestingly enough, in the books dealing with Rhetoric, we find the theme, *magistratus de confesso sumat supplicium,* "Let the magistrate inflict punishment on the one who confessed."[4]

Of even greater significance is Cato's argument with regard to the confessing Catilinarians:

> Let those who have confessed be treated as though they had been caught red-handed in capital offences, and be punished after the manner of our forefathers.[5]

On the basis of these and similar passages, Theodor Mommsen has pointed out that the private law equation of *confessus* with *iudicatus* was transferred not only to matters of private delict but also to public criminal law, in actual practice as well as in theory.[6]

What prevented the Rabbis of the Talmud from making this transfer, or from applying one rule to both criminal and monetary cases?

The problem may be formulated in the following fashion. It has been pointed out that a man's statement concerning his criminal act cannot attain the status of "testimony." He cannot be a "witness" against himself. Should there not be another status that we could attribute to his statement, namely that of a "confession"? Should not a man's "confession" of criminal guilt be accepted as valid and convincing in and of itself?

It was left to post-talmudic rabbinic scholars to propose explanations for this unique rejection of the criminal confession and to suggest possible reasons for the distinction between criminal and civil cases.

(3) Nowhere do the Rabbis of the Talmud explicitly face the contradiction between their law against self-incrimination and the scriptural narratives which indicate that criminal confessions were accepted and were effective in bringing about the conviction and execution of the confessant. Here, too, it was left to medieval Jewish thinkers to cope with the problem.

THE GEONIC PERIOD (ca. 500–1000)

The geonic literature[7] contains the earliest explicit extension of the rule against self-incrimination to non-capital criminal cases, in which a verdict of guilty leads to the punishment of flagellation.[8] The significance of this information is not the fact of innovation on the part of the *Geonim*. On the contrary, inasmuch as the *Geonim* were the heads of the Babylonian Academies during the period following immediately after the redaction of the Talmud, they were undoubtedly the repositories of authentic talmudic traditions; and so it is a likely possibility that this extension of the rule to cover crimes punishable by lashes was already implied in the Talmud itself and was merely made explicit by the *Geonim*.

The *Geonim* further ruled that a confessant is not only not to be punished on the basis of his confession, he is not to be excommunicated or ostracized either.[9]

MAIMONIDES (RABBI MOSES BEN MAIMON, *RAMBAM,* 1135 SPAIN–1204 EGYPT)

Maimonides offers the following explanation for the in-admissibility of self-incriminating statements: They may very well not be true; it is quite likely that they have been made because of some unknown, ulterior motive. Thus, he writes in his Code:[10]

It is a scriptural decree that the court shall not put a man to death or flog him on his own admission (of guilt). This is done only on the evidence of two witnesses. It is true that Joshua condemned Akhan on the latter's admission[11] and that David ordered the execution of the Amalekite stranger on the latter's admission.[12] But those were emergency cases,[13] or the death sentence pronounced in these instances was prescribed by State law.[14] The Sanhedrin,* however, is not empowered to inflict the penalty of death or flagellation on the admission of the accused. For it is possible that he was confused in mind when he made the confession. Perhaps he was one of those who are in misery, bitter in soul, who long for death, thrust the sword into their bellies or cast themselves down from the roof. Perhaps this was the reason that prompted him to confess to a crime he had not committed, in order that he might be put to death. To sum up the matter, the principle that no man is declared guilty on his own admission is a divine decree.†

* The Jewish court whose procedure is exclusively according to Torah law.

† Maimonides appears to be the first rabbinic scholar to offer this explanation of the Talmud's rejection of confession. This may lead us to suspect that perhaps he was influenced by Islamic thought. On this matter, I should like to quote the opinion of Professor Joseph Schacht of Columbia University (in a private communication):

"There is no doctrine in Islamic law parallel to the theory proposed by Maimonides. Confessions in criminal cases implying *hadd* punishments are discouraged, it is true, may be withdrawn, etc., but once validly made must be acted upon by the cadi. The idea that a confession may be a

The scriptural decree mentioned by Maimonides would appear to be the dogmatic disqualification of a kinsman, including the defendant as his own nearest kinsman, from acting as a witness, coupled with the passage from Deuteronomy (19:15–16), cited *supra,* pp. 40–41, which requires the testimony of a minimum of two eyewitnesses in order to convict a man for a crime. Talmudic exegesis of these verses considers such testimony as the *sole* type of acceptable evidence. For according to the Rabbis, not only is the testimony of one witness excluded—as is evident from the Bible itself—circumstantial evidence[15] and hearsay are also unacceptable;[16] and, finally, the criminal's own confession of guilt is equally unacceptable.[17]

Maimonides' interpretation of the Talmudic law against self-incrimination as being based upon serious suspicion of the veracity of statements made by an individual concerning himself evidently did not satisfy Maimonides himself. This is indicated by his initial appeal to "scriptural decree" and becomes obvious from reiteration, after having presented his interpretation, that it "is a divine decree"—a sure sign that he considered the rule nonrational. Moreover, he makes no allusion to this interpretation when he discusses elsewhere[18] the legal inability of a man to incriminate himself to the extent of disqualifying himself from acting as a witness. One of the commentaries on the Code[19] points out that his interpretation is inappropriate for the rule against self-incrimination concerning crimes the punishment of which is flogging.

With the aid of modern psychiatry and its new insights, however, we might follow the line of reasoning delineated by Maimonides and submit that self-incriminating state-

---

means for committing suicide is completely lacking. So Maimonides cannot possibly have been influenced here by Islamic thought." Cf. further J. Schacht, *Introduction to Islamic Law,* p. 176 f.

ments may be made falsely to satisfy a masochist's desire for corporal punishment or public humiliation.[20] A guilty conscience may be seeking ways to do penance.*

Moreover, as various Jewish authorities have pointed out, a man may have ulterior motives for using the stratagem of having himself declared disqualified from acting as a witness: He may have been present at certain business

---

* To what extent can voluntary confessions be trusted? This question elicited the following answer from a prominent psychiatrist:

"No matter what conscious or unconscious fantasies exist, a sane man without conscious ulterior motive will not confess to an actual crime which he did not commit. On the other hand, in the presence of mental illness such confessions are not uncommon. The melancholic patient, for example, will 'confess' that he has done immense irreparable damage to all about him and to the entire world. In fact, his confessions are generally so extravagant that they are utterly incredible to a reasonable observer. A schizophrenic individual who is depressed might produce even more bizarre confessions. I can imagine that an extraordinarily self-destructive masochist might put himself in a position for public humiliation by false confession. However, I should imagine, too, that such an event would occur rather infrequently. From a diagnostic point of view, perhaps one should include a hysterical episode as a possible predisposing condition for false confession. However, that again would be extremely unusual and one would have to be certain that there is no psychosis. In other words, a false confession is likely only in the case of an individual who is seriously disturbed. It is possible that the disturbance will not be visible to the untrained observer especially since most individuals under the pressure of apprehension, trial and possible punishment will feel themselves under considerable stress and behave in abnormal ways. . . ."

Proceeding from the false confession to self-destructive behavior in general, the psychiatrist made the following remarks: "There is the occasional individual whose self-destructive behavior can be recognized not only by his psychiatrist but also by his family and friends. Yet if he is not actually psychotic and if he will not respond to treatment, there is nothing that can be done to deter him" (Dr. Mortimer Ostow in a private communication).

It is clear from the doctor's response that only a small number of criminal confessions could not be trusted. On the other hand, The Temporary [New York] State Commission on the Constitutional Convention in a document entitled, "Individual Liberties: The Administration of Criminal Justice," states that "recent disclosures cast doubt upon the previously held belief that false confession cases are rare" (The New York Times, April 12, 1967, p. 35). According to Maimonides, we would have to say that the number of false confessions is large enough to motivate Jewish law to reject all criminal confession and to disqualify confessions as a legal instrument.

transactions or ritual ceremonies, and now, summoned to testify, he "confesses," to a sin which disqualifies him and thereby "escapes."[21] A confession to having committed a minor violation may furnish a man with an alibi for a major crime he perpetrated. Ulterior motives vary: from a desire to save a beloved friend from punishment to an attempt to obtain warm shelter and food in the winter[22]—the possibilities are limitless.[23]

The concern of the judicial authorities with regard to the substantial possibility that a man confessing to a crime may be lying is restricted, however, to non-monetary matters, for if a man wishes to give away his money it is within his full legal power to do so; the courts have no right nor inclination to interfere.

In addition to containing an explanation of the inadmissibility of confessions in evidence in Jewish criminal law, the above-quoted Maimonidean passage represents the earliest explicit attempt to reconcile the scriptural accounts of Joshua and David, who accepted criminal confessions and acted on them, with rabbinic law. Two interpretations of their conduct are offered in justification.

The first interpretation is based upon the concept הוראת שעה, an emergency measure, and it is undoubtedly based upon the aggadic elaboration of the biblical dialogue between Joshua and Akhan which we have quoted verbatim, *supra,* pp. 42–43.

The rabbinic rationalism put into the mouth of Akhan was, of course, motivated by the obvious discrepancy between Joshua's resort to the Lot and normative rabbinic criminal procedure which rests exclusively on the testimony of two eyewitnesses.[24] It was inconceivable to the talmudic rabbis that Joshua, who was reckoned as a significant link in the chain of Jewish tradition which extends from Moses at Sinai to the last generation of *Amoraim,*[25] should have flagrantly violated laws that are derived from the Pentateuch itself. In rabbinic thinking it was axiomatic that Joshua was not only a law-abiding leader, but he himself served as a model whose actions and practices were to be emulated by succeeding generations.[26] His action with regard to Akhan was looked upon as הוראת שעה, an act of emergency, due to extraordinary circumstances—the violation of the *herem* and the challenge to the authenticity of the instrument whereby the Land would be divided—which may never be utilized as a precedent.[27]*

David, to whom Sacred Scripture ascribed authorship and/or editorship[28] of the Psalms and whom Maimonides regarded explicitly as one of the links in the chain of tradition,[29] was held in the same high regard as Joshua.[30] He, too, states Maimonides, was acting in accordance with the principle of *hora'ath sha'ah*. Maimonides, however, does not specify what the emergency was. A number of years later, Levi Gersonides[31] offered an explanation of what emergency may have motivated David. Describing the trial of the Amalekite stranger, he writes, "Though there were no witnesses and he had incriminated himself—on the basis of which, legally, he should have been acquitted—David did it as הוראת שעה, an emergency measure, so that people should not take regicide lightly."[32]

Gersonides' explanation commends itself on a number of grounds. That David sincerely believed in the inviolability of the body of the king is clear from his adamant refusal to allow any harm to come to Saul; when Saul, who is pursuing him as an outlaw, accidentally falls into his hands,

---

* The ordeal of the bitter waters to which a woman suspected by her husband of infidelity was subjected (Numbers 5:11–31) is obviously in a different class, for no human tribunal sat in judgment nor did any human hand carry out the penal execution. For our purposes, the procedure of "leaving her to heaven" makes the world of difference. Cf. R. de Vaux, *op. cit.*, p. 157 f.

David recoils with horror at the suggestion that he do away with "the anointed of the Lord."[33] Now, if this was true of David the subject, how much more so would it be true of David the king, whose awe of royal majesty was now reinforced by practical considerations of self-preservation; for if any king's life were esteemed lightly, his own, too, could easily fall prey to the knife of an assassin.[34] Since David had the religious conviction that no one could put forth his hand against the Lord's anointed with impunity, it is quite probable that his own political sagacity would teach him to beware of the awe in which a regicide, going about unpunished, would be held by the masses. The situation, created by the Amalekite stranger and by Rekhab and Ba'anah, which the "weak and newly anointed king"[35] faced, surely represented a clear and present danger to the stability of his rule and warranted his invoking of הוראת שעה, emergency measures to cope with it. Thus, such action could not be cited as precedent for normative Jewish law.[36]

The second interpretation given by Maimonides is that Joshua and David were exercising דין מלכות, their royal prerogatives.[37]

This extra-biblical system of the "law of the king" is explained by R. Solomon b. Adreth (*Rashba*) [38] as follows:

> And punishment is meted out by royal prerogative even on the basis of the testimony of relatives and even on the basis of the confession of the accused himself, and also where the accused was not given a prior warning; for royal justice seeks the truth only (regardless of procedure). For if you do not grant this but insist strictly upon Torah law as fulfilled by the Sanhedrin, the world would be destroyed.

Thus, although it was sometimes the source of invidious comparisons and although it may have been regarded as a necessary evil, this system of the secular law of the king, recognized by Jewish law, was, according to Maimonides, invoked by Joshua and David in the episodes narrated in the Bible.

RABBI SOLOMON B. SIMEON DURAN

R. Solomon b. Simeon Duran (*Rashbash*), an Algerian rabbi of the fifteenth century, is, to the best of my knowledge, the only Jewish authority who disagrees with the general interpretation of the rabbinic law against criminal confessions as presented in this study.

R. Solomon interprets Raba's dictum, אין אדם משים עצמו רשע, "No man may render himself a *rasha*," as, strictly speaking, concerned with and limited to the question of the disqualification of a person from acting as a witness.[39] As far as crimes punishable by death or lashes are concerned, however, he maintains that a man's confession *may* serve as the basis of his conviction. It would appear that R. Solomon here follows a type of reasoning found in B. Sanhedrin (40b) whereby the more serious the crime, the greater the willingness of the law to dispense wih procedural safeguards.

In addition, he points out correctly that not only does the Talmud not cite this dictum in any other connection, but Maimonides, too, applies it only to the laws of witnesses.[40] With regard to criminal confessions Maimonides resorts to a vague "scriptural decree";[41] it would be farfetched to define this scriptural decree as the biblical verses upon which Raba's dictum is based.[42]

Indeed, according to R. Solomon, the Talmud clearly allows a man to be punished on the basis of his confession to a violation of the law; he cites two passages in support of his position:

(1) The first is an earlier piece of mishnaic legislation:[43]

> At first the authorities allowed three categories of women to sue for divorce and to receive their alimony: The one who said to her *kohen* (priest) [44] husband, "I have been violated and I am therefore forbidden to you". . . .[45] Subsequently, however, they revised the law so that no woman, having fallen in love with another man, could deceive her husband into granting her a divorce; and they ruled that if a woman says to her husband, "I am forbidden to you," she must bring proof for her statement.

The earlier law is the normative one; the revision is merely an emergency measure. Thus, legal principle is clear: Where disqualification to act as a witness is not at stake, a person's confession of unfitness is accepted.

(2) The second passage[46] is an actual judicial decision rendered by an *Amora* and viewed by R. Solomon as adequate precedent, for corporal punishment is inflicted on a man on the basis of a self-incriminating statement uttered.

The case concerned a young man who complained to the authorities that his bride was not a virgin. His expertness in sexual matters however, convinced R. Naḥman, the presiding judge, that he must have led an immoral life and had much experience with the local harlots. On the basis of his self-incriminating complaints, the young man was sentenced to lashes for dissoluteness.[47]

R. Solomon's conclusion, based on these passages, is unique. The ability of a woman to have herself declared unfit to remain married to her priest-husband, as described in the Mishnah, is explained in the standard commentaries by the metaphoric statement that "she has rendered herself a piece of forbidden food," which may, in this instance, be looked at from two points of view. If her allegations were false, she still retains the power the Torah has given anyone—along the lines of a vow—to render permitted acts forbidden. If her statements are indeed true, then we cannot force her to continue to live with her husband in violation of the Torah; for it is established rabbinic principle that a consistent application of the law against self-incrimination is not to be pursued where it would cause the confessant to perform a sinful act or prevent her from fulfilling her sacred obligations.[48]

R. Naḥman's decree of lashes for the promiscuous young man is an approved departure from normal criminal procedure in the interests of preserving morality. It is in line with the general rabbinic practice of invoking emergency measures when public mores are at stake and matters appear to be getting out of hand.

> It has been taught: R. Eliezer b. Jacob said: "I have a tradition from my teachers that the Beth Din (the Jewish Court) may, when necessary, impose flagellation and pronounce capital sentences even when not warranted by the Torah; yet not with the intention of disregarding the Torah but, on the contrary, in order to safeguard it. It once happened that a man rode a horse on the Sabbath in the Greek period, and he was brought before the Court and stoned—not because he was liable thereto but because it was required by the laxity of the times. Again it happened that a man once had intercourse with his wife in public, under a fig tree. He was haled into court and flogged—not because he merited it but because the looseness of the times required it."[49]

Thus, far from being normal criminal procedure, R. Naḥman's sentence is almost universally regarded as another example of the הוראת שעה clause[50] in operation.

This contrast between normal criminal procedure and emergency measures to cope with gross breaches of public morality is made explicit in a responsum of Rabbenu Asher.[51]

As to the question you asked me, I will answer you what, according to our law, the rule is regarding one who obligated himself under oath to do something and subsequently stated, "I violated my oath, and I did do what I had sworn not to"; and the matter cannot be proven by witnesses that he in fact had violated his oath, only by his own admission.

He does not become disqualified from ever testifying or taking an oath in court, and he is not to be punished, for no man may render himself a *rasha*.

Now, this man took an oath that he would keep the accounts as honestly as he could. If he now admits that he has acted fraudulently and maliciously, we do not believe him. Therefore, according to our law, he is not to be punished, since it cannot be established that he deliberately violated his oath; indeed, perhaps he did act with the best of intentions.

However, if in your opinion he should be punished for having acted brazenly and having stated that he violated his oath, inasmuch as he deserves it, mete out the punishment you deem proper.

Written by Asher, the son of Rabbi Yeḥiel of blessed memory.[52]

Thus, the sources invoked by Rashbash to establish his thesis lend themselves most easily to a markedly different interpretation. The tannaitic statements which we have studied, from Siphrei and the Tosephta, are a direct contradiction to his position. He may have not seen these tannaitic statements; or, having seen them, put a different construction upon them; or, more likely, have felt that, inasmuch as the statements are not cited in the Talmud, they carry no authority.*

---

* Thus, Rabbenu Asher writes in his work on Ḥullin, Ch. II, paragraph 6: "It stands to reason that any Tosephta that was promulgated after the Talmud was edited is not authoritative. For it is most likely that since the Sages of Israel desired to compose an authentic, lasting work, they searched out and investigated all the manuscripts that contained rabbinic

What is mystifying, however, is how R. Solomon could maintain his thesis in the face of the clear ruling of Maimonides[53] whom he revered. This ruling, cited verbatim earlier in this chapter,[54] he himself quotes; its meaning is clear: a criminal confession has no place in a rabbinic court![55]

Thus R. Solomon is not only alone in his opinion on self-incrimination. His proof-texts are not convincing, and the weight of the traditional literature is in direct opposition to him. No later authority takes up his position, and no later decision follows his line of reasoning.

RABBI DAVID BEN ZIMRA (*RADBAZ*)

Rabbi David ben Zimra (sixteenth century, Safed; known as Radbaz) [56] declares that a man may decide the destiny only of those things that are his. Since man's life does not belong to himself but rather to God, as it is written, "Behold, all souls are Mine" (Ezekiel 18:4), a man cannot make a confession about himself in capital offences. On the other hand, continues Radbaz, an admission of liability in monetary matters is accepted, for a man's money is his own possession. Indeed, possessions of a man may be looked upon as those things which are in his power to the extent that he is the sole or main decider as to what fate shall befall them.

Following Radbaz's line of reasoning we may say that not only is a man's life not his own,[57] his body is also not his

---

teachings, choosing those teachings that were authoritative and thereby created the Talmud. Therefore this passage from the Tosephta is not dependable since the editor of the Talmud did not give it his stamp of approval."—A kind of extension of the talmudic warning that any extra-mishnaic statement that had not been approved by the Academies of R. Ḥiyya and R. Oshaia was not authoritative and may not be invoked in debate (B. Ḥullin 141a bot.) .

own. He may not do with it as he wishes: he may not inflict any injury upon it though he may wish to do so;[58] he
may not even feed it as *he* wishes.[59] This is implied in the
very verse from Ezekiel cited by Radbaz, for the Hebrew
word for soul, *nephesh,* implies the whole living organism,
both soul *and* body.

Thus, a confession of guilt that would affect his physical
body adversely, causing lashes to be inflicted on it, is also
beyond his power. Compare this to a man's power to alien-
ate his property by giving a gift, declaring it ownerless,
abandoning it or destroying it—and the contrast is evident.
In this connection, it is well to point out that when the
Talmud states that he who admits that he is guilty of a
crime which is normally punishable by a fine is exempt
from that fine, it does not offer the rule against self-incrimination as its reason. Rather, the Rabbis had to resort
to a special scriptural decree;[60] for a man's money *is* his
own, and a confession of guilt affecting his possessions
would otherwise have been recognized.

In the light of what has been said, let us examine the
following passage summarizing rabbinic law on the disqualification of witnesses on grounds of criminality and
sinfulness:

> No man becomes ineligible on his own admission of
> religious delinquency. For example: if a person appears in
> court and says that he has stolen or robbed or loaned money
> on interest,[61] although he has to make restitution on his
> own admission,* he is not disqualified as a witness. Likewise,
> if he says that he has eaten *nebelah* or cohabited with a
> woman forbidden to him,[62] he is not disqualified—unless
> there are two witnesses who testify against him—for no man
> can incriminate himself.[63]

---

* For as far as monetary restitution is concerned, a man's own admission of liability has the power of one hundred witnesses.

We must conclude, therefore, that not even his own reputation is his to be debased and defamed by himself![64]

Thus, even if a man may be telling the truth, no utterance he may make in court concerning himself has any legal status; juridically it does not exist.[65] Emphasis should be put, of course, on the words, "concerning himself"; for it is when a man is speaking concerning himself that his statements carry the most weight and his listeners have the strongest tendency to give his words the greatest credence.[66] It is this overpowering psychological force that a man's confession carries with it that the Halakhah rejects on philosophical grounds, namely that in criminal court procedure—where evidence duly established leads to inexorable consequences of the utmost seriousness—no man should be allowed to wield such power over something that is not his—*i.e.,* his life, his body, nay, even his good name. On the other hand, where a man is speaking as an outsider, as an objective law-abiding adult citizen who is swayed neither by considerations of self-interest nor by feelings of kinship, his words do not carry such overwhelming influence; on the contrary, the listener is on his guard, weighing cautiously the allegations of the speaker and checking for inaccuracies and discrepancies. He is not speaking "concerning himself"; he is a "witness," his words become items of "evidence"; the verdict is indirectly and partially a result of his testimony—it is only in such a context that a man is heard in a rabbinic court.[67]

The depth of religious feeling that permeates the words of Radbaz is self-evident. No wonder, then, that it has caught the imagination of those few students of American law who have been exposed to it. Thus, we find one of them writing as follows:

> To coerce a confession is to infringe upon one's personality. Perhaps it is also a violation of one's dignity to seek

to impose disabilities upon him out of his own mouth. If so, one must disallow all confessions, for it is a false notion of the meaning of personality to allow one to impose disabilities upon himself only if he knows what he is doing.[68]

We pause at this point to place in bolder relief the differences between the interpretations of the rabbinic law which rejects criminal confessions offered by Maimonides and Radbaz respectively. Following the interpretation offered somewhat hesitantly by Maimonides, we may say that the courts entertain serious reservations as to the truth of a man's allegations concerning himself, for suspicions of ulterior motives not connected with the substance of these allegations are everpresent in the minds of the judges. According to R. David ben Zimra, a man's arbitrary power and full control are limited to his property, to that which he truly possesses; his life, body and good name are not his, however—they belong to his Maker—and so he may not do with them as he pleases.

These two divergent interpretations, the psychological one of Maimonides and the philosophical one of Radbaz, lead to certain practical differences.

For example, there is on record the following case which took place at least a century after the death of Radbaz:

Each member of an association of liquor manufacturers obligated himself by an oath to register with a designated trustee the amount of grain he intended to use; failure to do so would mean a fine of twenty gulden. Subsequently, one of the members failed to do so, and so his associates filed suit with the rabbinical court. Summoned to appear, the defendant freely admitted to having violated the conditions that had been agreed upon and then proceeded confidently to defend himself on the basis of extenuating circumstances that justified his course of action. The court found his defense inadequate, and he was fined.

Moreover, inasmuch as he had violated his oath, he was declared disqualified thereafter to act as a witness or to take an oath in court.

Now, there were authorities who disagreed with the sentence of the court. Since the only witnesses who testified were the other members of the association, men who were interested parties (for each one stood to gain a share of the fine as well as a share of the hidden liquor), their statements were inadmissible as testimony. Moreover, those authorities felt that no man's statements in court may be used against him to render him a *rasha*.[69]

It seems to me that the controversy of these authorities with the court's decision can best be explained on the basis of the divergent interpretations of Maimonides and Radbaz.

The court, apparently, had accepted Maimonides' line of reasoning. Ordinarily—they maintained—we will not accept a man's self-incriminating statement, for we are apprehensive lest he be lying for some ulterior motive. In this case, however, it is clear that the man was telling the truth; he even defended his action and was confident that the court would exonerate him from any guilt. A confession which is made indirectly and which is intended to be used as a basis for a defense is admissible.

The authorities who rejected this approach probably based their thinking upon the philosophical grounds of Radbaz, according to which a confession is absolutely inadmissible regardless of its directness or indirectness and regardless of the intentions of the one uttering it.

There would be a similar practical difference between the approaches of Maimonides and Radbaz, where there was corroborating evidence (but not that given by two eyewitnesses) supporting the self-incriminating statements.[70]

In the foregoing cases, those who agreed with the Maimonidean idea—that confessions are unacceptable because we suspect that the confessant, out of some ulterior motive, is lying—would accept his self-incriminating statement that either made unwittingly or that was corroborated by other evidence; for under such circumstances we are assured that his confession is truthful. Those who agreed with the interpretation of Radbaz were unaffected by the truthfulness of the confession; the prohibition of admitting a man's self-incriminating statements was in their eyes absolute.

It must be emphasized, however, that the conflicting decisions in the foregoing cases are limited to the disqualification of acting as a witness. Both interpretations are fully agreed, however, that under no circumstances can a man be punished, capitally or corporally, on the basis of his own statements, for this would be a direct violation of the biblical rule of evidence, "At the mouth of two witnesses . . . shall a matter be established" (Deuteronomy 19:15).

THE LATE MIDDLE AGES

The scholars of the late Middle Ages held their predecessors in extreme reverence. Hence, whatever we may record in the subsequent theoretical development of the rabbinic law of self-incrimination that is of basic significance is usually formulated as having been implied in the teachings of earlier authorities.

Thus Rabbis Solomon Luria (sixteenth century, Poland) and Zebi Ashkenazi (1658–1718, Germany, Holland, Poland) look upon themselves as doing nothing more than articulating the tacit assumption of all the previous generations of authorities when they declare the inapplica-

bility of the law against self-incrimination where the confessant's presumption of innocence has been destroyed.
The details of this declaration will be discussed later.[71]

A number of rabbinic scholars offered varying suggestions as to how the rule that in monetary matters a man's
admission of liability had the power of one hundred witnesses may be understood.

R. Joseph ben David ibn Leb (sixteenth century, Tur-
key),[72] known as Mahari ibn Leb, is of the opinion that
when a man confesses that he is liable on a monetary claim
which has been lodged against him and the courts condemn
him to render compensation on the basis of his admission,
it does not mean that the courts thereby have necessarily
accepted his version of the facts. His alleged loan, delict
or theft may have actually never taken place. His confession
is ultimately construed as an act of התחייבות on his part,
a manifestation of his willingness to obligate himself to
pay the other party the specific sum to which he has
"confessed"—*as if* he were paying a debt or giving a gift.
Such an obligation is enforceable in the courts in the same
manner that any voluntary obligation is enforceable in
the event that the interested party subsequently lodges a
formal claim.[73]

Thus, according to Rabbi ibn Leb, even in money matters a man's admission of his own liability does not constitute self-incriminating "testimony," nor does "confession" have any special status in court. For, he maintains,
were his credibility the basis, he could not be believed:
inasmuch as he has been placed in the general category of
"kinsman," his testimony would be rejected regardless
whether he was testifying to his advantage or to his disadvantage.

R. Sabbetai Cohen (seventeenth century, Poland) argues against this line of reasoning by distinguishing between a litigant himself and "other" kinsmen. The former loses the status of a "kinsman" when he testifies to his own disadvantage for he has thereby removed all positive interest in his testimony, whereas the latter's disqualification is dogmatic and independent of the nature of his testimony —whether it be favorable to his kinsman or not.[74] (We have in these words of R. Sabbetai Cohen further corroboration of the *metaphoric* character of the Talmud's classification of a litigant-defendant as a "kinsman to himself."[75])

The argument of R. Aryeh Leib HaKohen (d. 1813, Galicia) against the position espoused by Mahari ibn Leb is even weightier, although its substance does not concern us. What does concern us is his conclusion: The power of a man's admission of liability is an independent, axiomatic principle of Jewish law; just as the Torah has commanded any Jewish tribunal to accept as final and as definitive the testimony of two unrelated, unbiased and uncorrupted eyewitnesses, so must it accept and grant similar status to the self-admitted liability of a litigant.[76]

Rabbi Jacob Algasi (eighteenth century, Jerusalem), on the basis of the works of earlier commentators, has an entirely different approach. It may be presented in the following way:

The Bible forbids the eating of *ḥeleb,* certain portions of the fat of oxen, sheep or goats.[77] The punishment ordained for wilfully violating this prohibition was *kareth.* One who does so unwittingly, however, was blameless and was granted the privilege of expiation in the form of a sin-offering to be brought to the Sanctuary.[78] Scriptural law makes it an obligation for one to take advantage of this privilege of expiation; he *must* bring the sin-offering.

It is in connection with this biblical prohibition that

the Mishnah raises the following problem: Two witnesses declare that a certain man has eaten the forbidden fat-portions (apparently unwittingly) and so he must bring the sin-offering; he counters however that he did so *deliberately* and so is exempt from the required offering. In such a case, concludes the Mishnah, we would have to accept his statement.[79]

The medieval commentators point out the consequences of the Mishnah's conclusions, namely, that by doing so we are allowing him to render himself a *rasha*, a wicked man. This, they explain, is unavoidable, for otherwise we would be in the position of coercing a man to bring an offering to the Holy Temple, which according to his own testimony has neither sanctity nor validity. True, the rabbinic court would not administer the lashes that Jewish law metes out to one who eats such fat deliberately;[80] nor is he considered to have incriminated himself sufficiently to have disqualified himself from being accepted as a witness in a judicial proceeding. Nevertheless, as far as the sin-offering is concerned, his self-damaging confession is accepted; for it is forbidden to have an unsanctified and an unnecessary offering brought to the Temple.[81] Or, better still, should we not regard him as a repentant sinner who does not *wish* to bring an unsanctified offering to the Temple?[82]

Thus, a consistent application of the law against self-incrimination is not to be pursued where it would force the confessed criminal to perform a sinful act or prevent him from fulfilling his sacred obligations.

By extension of this view, R. Jacob Algasi declared that any person confessing to a monetary obligation must be believed, for we look upon him as a repentant sinner desirous of returning money not rightfully his.[83]

In response to the query as to why the rabbinic rule, "A

man's own admission of guilt has the power of one hundred witnesses," was limited to monetary cases, the replies of both R. Jacob Algasi and of R. Joseph ibn Leb agree that this admission is not based on any credibility attributed to the confessing litigant and that therefore juridically it is not considered as a method of clarification subsumed under "evidence." The position taken by R. Aryeh Leib HaKohen is, however, that we have in this rule a fundamental and axiomatic method whereby a court may arrive at its decision.[84] Following R. Aryeh Leib, one would have to resort to either the rationale of Maimonides or to that of Radbaz in order to explain a man's credibility in money matters in contradistinction to his lack of credibility in criminal matters.

CHAPTER **VI**

Medieval Rabbinic Criminal Procedure

It is almost a superfluity to state that all the rabbinic jurists of the Middle Ages were steeped deeply in the talmudic tradition and faithfully continued the laws and practices of the Halakhah. Yet, despite the great reverence in which talmudic law was held, changes due to different political and economic conditions were inevitable. Halakhic adaptability and flexibility were greatly facilitated by the *hora'ath sha'ah,* "emergency" clause in B. Sanhedrin 46a.[1] Although this clause cannot explain adequately some of the wide departures of the rabbinic law of the Middle Ages from the rules contained in the Talmud itself—the new practice of putting witnesses to the oath, the serious modifications of a husband's (biblical) right to inherit his wife, the admissibility of testimony given by relatives, wives, and minors—it did serve as the underlying principle justifying startling innovations and drastic measures in criminal matters.

In a Hebrew volume entitled *Punishments After the Redaction of the Talmud,*[2] R. Simḥah Assaph has collected numerous passages illustrating the Jewish criminal law of medieval times. In his Introduction, the author points out the phenomenon of capital punishment even though capital jurisdiction had been suspended, according to the Talmud, forty years before the destruction of the second Holy Temple of Jerusalem, and the practice of levying fines in spite of the fact that the Talmud withholds such power from Jewish judges outside of Palestine. Modes of punishment were occasionally introduced that were previously unheard of in Jewish annals, such as the tearing off of a limb,[3] branding, and the shaving of head and beard; for the first time, we hear of prison sentences as a punishment,[4] debtor's prison and house arrest.[5]

Not mentioned in the Introduction, but of great significance to our study of the rabbinic law of criminal confessions, is a responsum of Ribash[6] (R. Isaac b. Shesheth Barfat [Perfet]: 1326 Valencia, Spain—1408 Algiers).[7] In order (1) to understand the responsum correctly, (2) to utilize it effectively as an accurate reflection of the place and time in which it was written, and not to be misled into dismissing it as a bizarre and rare exception, and (3) to enable us to draw the proper conclusions for the purposes of our study, we append the following brief historical introduction.

The law governing Spain of the fourteenth century was a hodgepodge of diverse codes, each code governing a different segment of the population: nobility and clergy, middle and lower classes, urban and rural populations, Jews and Moors. Each group comprised a different class, each class was governed by a different code, and each code had its own historical, legal and religious antecedents.

By royal authorization, all Jewish residents in a district —village, town, or city—were, with a few exceptions, compulsory members of the *aljama*, the Arabic-Spanish designation for an organized community (Hebrew: *qahal*). In the larger cities, the *aljamas* were well-organized, having a legislative council, judicial magistracies and executive officials, who were generally empowered by the sovereign to order and regulate the political, social and religious lives of their constituents, and who were permitted to exercise jurisdiction in cases of civil, criminal and ecclesiastical law.

The Jews were subject to a double system of legislation and control. On the one hand, the royal legislator or jurist freely admitted whole elements of talmudic law into the legal system that was to prevail within the *aljamas;* on the other hand, in relation to the remainder of the population and the sovereign, the general law, molded by the historic Roman, Visigothic and Canon influences and often seriously modified by the all-important local charters (*fueros*) of the cities and rural localities, reigned supreme. This does not mean, however, that each Jewish community was subject to the same law, for although the talmudic tradition was stable and essentially one to all of them, each *aljama-qahal* was subject to its own local charter often very different from that of another community. Jewish autonomy, although real and substantial, was always subject to royal control and limitation and often subject to royal scrutiny and interference.[8]

Rabbi Judah ben Asher, one of the leading authorities of the time, explains that Jewish courts trying capital cases serve two purposes: (1) They obviate the need for trial by a Gentile court and thereby save the life of many an accused who would otherwise have been sentenced to death. (2) They bring about the death of those who would have escaped under Spanish law, such as informers and the like.[9]

"The most dangerous criminal in the Spanish *juderia* [Jewish community]," writes a modern historian, "was the informer, or *malsin*. He was despised as a traitor and

dreaded as an enemy of society. The hatred which he in-
spired can be explained only by the panicky state of mind
of a community which lived in constant dread of lurking
danger. The informer, *malsin,* was essentially one who be-
trayed his people by denouncing the community or its
representatives to the general authorities; but the term
was broadened to include anyone who reported a violation
of the law, actual or alleged, to the government officials
and thereby jeopardized the person or property of his fellow Jew. The truth or falsity of the charge [of the in-
former] was not always material, nor even the good or bad
faith of the informer. The flagrant offense lay in dragging
in an outside jurisdiction, which notoriously had no sense
of mercy or justice where Jewish life and property were
involved. The hateful name, therefore, covered many
types. It included spies and sycophants. It embraced con-
spirators, high in the social and political scale, and malicious creatures of a more common brand. But it also included the person who aired his grievances in public and
sought justice and vindication from the general authorities instead of the Jewish courts and communal officials. . . .

"The curse of the informer plagued the life of the
juderia throughout its history and followed the unhappy
exiles in their wanderings after the final expulsion. No
one was too highly placed to be beyond his poisoned fangs.
Men of leading importance in their communities—Jewish
bailiffs, court physicians, diplomats and ministers of fi-
nance; distinguished rabbis who were universally beloved
and revered, like Alfasi, Nissim Gerundi, Barfat [Ribash]
and Hasdai Crescas—were the targets of venomous denun-
ciation. They were thrown into prison, their lives were in
grave danger and, with their fate, the existence of their
communities was at stake. . . ."[10]

It was these informers who brought about the most drastic departures from normative criminal Halakhah on the part of the rabbinic authorities, and the emergency measures invoked by these authorities represent the most persistent application and the widest extension of the *hora'ath sha'ah*, emergency principle.[11]

The case that R. Isaac b. Shesheth Barfat was called upon to decide was submitted to him by the *muqdamim* of Teruel. The *muqdamim*, corresponding to the *adelantados* (or *adenantades*) in the Spanish-Latin sources, were the officials of the administrative board of the Jewish community;[12] Teruel was a city in the province of Aragon.[13]

It appears that Reuben and his son were arrested by officers of the king on charges of theft and were handed over to the Jewish *muqdamim* for trial. Simeon, whose sister had been the victim of the theft, had undoubtedly initiated the charges against Reuben and his son for the crime and demanded their death. When judgment was delayed, he demanded vociferously that the trial be conducted by royal officials and (non-Jewish) city councilors; he thereby slandered the Jewish *muqdamim* and caused much (unspecified) damage to the Jewish *aljama-qahal*. The punishment that the heads of the Jewish community sought to mete out upon Simeon, the informer, was death, a penalty they were empowered to inflict under the royal "privileges" granted to them.[14] Although it was possible that Simeon was branded as an informer because he had Reuben and his son arrested by officers of the king rather than by officers of the Jewish community, it was more likely that his crime consisted in having aired his grievances in public with the specific intention of seeking justice and vindication from the general authorities instead of from the duly constituted Jewish courts and communal officials.[15] In any event, Simeon confessed to having sought to enlist "outside" help.

The following are extracts from the reply of Ribash:[16]

The first question. You are in doubt whether to listen to the informer's verbal confession before you admit the testimony of the witnesses testifying against him, and whether it makes any difference whether you accept his confession at all.

It is clear that in monetary cases we do not admit witnesses until the defendant has answered the charges of the plaintiff, for if the defendant admits liability he is rendered obligated to pay by his own acknowledgment of indebtedness. . . . Why then should the Court bother to listen to witnesses before it has heard the response of the defendant to the plaintiff? . . .

In capital cases, however, according to the strict letter of the law no heed is paid to a confession, for no one may be convicted and sentenced to death on the basis of his own words—only on the basis of the words of witnesses—and his confession makes no difference. . . . In these days however the Jewish Court is not permitted to judge capital cases except by authorization of the king,[17] and so *it is necessary to verify our verdicts also in the eyes of the non-Jewish judges of the land*[18] so that they should not suspect us of trying cases unlawfully and unjustly. Moreover, the fact that we do judge capital cases in these times, although capital jurisdiction has been suspended [talmudically] is due to the emergency needs of the times (צורך השעה), for the Jewish court may impose flagellation and pronounce capital sentences even when not warranted by the Torah when the times demand it (לפי צורך השעה)—even without full [talmudically required] evidence as long as there is convincing proof that the accused committed the crime. *This, then, is the reason we have been accepting confessions of criminals even in capital cases,* namely in order that the matter be clarified by his own statements in conjunction with additional items of proof although they do not constitute what the Talmud ordains as fully acceptable evidence. . . . It seems to me, therefore, that it is preferable that we listen to the confession of the culprit before we admit the witnesses so that we will then be able to question the witnesses concerning the details contained in words of the criminal . . . but this is not strictly required. . . .

As to the other parts of this question, namely if taking the confession of the accused incurs the suspicions of an *inquisitio,* it seems to me that you are hesitant, in view of the law which forbids an *inquisitio* in Aragon. My opinion is that inasmuch as there is an accuser [*i.e.,* Reuben] the law has not been violated, for *it only applies to the institution of an* inquisitio *against someone in the absence of an accuser.* . . . And I have seen here[19] that the heads of the community[20] have accepted the confession of an accused a number of times—as long as there was an accuser. Do not, however, rely on me in this matter since this is not my decision inasmuch as it is not ordained by the law of our Torah; *ask the Gentile scholars.* For if you are apprehensive in this matter, the decision is theirs and let them render it. Similarly, with regard to your question whether the "document under seal" (*privilegio*) of His Royal Highness suffices for the proceeding or not without incurring any danger to the [Jewish] court or the *qahal,* this, too, is their decision.

The second question. Is the court obligated to provide an informer with an attorney (טוֹעֵן) to prepare his defense or to appoint an authorized representative (מוּרְשָׁה); and, if so, should he be so provided before his confession or after? For he has requested an attorney just as his opponent has one.

In monetary cases there is a dispute among the *Geonim* of blessed memory whether a defendant may appoint an אַנְטְלֵר, which is an attorney or authorized representative. . . . Anyway, this seems to be the case only in money matters where there is a distinction between plaintiff and defendant. . . . In capital cases, however, if a distinction is to be made, the opposite would be true, namely that the accuser

may not appoint an advocate since he is not making any
monetary demands that may be transferred by legal authorization; the accused . . . however, may appoint an advocate
who would argue in his behalf and defend him for we always
pay heed to anyone who comes in defense of the accused[21]. . . .
However, nowadays that we have been accepting confessions
made by people accused of crimes, *if the court decides to
listen to the confession before an attorney is appointed, so
that he should not instruct his client to make false statements, it may do so.* . . .

In answer to the third question, R. Isaac b. Shesheth
does not agree to the release of the alleged informer from
prison upon the putting up of satisfactory bail. In answer
to the fourth question, the point is made that one accused
of informing need not be confronted with his accusers. In
his fifth answer, R. Isaac warns the *muqdamim* that, although they have the *privilegio* of trying cases in accordance with Jewish law, they should be careful not to do anything that could serve as a pretext for the Gentiles to cause
any trouble to them or to the Jewish community.[22] Incidentally, after his most illuminating discussion of the
Jewish-Spanish practice, R. Isaac came to the conclusion
that the accused had committed no act of informing for
which he should be put to death, for his appeal to the
king's judgment could be looked upon as justified. "Nevertheless, since the consequences of his act have caused harm
and expense to the community, . . . he cannot be acquitted of having disturbed and injured the public welfare,
. . . and he deserves to be punished as the court sees fit,
whether by flogging, excommunication or bans, or by financial penalties and prohibition. . . ."[23]

In quoting the reply of Ribash, Assaph has with good
reason italicized the words, וצריך לאמת הדין אף בעיני שופטי
הארץ שלא מבריתנו, "and so it is necessary to verify [or,

justify] our verdicts also in the eyes of the non-Jewish judges of the land." In granting the Jewish courts the power to punish offenses against morality (with specific concern regarding sexual transgressions between Jewish men and Christian women) and to combat the plague of informing, the royal edicts[24] laid down detailed rules of procedure and defined the categories of capital and corporal penalties. Cases were to be recorded in the Catalonian language; sentences were executed by the Gentile bailiffs and their police. Where actual rules of procedure are not given, the judges were instructed to act in accordance with reason and law. Inasmuch as the rules of procedure decreed were the product of the Roman, Canon and Spanish legal systems, and "reason and law" were defined in accordance with the standards[25] of fourteenth century Spain, it is of little wonder that elements of Spanish inquisitorial legal procedure play so prominent a role in Jewish-Spanish court practice and modes of execution.

Thus, in a murder trial in which there was much circumstantial evidence against the accused although insufficient legal testimony according to talmudic standards to warrant a conviction, R. Judah b. Asher instructed the Jewish court of Cordova that the defendant should be punished in one of a number of ways, depending on the weight of the evidence. If the murder could be fully established, with legal testimony, the defendant should be sentenced to die. If the testimony was reliable but technically blemished, both his hands should be cut off. If the witnesses were disqualified because of kinship, his left hand should be cut off. If all the witnesses were invalidated, but it was public knowledge that he was guilty, he should be banished from the community.[26]

Indeed, in another responsum of R. Judah b. Asher, we

approach the closest approximation of torture as a judicial tool ever administered by a court of Jewish authorities. He records the following decision rendered by his father, Rabbenu Asher (*Rosh*) :

> Question: Whether we may punish crimes on the basis of one witness or not.
>
> It is well known that according to Torah-law they cannot be put to death; but since the times demand it we impose flagellation and pronounce capital sentences even when not warranted by the Torah, not with the intention of disregarding the Torah but in order to safeguard it [B. Sanhedrin 46a]. Certainly this is true with regard to the woman with whom you are dealing who is known to have played the harlot previously; she is to be punished on the basis of persistent rumors that cannot be denied. This holds all the more true if there is one witness who corroborates said rumor; for we find in the Talmud that a rumor carries weight like one witness, so that we have two "witnesses." Moreover, we may justifiably whip her till she expires; perhaps thereby the words of the one witness will be corroborated. This is all the more true inasmuch as the long-standing practice in Toledo has been to flagellate and to whip, not in accordance with Torah-law, to safeguard the Torah and to remove evil. The decision is the same for the adulterer as for the adulteress to inflict upon them bodily pain on the basis of persistent rumor; *a fortiori* when one witness corroborates said rumor, it is proper to remove evil from your midst as I have written in another responsum.[27]

This responsum of Rabbenu Asher is all the more interesting for it teaches us that the *hora'ath sha'ah* principle was not limited in application to emergency measures against informers; it permeated the judicial procedure of the authorities combatting crimes which were regarded as serious breaches of morality and public order. Moreover, when certain practices typical of the inquisitorial procedure were eschewed, it was apparently because they were forbidden by the Gentile authorities. In the responsum of R. Isaac b. Shesheth to the *muqdamim* of Teruel, mention was made of instituting proceedings against someone without a specific accuser as being an *inquisitio;* this had been forbidden under the *Privilegium Generale* of 1283 and by the *fueros* of Aragon, although both the kings and their officials themselves broke these laws from time to time. And when specific criticism of illegal forms of inquisition is levelled by R. Judah b. Asher himself—he rejects the prouncing of a *ḥerem* (ban) on anyone who knows anything reflecting upon the acceptability of the witnesses so that he come forth and testify, for such procedure is characteristically inquisitorial and forbidden—this criticism seems to stem from certain limitations placed on the Jewish courts by Spanish law.[28]

It is remarkable, however, that even during this period, when inquisitorial elements found their way into Jewish courts, almost every responsum contains a reminder to the questioner of the differences between the revered talmudic tradition and the present Spanish-Jewish practices. Moreover, this talmudic tradition remained the norm both in theory and in practice in all other Jewish communities throughout the Middle Ages, as we shall see from the numerous cases to which it was applied in the Responsa literature, codes and commentaries, which will be cited frequently in the ensuing chapters.

PART THREE
A JURIDICAL PRESENTATION

CHAPTER **VII**

Range of Applicability

In Jewish law, the rule against self-incrimination is remarkable not only in the uniqueness of its extreme position but in the pervasiveness of its applicability as well. It applies both to biblical and rabbinic law, to female as well as male defendants, and to the whole gamut of violations of the law from the severest of felonies to the lightest of infractions.

BIBLICAL AND RABBINIC LAW

We have had occasion[1] to refer to the distinction in Jewish law between biblical law, explicitly stated in the Torah or the product of rabbinic exegesis of Scripture,* and rabbinic law, the positive enactments and the negative precautionary measures that the Rabbis themselves legislated.[2]

There are, for example, a large number of acts that are biblically permitted but have been rabbinically proscribed either to protect the spirit of scriptural law, or for other

---

* Also included are *"halakhoth* to Moses from Sinai," oral Sinaitic traditions with no basis in the text of Scripture.

cogent reasons. A person who commits such acts would, according to biblical standards, not come under the category of a *rasha,* a violator of the law who is thereby rendered unfit to give testimony in court. However, he is disqualified by the standards of rabbinic law, which, though of lesser sanctity, are invariably of a stricter nature.[3]

Numerous authorities have pointed out that (1) not only does a man's confession to having committed a crime not render him a *rasha,* according to biblical law; it does not render him a *rasha,* disqualified to act as a witness, according to the stricter rabbinic standards.[4] Moreover, (2) this holds true for confessions of having violated biblical as well as rabbinic precepts.[5] In all cases אין אדם משים עצמו רשע, "No man may render himself a *rasha.*"

MALE AND FEMALE DEFENDANTS

A woman, too, cannot incriminate herself. This is the unanimous opinion of all rabbinic authorities who deal with the question directly or indirectly.[6]

The reason for the blanket application of the law against self-incrimination is rather obvious. Whether (1) the law which was violated is biblical or rabbinic, or (2) the disqualification is of biblical or rabbinic force, or (3) the accused is male or female, the rules of evidence remain the same. The question facing the court is whether the law was in fact violated; this question may be answered juridically only by two qualified witnesses. A person, man or woman, is not qualified to testify concerning himself.[7]

THE LAW OF THE NON-JEW

According to the Rabbis, the Divine Torah legislated for the Gentile world as well as for the Jewish people. In some respects, it was more lenient with the Gentile; in other respects it was stricter. Thus, on the one hand, in contrast to the Jew who was commanded to obey 613 precepts, the Gentile was subject to only seven, the so-called "Noahide," commandments: (1) not to worship idols, (2) not to blaspheme, (3) to establish courts of justice, (4) not to kill, (5) not to commit adultery and incest, (6) not to rob, (7) not to eat flesh cut from a living animal.[8]

On the other hand, it was easier to convict a Gentile of a crime than it was to convict a Jew. Thus, the Talmud,[9] quoting from the *Book of Agadatha* of the School of Rab, describes the following court procedure for the Gentile world:[10]

"A Noahide is sentenced to death by a court consisting of one judge"—as opposed to twenty-three judges for a Jew; ". . . by the testimony of one witness"—as opposed to two for a Jew; ". . . without a warning prior to committing the crime"—indispensable in order to convict a Jew; ". . . even through the testimony of a kinsman"—who would be disqualified to testify were he and the defendant Jewish.

Could a Gentile be executed on the basis of a self-incriminating confession?

Rabbi David Frankel of Dessau, in his famous commentary, *Qorban HaEdah,* records a reading in the Palestinian Talmud[11] which states that Rabbi Judah ben Pazi added another detail in which the judicial procedure in the trial of a Gentile was different from that of a Jew, namely, he could be sentenced to death on the basis of his own testimony in court. This reading appears to be unique, finding no parallel or corroborating statement in any part of both Talmuds, nor is it recorded in Maimonides' Code. Indeed, the only early authoritative work which states explicitly that a Gentile may incriminate himself is the *Sepher HaḤinukh* (Precept 26).[12]

Logic, however, does support the *Ḥinukh.* To convict a

Jew, we must have the testimony of two witnesses; moreover, a relative is disqualified. Thus, a Jew could never
be convicted on the basis of his own testimony. A Gentile,
however, may be convicted on the basis of the testimony of
one witness, and the witness may be a kinsman; hence, he
himself, his closest "kinsman," could also testify against
himself.

We may counter, however, and say that regarding himself, a man is never considered a "witness"; and, since the
Talmud does insist that a Gentile, too, must be convicted
on the basis of the testimony of a "witness," though it be
one, a "witness" it must be.[13] Thus, a Gentile, too, may
not incriminate himself.[14]

Or, perhaps we may say that if the courts are to accept
the testimony of a Gentile against himself, their action is
self-defeating and can never lead to conviction; for he has
thereby rendered himself first a *rasha,* and a *rasha* is disqualified from acting as a witness.[15]

Though there does not seem to be any authority who
disagrees with *Sepher HaḤinukh* explicitly, it seems to me
that R. Levi Gersonides (*Ralbag*), by implication, maintains that the Halakhah is not as the *Ḥinukh* has said it is.

Gersonides[16] explains that David had the Amalekite
stranger put to death on the basis of his own admission to
having killed Saul *not* in accordance with Talmudic law,
but, rather, as an emergency measure—"so that people
should not take regicide lightly." Now, according to Gersonides, the Amalekite stranger was a Gentile. If this is
so, we may ask, why does Gersonides characterize the
Amalekite's conviction based on his own admission of
guilt as contrary to Talmudic law? It is clear that Gersonides held the opinion that Talmudic law did not accept
self-incriminating testimony as a valid basis for the conviction of a Gentile. A Gentile court which executed a

man on the basis of his own confession would, in his opinion, be violating God's law.

SUBJECTION TO AN OATH

The role of the oath in Jewish legal procedure is an intricate one, and the delineation of its place in judicial proceedings would take us far beyond the scope of our present study. Suffice it to say that there are a number of situations where the litigant is subjected to an oath to his advantage, *i.e.,* usually with the result that, having taken the oath, he is acquitted of all obligation to pay. With regard to such oaths, Maimonides' summation of talmudic law is important for our purposes.

> He who is *suspect* with regard to an oath may not be subjected to an oath, whether pentateuchal or rabbinical or informal. Even if the plaintiff wishes to have the defendant who is so suspect subjected to an oath, no heed is to be paid to him. . . .
>
> A man does not become suspect until witnesses come and testify that he has committed a transgression which disqualifies him. But if one confesses by his own mouth that he is suspect and that he has committed a transgression which disqualifies him, although his confession may not be altogether disregarded and it is improper to constitute him a witness *at the outset,* if he has become liable to an oath he is subjected thereto, since we may say to him, "If what you say is true, swear, the fact that you have committed a transgression notwithstanding, there being no prohibition against you to swear to the truth; and if what you say is false, make an admission to your adversary."
>
> But he who has become suspect through testimony of witnesses may not be trusted to swear (italics supplied) .[17]

Thus, "suspect with regard to an oath" and "disqualified from bearing testimony" follow the same rules in matters of self-incrimination.[18]

The *Aharonim*, later medieval authorities,[19] explain that the expression "at the outset" means that a confessed sinner or criminal will not be approached and invited to act as a witness to a legal act which requires the presence of constitutive witnesses, *e.g.*, a wedding ceremony or divorce proceedings. But if *de facto* such a man did act as a witness, his attestation is valid and his testimony is acceptable.

The earlier medieval authorities[20] modify the law by distinguishing between one who takes an oath and thereby exempts himself from payment and one who takes an oath and thereby collects:[21]

> Moreover, when do we not believe a man who confesses that he is suspect with regard to an oath? If he was to have taken the oath and been exempt from payment. But if he was to have sworn and collected, we believe him; for he is thereby causing himself a monetary loss, and in such matters a man's acknowledgment of liability has the power of one hundred witnesses.

PENALTIES AND COMPENSATION

We have already seen[22] that pecuniary cases are divided into two types: regular civil cases and those in which fines are involved. In the former, the Halakhah declares that the testimony of a litigant to his own detriment has the same power as the deposition of one hundred witnesses. In the latter, however, the infliction of penalties is a manifestation of judicial power. Such judicial power must be exercised in accordance with the rule controlling court procedure, מודה בקנס פטור, "He who confesses to an act the commission of which makes one liable to a fine is exempted from paying the penalty."[23]

Thus, the exclusionary principle under discussion, that a self-incriminating statement on the part of the defendant may not be used against him, also comes into play in cases involving penalties, *i.e.,* cases in which the award against the defendant is not equal to the debt he incurred or the damages he inflicted—indicating that the payment ordered by the court (which in Jewish law is to be paid to the plaintiff) is penal and does not represent the loss suffered by the plaintiff.

In cases where the component parts are both civil and penal, a confession of guilt would render the confessant liable on the civil aspect of the case and exempt from liability on the penal aspect. Typical of these cases is theft. Conviction for theft renders the thief liable for double the value of the stolen article.[24] Admission of guilt on the part of the thief exempts him from paying the fine. He is, however, obligated either to return the stolen article or, if lost or destroyed, to pay for it. This latter obligation is a compensatory one and not a penal one; hence his confession concerning it has the power of one hundred witnesses.

This distinction between compensation and penalty is further sharpened and clarified by the following passage in Maimonides:[25]

> The rule that he who made an admission with respect to a penalty is quit applies only where he admitted the claim which made him subject to the penalty, as where he said, "I inflicted personal injury upon this man."
>
> But if he said, "I inflicted personal injury upon this man and he produced witnesses against me in court and I was adjudged liable to pay him so much for his injury," he is liable to pay.

Once the defendant was adjudged by the courts as liable to pay his victim for the injury inflicted, the penalty becomes a debt which he now owes the injured party. Acknowledgment of indebtedness, regardless of the source of such indebtedness (*i.e.*, even if the source was penal), is regarded as ממון, compensatory; hence, the rule הודאת בעל דין כמאה עדים, *i.e.*, that the confession has the power of one hundred witnesses, applies.[26]

(The Talmud[27] reports a controversy concerning the status of a man who first confessed to an act the commission of which makes one liable to a fine and subsequently was charged with the crime by witnesses. Rab holds that the exemption the man achieved by his confession persists even in the face of witnesses, and Samuel is of the opinion that the exemption is thereby overturned. It has been suggested that their disagreement hinges on their respective interpretations of the man's confession. Rab construes the confession as an act of repentance[28] and therefore obviates any need for a penalty. Samuel looks upon the exemption as stemming from the traditional view of confession as insufficient for judicial conviction;[29] hence, when two qualified witnesses arrive and supply sufficient grounds for a conviction, the exemption falls away.)[30]

Incidentally, it appears that, according to Rashi, the death sentence and the infliction of lashes are also "penalties," and therefore the biblical exemption of a confessant criminal applies equally to the penalties of death and flagellation. The Tosaphoth point out that this interpretation of the Halakhah's refusal to punish a man on the basis of his confession[31] is fraught with difficulties. The most obvious one is based upon the acceptance of Rab's ruling that the man, having once confessed, may never be penalized even if two witnesses were to come subsequently to attest to his criminal act.[32] Murderers, by confessing, could thus escape prosecution forever—this is unheard of.[33]

CONFLICTING PRINCIPLES

We have seen that Jewish law divides the entire area of jurisprudence into two parts, each governed by a different principle: (1) In criminal law (including fines and penalties), the basic principle is that a man's statements regarding himself cannot be used to bring about his conviction and punishment (by death, lashes or fines) and to disqualify him from acting as a witness or from taking an oath in court. (2) In civil law (concerned with problems of *mammon,* monetary compensation), the basic principle is that a man's admission of guilt-liability has the power of one hundred witnesses.

Should these two principles conflict, their immutable character is such that each must be given its due consideration regardless of the logical implications of the other.

For example, if a man confesses that he has committed an act such as theft which renders him a *rasha,* and, as a consequence thereof, he is liable to pay his neighbor compensatory damages, the criminal code frees him from any taint of character at the same time that the civil code obligates him to pay or restore the stolen article. Again, if a man admits that he committed arson on Yom Kippur and destroyed his neighbor's house, though he will go unpunished for the crime of violating the sacred day and will not be disbarred from acting as a valid, untainted witness, nevertheless he must compensate for the damage he has caused,[34] even though the criminal and civil elements are interconnected and the civil liability is a direct consequence of the criminal act.

In order to clarify this procedure of "splitting the confession," we present extended extracts from a case that took place in a Rabbinical Court[35] in modern Israel.* It will incidentally serve as an apt illustration of capable application of rabbinic law to modern problems.

Case No. 226
District Court of Tel Aviv/Jaffa

Mr. A., the defendant, and Mrs. B., the plaintiff, both admit that they lived together as man and wife from 1941 to 1951 although they were never legally married to each other, and although Mrs. B. had not been divorced from her legal husband, Mr. B., until 1947. (Mr. B. was a resident of Tel Aviv until 1948. From 1941 to 1948, he would occasionally meet with Mrs. B. to discuss problems relating to their child. In 1948, Mr. B. moved to the United States.) In 1945, Mrs. B. bore Mr. A. a daughter. All these facts are openly admitted by both litigants; some are attested to by legal documents.

Mr. A. and Mrs. B. have since separated. Plaintiff demands financial support for her (their) child, but refuses to grant the father visiting rights because he had deliberately revealed the illegitimacy of the daughter and thereby ruined her reputation and made her chances for marriage much more difficult. The court found itself confronted also with the problem of clarifying the status of the daughter.

The court decided that without a corroborating statement from Mr. B., the legal husband of Mrs. B. at the time that she gave birth to the child, the statements of Mr. A. and Mrs. B. are not sufficient to render the child a bastard. This is especially true inasmuch as there exists the possibility, no matter how remote, that she had actually been fathered by Mrs. B.'s legal husband.

Now, in monetary matters a man's acknowledgment of obligation is equal to the testimony of one hundred witnesses. His statement that the child is his daughter is tan-

---

* The rabbinical courts have jurisdiction over cases involving the personal status of the Jewish citizens of Israel.

tamount to a confession that he is obligated to support her financially. At this point, however, the difficulty arises that a statement that the child is his daughter is simultaneously a confession that he committed adultery—and no man can render himself wicked.

Citing Ran, Kethuboth 72a; Ritba, *ibid.* and Makkoth 3a; Rashba, Resp. 231 (Vol. II) ; and *Beth Yoseph, Ḥoshen Mishpat* 34 quoting *Sepher HaTerumoth (Sha'ar* 21, Pt. B, para. 3), the court made a distinction between testimony and disqualification on the one hand, to which the injunction against self-incrimination does apply, and claims and admissions on the other hand, in which such an injunction does not apply and in which the self-incriminating acknowledgment of monetary obligations was nevertheless valid and binding.[36]

Our case is more complicated, however. How can we obligate Mr. A. to support the child on the basis of the acknowledgment of paternity which the court itself has rejected? We are faced with an inner contradiction: We have assumed that she is not his daughter since his statement to that effect is unacceptable. On the other hand, we are obligating him to support her because he has admitted that she is his daughter. If she is his daughter, she is illegitimate—this we have refused to accept. Now if she is not illegitimate and not his daughter, there is no basis upon which to obligate him to support her. Can we accept a confession of monetary obligation based upon a relationship which itself is rejected?

Indeed we can. On the basis of Maimonides, *Nashim— Yibbum* 3:4, the comments thereon by *Maggid Mishneh,* and *Responsa of Maharashdam, Eben HaEzer,* Resp. 233, we may say that although the man's declaration of paternity is not accepted, we are not prevented from placing upon him a financial obligation based upon that very declaration.

Such legal reasoning, apparently self-contradictory *ad absurdum,* is best explained by an analysis of the interpretation Jewish law places on a man's confession to financial obligation.

When a man admits in court that he owes someone money, he is obligated to pay even though his admission is not a true one, nay even though the court knows that such an obligation never existed; Ritba, Kethuboth 102a, Baba Meẓia 46a; *Nimmuqei Yoseph,* Baba Bathra 149a.

The *Qeẓoth HaḤoshen,* 40:1, identifies this as the form of transfer of ownership mentioned in the Talmud, Baba Bathra 149a, as *Oditha,*[37] whereby the confession itself constitutes one of the recognized methods of acquisition or alienation of property. If this is true, the question of the "truth" of the confession is a moot one.

Moreover, even if we do not accept the explanation of *Qeẓoth HaḤoshen,* the patent falsehood of a confession would nonetheless render the confessant financially liable. For in financial matters a man's confession is the greatest source of certainty and the most powerful basis for proof, greater than any other proof which contradicts it and more powerful than any other fact or source of information available. When a man declares that he is liable, the obligation is absolute—nothing can controvert it. Thus, the rule that a man's admission of guilt in a monetary matter has the power of one hundred witnesses really means that it is of *greater* power than the testimony of one hundred witnesses (*Responsa of Rashba,* Vol. III, Resp. 67; Rema, Ḥoshen Mishpat 79:1.) [38]

Thus, since even in the event that the known facts of the matter oppose the words of the confessant the obligation based upon the confession nevertheless stands, then it follows *a fortiori* that where there is a contradiction to the confession the obligation based upon that confession will certainly stand; for no contradiction can be greater than that of a known fact. Therefore, in our case, the above-mentioned contradiction does not prevent an award of support to the child based upon the confession of the defendant.

The decisions of the court were: (a) According to Jewish religious law, the child is to be considered legitimate. (b) The defendant must provide sixty Israeli pounds monthly support of the child. (c) On the grounds explained by the court, the defendant's plea for visiting rights with the child was denied.

November 11, 1954

MINOR INFRACTIONS

We have thus far described how a man's "testimony" against himself cannot be used to convict him of a capital crime, to sentence him to lashes, to debar him from ever acting as a witness, to disqualify him from taking an oath in court, and, finally, to render him liable to pay a fine.

It remains for us to point out that rabbinic law goes even further; it will not allow a man to "testify" to his own detriment *in any manner whatsoever*.[39]

(1) In Jewish law, deceiving one's fellow-man—without, however, perpetrating an actual act of theft or embezzlement—is regarded as a religio-moral offense outside the jurisdiction of the courts. Nevertheless, a man's admission to an act of deceit is unacceptable.[40] Of course, according to those authorities who maintain that such acts brand the deceitful person a *rasha,* an out-and-out sinner,[41] the rule against self-incrimination obviously applies to him with all its force.

(2) "Witnesses, whose signatures are affixed to a note, who state that the debtor was a minor at the time of the loan are not believed; for since the law is that witnesses are presumed to have signed only if the loan was made by an adult and it is incumbent upon them to make proper inquiry, among other things, whether he is in fact an adult, any witnesses who did not so investigate are blameworthy.

Hence, they are not to be believed, for no man may render himself a *rasha*."[42]

(3) "The ancients placed the ban of excommunication upon any Jew who should deceive his fellow-Jew by means of pawns for security, claiming that they belong to a Gentile (and thereby obtain a loan on interest—otherwise forbidden). Therefore, no man is believed when, desiring to evade the payment of interest, he says to his creditor at the time of payment, 'I deceived you; the pawn is mine, and so the interest I owe you cannot be legally recovered,' for no man may render himself a *rasha*."[43] Thus, no man may testify to his own detriment even to incur upon himself the ban of excommunication.

(4) No man may be rendered subject to any punishment or any stigma attached to his name as "informer" on the basis of his own confession. He is, of course, liable to pay for all *monetary* damages his act of informing incurred; for where money is involved, his admission of guilt has the power of one hundred witnesses.[44]

(5) No man may lower himself in the eyes of others by admitting that he did not perform a ritual act in the most preferable manner, though such laxity carries with it neither legal nor religious sanctions.[45]

(6) A man may not admit that he was unable to lay down his life as an act of supreme sacrifice in the name of his religion; he may not confess that he succumbed to threats of force and, for fear of his life, violated the laws of God. Now, succumbing under such circumstances, surely does not render him a *rasha* whose testimony will no longer be acceptable in court. Yet, inasmuch as such words would tend to lower him in the esteem of his fellow Jews, for he did not live up to the standards set up by Torah law (indeed, standards for saints and martyrs), he may not utter them against himself.[46] This extreme posi-

tion, however, is seriously questioned and rejected by many authorities.[47]

SELF-INCRIMINATION AND THE IMMUNITY OF WITNESSES

The inadmissibility of self-incriminating statements in court raises the following problem: If a witness in the course of his testimony incriminates *himself*, what is the status of this testimony of his? Is it acceptable or not? This problem, raised in the Talmud,[48] was the subject of controversy among the *Amoraim:*

> Two witnesses testified against Bar Binithus. One said, "He lent money on interest in my presence." The other said "He lent me[49] money on interest." Raba thereupon disqualified Bar Binithus from ever acting as a witness (and punished him for his infraction as well).
>
> But how could Raba have rendered such a decision? Did not he himself rule elsewhere that a borrower on interest is unfit to act as a witness? Consequently the second witness himself is a transgressor and the Torah said: "Do not accept the wicked as a witness."[50]
>
> Raba, in accepting the second witness' testimony against Bar Binithus, was acting in accordance with another principle of his; for Raba said: "Every man is a kinsman unto himself, and no man may render himself a *rasha.*" (Consequently his evidence is valid only with regard to the lender but not to himself, on the principle that we consider only half of his testimony as evidence.)

R. Joseph (B. Sanhedrin 9b) and the anonymous *Amora* of the above passage maintain that if we are to believe the words of the witness who has included a self-incriminating statement in his testimony, he has rendered himself a *rasha,* a transgressor, and has consequently disqualified himself from acting as a witness. If, on the other hand, we refuse on general principles to accept self-incriminating statements, then obviously we must reject his testimony. Thus, in any event, his testimony is completely inadmissible.[51]

Raba proposes a novel solution to our dilemma: פלגינן דיבורא, "we split his speech"—we divide his testimony into its two component parts: To the extent that it deposes that the defendant committed sodomy or lent money on interest, the testimony is valid and acted upon; to the extent that the witness is incriminating himself as a party to the crime, it is stricken from the record.[52] The witness thereby retains his credibility on the one hand, and on the other hand he remains immune from prosecution as long as two independent eyewitnesses do not appear in court to testify against him.[53]

Raba's approach, as opposed to that of R. Joseph, prevails in Jewish law. Thus, in the Code of Maimonides,[54] it is written:

> If A testifies that B loaned money on interest, and C testifies, "He (B) made a loan to me on interest," B is disqualified on the evidence of A and C. As to C, though he admits that he contracted a loan on interest, he cannot incriminate himself (literally, he cannot render himself a *rasha*). He is accounted trustworthy with regard to B but not with regard to himself.

We have thus arrived at a form of immunity of witnesses in the Talmud. This immunity, we must be careful to point out, however, is a limited one, for a man is immune from prosecution based on his testimony concerning others; it falls away should other witnesses come to testify. This is in marked contrast to American legal procedure in which the law against involuntary self-incrimination has been invoked innumerable times to protect a witness from being forced to testify concerning others.[55] "I refuse to testify concerning *him* on the grounds that my testimony may tend to incriminate *me*" has become a refrain familiar to the ears of investigating Congressional committeemen. In accordance with rabbinic law, such statements could never be made. On the contrary, witnesses are duty-bound to tell all they know;[56,57] any self-incriminating details will simply be disregarded by the judges.

The principle of "splitting the speech" is a highly intricate one, and a thorough examination of it would take us far beyond the scope of this study. For our purposes it is sufficient to cite one example of testimony that cannot be divided into its component, valid and self-incriminating parts. We shall see that in such an eventuality, Raba would agree with R. Joseph that the entire testimony is inadmissible.

> Mishnah: If witnesses said, "The signatures on this document are ours, but we were forced to sign, we were minors, we were disqualified witnesses,"* they are believed. (Since it is they who at the first instance confirm their signatures, they are also believed in the attendant reservation made by them in regard thereto.) [58]
>
> Gemara: . . . Rami b. Ḥama said: This Mishnah holds true only when the witnesses said, "We were forced to sign by threats on our lives," but if they said, "We were forced to sign by threats against our money," they are not believed, because no one may render himself a *rasha,* a wicked man.[59]

The point of Rami b. Ḥama's distinction is that although the commandments of the Torah are generally suspended when a man's life is in danger, they must be observed when a man's property is threatened. To have

* Because of kinship or criminal conduct.

falsely affixed their signatures on a document and thereby aided in the unlawful deprivation of a man's property in order to save their own money is a criminal act, and their confession to having done so cannot be accepted by the courts. As a matter of fact, R. Joseph Qaro[60] notes that such a confession is rejected even if the witnesses expostulate and claim that it is being made as an act of repentance.[61] Acts of repentance and their genuineness, it is felt, are not within the province of a human tribunal to judge and evaluate, "for man looketh on the outward appearance, but the Lord looketh on the heart" (I Samuel 16:7).

As far as the procedure of "splitting the speech" is concerned, R. Nissim b. Reuben (*Ran*) points out that it is inapplicable in this case. One cannot accept the first part of the statement of the witnesses, "The signatures on the document are ours, but we were forced to sign," and reject the second part which contains the self-incriminating detail, ". . . by threats against our money"; for how can their declaration that they were "forced" be allowed to stand alone? "Forced" is meaningless unless we know whether they were forced to sign falsely under the threat of death—in which case the Torah permits them to have done so—or whether they were forced by threats of loss of money—in which case the Torah forbids them to have done so and brands them as *reshaim*, "wicked," and unfit to act as witnesses. Thus, "forced . . . by threats against our money" is one statement, indivisible and "unsplittable." Under such circumstances, Raba, too, would agree that their entire testimony carries no weight in court.[62]

CHAPTER VIII

Confessions Accompanied by Corroborating Factors

Hitherto we have discussed the Jewish law against self-incrimination in general terms, that is under the general assumption that the only basis upon which the defendant's own guilt may be established is his own admission of blame or his own confession to the crime. We must now turn our attention to cases where there are circumstances or indications which substantially strengthen the probability of his guilt. These indications may contribute to the positive corroboration of his own guilt. For example: (1) there is the corroborating testimony of *one* witness, or (2) there are factors which give a reasonable indication of the sincerity and authenticity of the defendant's admission of guilt.

In addition, there may be circumstances which, though they may not serve as positive corroboration of the confession, tend to weaken any basis for *not* accepting the defendant's confession. For example: (3) the defendant's presumption of innocence has been seriously shaken, or

(4) the confessant's present status is not affected by his statements.

Does the law against self-incrimination obtain in these cases also?

THE CORROBORATING TESTIMONY OF ONE WITNESS

Some authorities maintain that the rule against self-incrimination does not apply where the self-incriminating statement is supported by the testimony of a single witness. The question comes up in the context of cases where a person confessed to having committed an act which renders him a *rasha,* unfit to act as a witness, and then is subsequently called upon to testify in an unrelated matter. If his original confession had been corroborated by the deposition of a single witness, he is thereafter truly disqualified. For though one witness alone could not disqualify him nor could he be disqualified on the basis of his own statements, the combination of both does have such power.[1] The matter, however, is disputed,[2] and we have already presented our interpretation of the dispute.[3]

Under no circumstances, however, could a man's confession be combined with the testimony of a single witness to convict him of a capital crime.[4]

For purposes of protecting public morals, however, extra-halakhic measures were sometimes taken. In Babylonia of the eighth century we find the following decision:

> If a man and a married woman admit that they have sinned, we pay no attention to them, for they are conspiring to arrange for her divorce in order that they may get married.[5] The man, however, should be put to the lash; but not the woman. She must remain married to her husband, and

were she to undergo lashes she would be forbidden to continue to live with her husband.[6]

If a witness, even *one* witness, were to corroborate the statement made by the man who confessed to having sinned with his neighbor's wife, the husband must divorce his wife. The adulterer is given unlimited lashes as prescribed by rabbinical (not biblical) law, and his beard and head are to be shaven; the head of the woman is also to be shaven, and she, too, is to be given (rabbinical) lashes.[7]

FACTORS POINTING TO THE AUTHENTICITY OF THE CONFESSION

(1) We consider first the case of men who confessed to an act which could render them *reshaim,* unfit to testify. The judges are convinced of the truth of their allegation concerning themselves, for inasmuch as the confession is irrelevant to the confessants they see that there was no reason to lie. Are they to be declared *reshaim* and is their testimony with regard to others to be rejected?

The question arises in the following case:

Reuben produces a promissory note in court; the signatures of the witnesses have as yet not been validated. The witnesses, summoned to appear in person, state that they recall the loan made by Reuben to Simeon and attest to the authenticity of their signatures. They add, however, that at the time they had affixed their signatures, they were technically *reshaim* due to criminal acts they had previously committed. But they are confident that this will have no bearing on the validity of the document in question, for they have proof (which they produce) that they have since repented of their crimes, made full restitution, and have subsequently been readmitted into the good graces of society.[8]

Now, the judges are convinced that the intention of

these men is to attest to the validity of the note. The fact that they bring proof that they are now respectable and law-abiding citizens indicates that they are certain that their attestation is valid. Untutored in the law, they do not realize that their statements which seem to them to be irrelevant to the case tend to actually *invalidate* the document.

Should they be believed?

R. Joseph ibn Migash answers in the affirmative. When do we say that no man may render himself a *rasha?* When we do not know his motives, and we fear lest his purpose be to destroy either the validity of the note or his own reputation. But when it is clear that he is telling us the truth (as in our case, for the witnesses could have achieved the validation of the note by merely keeping silent concerning their former criminal status), then it behooves us to accept his statements and to invalidate the document.[9]

R. Moses Naḥmanides (*Ramban*) and R. Aaron HaLevi (*R'ah*) demur. Truth and certainty do not enter into the matter. No man's statement rendering himself a *rasha* can have any status before the judicial bar; Jewish law simply throws it out of court. The document is valid.[10]

It should be borne in mind that R. Joseph ibn Migash, a disciple of Alfasi, was the teacher and master of Maimonides' father. It is therefore most likely that it was to the aforementioned position taken by ibn Migash that Maimonides was indebted* for his psychological interpretation of the law against self-incrimination presented in Chapter V of this study.[11] Conversely, it would appear that the position taken by Rabbis Naḥmanides and Aaron

---

* Concerning ibn Migash, Maimonides writes, "To anyone who studies his words and the depth of his mind, the man's understanding of the Talmud is terrifying (awe-inspiring), so that one may almost say about him, 'There was never any king like him' (II Kings 23:25) in his method of interpretation and his type of exegesis" (*Introduction to the Mishnah*).

HaLevi is best explained along the philosophical lines taken by Rabbi David ben Zimra.[12]

(2) A man's self-incriminating statement may be accepted in court if he made it for the purpose of bolstering his monetary claims and winning his case. Thus, it happened in Prague that Reuben gave Simeon, his agent, money to buy certain wares for him. Simeon, however, used the money to buy other merchandise and subsequently declared in court that the purchases were for himself.

R. Isaac b. Meir (*Ribam*) awarded all the profits that accrued from the purchases to the agent on condition that he swear to the truth of his statement, *i.e.,* that the purchases had been indeed made for himself. He did so despite the fact that by taking the oath the agent was solemnly admitting that he had committed an act of theft by utilizing Reuben's money for his own purposes without authorization.[13]

Other authorities disagree and maintain that we may not accept confessions made even out of profit-making motives.[14] In this case, however, we do believe Simeon the agent, for laboring under the (false) impression that since he was going to repay Reuben he was committing no evil, he has not rendered himself a *rasha*.[15]

In later times, a formula was worked out whereby a self-incriminating statement would be accepted if made with the intention of protecting one's holdings; it would not be accepted if made with the intention of bolstering one's claims and of winning money from others.[16]

(3) A most potent factor leading to the admissibility of a confession is the rabbinic awareness of the substantial possibility that it may constitute an act of repentance, a sincere desire to rectify a wrong. This interpretation has already been presented.[17]

Thus, a *kohen* (priest) whose duty it is to deliver the

traditional priestly benediction,[18] cannot be compelled to do so if he refuses on the grounds that he has committed murder and thereby disqualified himself from participation in the rite;[19] similarly, the wishes of a *hazan* (cantor) who refuses to lead the congregation in prayer because, according to his words, he is guilty of theft, must be respected. If, however, the *kohen* or *hazan* had been accused of these crimes and confessed to them only after prolonged questioning and/or the appearance of witnesses, the confession has no legal status inasmuch as it was obviously made with no penitential intention.[20]

Again, a *shohet* (ritual slaughterer) declared an animal kosher and even took a portion of the meat for himself. Two days later he publicly admitted that his previous declaration of kashruth had been false: that the act of ritual slaughter that he had performed had been faulty, and that the meat was *nebelah*, unkosher. Rabbi Jacob Reischer[21] ruled that the *shohet's* second statement may be accepted because it may be viewed as an act of repentance, *i.e.*, the *shohet* does not wish to mislead the Jewish public into eating forbidden food. Indeed, continues R. Jacob, he may not be damaging himself at all, for he may have an excuse or an explanation which could exonerate him, *e.g.*, that he had slaughtered another animal on the same day and the two were interchanged; it is only now that he realized which animal was not kosher.

It remains to be pointed out, however, that where a man's self-incriminating statement is accepted because it may be construed as an act of repentance, it is not accepted as far as others are concerned and cannot affect any other party adversely.[22] Thus, if a *sopher* (scribe) confesses that he copied a Torah scroll without entertaining the devotional thoughts (*kawwanoth*) prescribed by ritual law for the transcription of the Divine Names (*azkaroth*), he is to be believed, for his confession is to be looked upon as an act of repentance. He also forfeits any claims for the fee due him for his labor.[23] People, however, who made use of the Scroll to discharge their religious obligations remain unaffected by his confession.[24] Moreover, anyone in need of his testimony may make use of him as a witness, for his confession, although respected, cannot disqualify him from acting as a witness in court, *i.e.,* it cannot affect others adversely.[25] On pages 115–116 *supra,* we have seen that this matter is the subject of a dispute among the earlier medieval authorities (*Rishonim*).

In accordance with the principle of the acceptability of confessions for the purposes of repentance, a number of authorities have ruled that, though the court will not punish a man who appears before it and says, "I have committed a sin the punishment of which is lashes; lash me!",[26] it will accede to the request of a man who begs for lashes to effectuate his personal atonement.[27] From this last point R. Levi ibn Ḥabib dissents. The obvious desire of the confessant is to avoid punishment in the world-to-come by paying in this world for the penalty of his misdeeds. Inasmuch, however, as a court administering lashes on the basis of a sinner's confession is acting illegally, the flagellation may not be properly construed as "punishment." Hence, maintains R. Levi, the court may not do so, for in any event it cannot effectuate his personal atonement.[28]

(4) An interesting, albeit limited, exception to the Jewish law against self-incrimination arises out of the scriptural power granted to man to render permitted acts forbidden to him by the taking of vows.

The legal reasoning underlying this exception may be presented in the following manner:

The Mishnah teaches:[29]

If a man says to a woman, "I betrothed you," and she denies it saying, "You did not betroth me," unless there are witnesses to prove his statement, they are not considered betrothed. Nevertheless, he is forbidden to marry any of her relatives who would have been forbidden to him had he in fact betrothed her, *e.g.*, the woman's sister or mother; whereas she is permitted to marry his relatives who would have been forbidden to her (even after the death of her "husband") had the alleged betrothal taken place, *e.g.*, the man's brother or father.

Why these apparent inconsistencies? If the betrothal is not recognized, why is he forbidden to marry her relatives? If he is forbidden to marry her relatives, why is she permitted to marry his?

The betrothal is not recognized because compounded with the woman's denial is the absence of witnesses. He nevertheless is forbidden to marry her relatives because by his confession of betrothal he has, at least as far as *his* person is concerned, "rendered himself as a piece of forbidden food."[30]

This power of "rendering oneself a piece of forbidden food," of creating for oneself a prohibition that according to the strict letter of the law does not exist, is sometimes construed as an offshoot of the rule that a man's admission of liability has the power of one hundred witnesses.[31] More often, it has been construed as an extension of the votive power the Torah has granted anyone, *i.e.*, to render something forbidden to oneself by taking a vow. For example, if a person declares, "I hereby vow not to drink wine for thirty days," he has thereby rendered wine a forbidden beverage to himself for thirty days (Numbers 30:3).[32]

On the basis of this votive power, R. Samuel Landau[33] has written that although there is the well-known exception to the rule that a man's admission of liability has the power of one hundred witnesses—namely, if such admission works to the detriment of others[34]—if a man's confession is accepted to bring upon himself a prohibition as "a piece of forbidden food," it will also be accepted even if it affects others adversely; for then the assumption is that his purpose is neither to render himself a *rasha* nor to cause harm to others, but rather to mend his ways by rectifying the wrongs he has committed, and, incidentally, to prevent others from sinning. Thus, if a scribe confesses that he wrote a Torah scroll improperly, he not only forfeits thereby any claims for the fee due him for his labor but he also disqualifies the Scroll for ritual purposes as far as others are concerned. We have seen that a number of authorities disagree with this position.[35]

On the basis of the rule implied in the above-quoted *mishnah*, R. Zebi Ashkenazi[36] makes the following distinction: A man may not incriminate himself as to what he already has done and may not disqualify himself from acting as a witness or taking an oath on the basis of past deeds. But his words do have a binding effect on his future status inasmuch as he has "declared himself a piece of forbidden food," *i.e.*, unfit in matters which belong to the realm of ritual where a man's status in the eyes of the courts is not at all as important as his actual condition vis-à-vis his Maker.

Thus, if a woman declares that she was unfaithful to her husband, in the absence of witnesses to her infidelity, she may not be punished nor is her legal status affected in any way. However, she must be divorced by her husband because she is ritually forbidden to him.*[37]

From this we may conclude that wherever full-fledged "testimony" is not needed, that is, in religio-ritual law (where the statements of one witness, of a woman, of a non-

---

* An adulteress may never again cohabit with her husband.

Jew speaking without any ulterior motive, or of a *rasha* are given credence) ,[38] a man's self-denigrating statements have sacral validity.[39]

To summarize, in rabbinic literature there appear to be four factors which point to the authenticity or, at least, acceptability of a confession:

(1) The ignorance of the confessant to the fact that he is really confessing; his obvious intention is to accomplish something quite removed from self-incrimination.

(2) The desire of the confessant to bolster his monetary claims.

(3) The confession as part of an act of repentance.

(4) The sacral validity of the confession derived from a person's votive power to render himself "a piece of forbidden food."

Whether the first two actually render the confession acceptable in court is the subject of a controversy among rabbinic authorities. As to the last two factors, opinion is well set that the confession is accepted; but most authorities limit this acceptability to the confessant himself—the confession is not allowed to affect others adversely.

THE DESTRUCTION OR WEAKENING OF THE DEFENDANT'S PRESUMPTION OF INNOCENCE

Every man is presumed to be an innocent and upright citizen and, until there is positive proof to the contrary, is qualified to testify or to take an oath in court. The rules whereby this presumption of innocence may be shattered have been summarized by Maimonides (*Judges–Evidence* 12:1) . On pages 77–78 *supra* we have already mentioned "the tacit assumption of all the previous generations of authorities" that the rule against self-incrimination, at least as far as rendering oneself a *rasha,* unfit to testify in court, applies only to those persons whose presumption of innocence was intact before they uttered their confession. Before we describe the context in which this assumption was articulated, we cite four cases in which allegations are made against witnesses, but inasmuch as these allegations are insufficient to shatter their presumption of innocence, the witnesses' own self-incriminating remarks are rejected and they are declared legally qualified to bear testimony.

(1) We begin our discussion with the following case that took place in Poland, *ca.* 1600 C.E.

The question concerns the validity of Bills of Divorcement that were written and executed in a certain community over a period of years, and now rumor has it that one of the witnesses who signed those documents is a thief. A number of women, on the basis of those documents, have already remarried* and given birth to children;† some of the women have as yet not remarried.‡ The rumor has been carefully investigated and the following has been discovered:

More than twenty years ago, someone deposited with said witness a briefcase containing one bag of money, banknotes and other papers; there were no witnesses to the deposit. The owner subsequently came for his belongings. Upon opening the briefcase, he discovered that the bag of money was missing.

The owner screamed, "I have been robbed! You took my money!" His screaming, however, was of no avail, for the depositee denied it and said, "I know nothing about it. Moreover, you are lying, for no part of what you deposited with me is missing."

The matter came before the magistrate, who ordered the depositee to be jailed, and then commanded the ser-

---

* Thus raising the possibility of unintentional adultery.
† Are they illegitimate?
‡ May they remarry or do they require new Bills of Divorcement?

vants, with the police, to search the house thoroughly. They did so and discovered the money bag with the money, both stuck in a hole in the wall of the depositee's house.

When the depositee was apprised of the fact that the stolen article had been discovered, he declared, "I do not know who did it; perhaps my wife or children stole and hid it without my knowledge."

All of this was related now by the servants, since the rumor was widespread that said witness, the depositee, was guilty of theft . . . more than twenty years ago, before he had signed the above-mentioned Bills of Divorcement. They also stated that at that time it was their opinion that the witness, the depositee, was indeed the thief, but there was insufficient proof on which to base their testimony.

Now, inasmuch as the witness, who had been signing the documents, was still alive, he was sent for and questioned concerning the rumor that had been spread about him and concerning the truth of the servants' allegations against him.

At first he made all sorts of excuses so that he not be considered a thief. Once he said that his wife or children had done it. Then he said that the owner of the bag of money had not repaid *him* the money he owed him—a debt equivalent to the amount of money in the bag. Finally he confessed and admitted that he had indeed stolen the money bag. He did however maintain that, before having signed the Bills of Divorcement, he had done penance as prescribed by Jewish law; and so he was qualified to act as a witness, and the documents he had signed were valid. . . .

What is the status of those women divorced on the basis of documents attested to by said witness?

The case, concerned with such serious questions as adultery and illegitimacy and involving so many women, attracted wide attention. Among the prominent legal authorities consulted were R. Benjamin Aaron b. Abraham Slonik[40] and R. Meir b. Gedaliah Lublin.[41] Both agreed on the following crucial points:

(a) The testimony of the witnesses, the police and the servants, who discovered the money bag in the house of the accused, does not, in and of itself, preclude the possibility (albeit remote) that the accused himself did not commit the crime. Thus, he could not have been disqualified on the basis of their testimony.

(b) His own confession cannot disqualify him either. The rule against disqualifying confessions applies even in this case, where circumstantial evidence points to the truth of the allegations of guilt.[42]

The authorities therefore concluded that the women who had already remarried had not committed (unintentional) adultery, that the children born of these second marriages were legitimate, and that the women who had not already remarried were permitted to do so.

(2) The eating of *heleb*[43] was a prohibition well-known in ancient Israel. The punishment ordained for wilfully violating this prohibition was *kareth*. One, however, who ate *ḥeleb* unwittingly was blameless and was granted the privilege of expiation in the form of a sin-offering to be brought to the Sanctuary. Scriptural law makes it an obligation for one to take advantage of this privilege of expiation.

The Talmud states that if a man were told by two witnesses that what he had eaten was *ḥeleb* and that he was therefore obligated to bring a sin-offering for expiation—were it not for certain tangential considerations[44]—he could not render himself a *rasha* by declaring that he had done so with full knowledge and intent. The obligation to bring a sin-offering, incumbent only upon one who sinned unwittingly, is derived in this case from the fact that, although the prohibition of *ḥeleb* is well-known, we assume that our defendant was unaware that the piece of fat he was eating was indeed *ḥeleb*. Thus, inasmuch as his presumption of innocence has not been affected by the testimony of the witnesses, the law against self-incrimination still obtains.[45]

(3) It is not generally known among the members of the Jewish community that not only does Jewish law prohibit the lending or borrowing of money on interest; it is equally sinful to even aid and abet such a transaction by acting as a witness thereto.[46] If a witness were to state that he had affixed his signature with full knowledge that it was sinful to do so, he would not be believed. Though we have the note before us and we see his signature thereon, there is nothing besides his self-incriminating statement to indicate that he had signed the document with full knowledge that it was forbidden to do so; hence his presumption of innocence is still intact. Thus, here, too, as long as a man's presumption of innocence is intact, his admission of guilt is rejected. Circumstantial evidence, such as his signature on the note, which tends to affirm the admission as genuine is insufficient to change the rule.[47]

(4) Where the act is generally known to be prohibited but the person asserts that he was ignorant of the prohibition (and there are no witnesses to the contrary), if the assertion appears reasonable it is accepted.[48] If the objective circumstances, however, are such as to cast serious doubt as to whether it could have been done through ignorance, there is a substantial possibility that the law against self-incrimination will *not* be held applicable; and if the defendant asserts that he acted willfully and knowingly, there are authorities who would accept his assertion.[49]

In the aforementioned cases, it has been explicitly stated that where a man's presumption of innocence is intact, his confession of guilt is rejected. Indeed, in the last sentence of case 4, the basis for the acceptance of the defendant's self-damaging statement is Maimonides' ruling[50] that ignorance of prohibitions that are well-known must be regarded as "close to willfulness"; hence even before the defendant confessed, his presumption of innocence had already been seriously shaken.

It was left to Rabbis Solomon Luria and Ẓebi Ashkenazi to formulate clearly the inapplicability of the law against self-incrimination where the confessant's presumption of innocence had been destroyed.[51]

Thus, a married woman who is pregnant is not believed at all when she declares that she has been unfaithful to her husband. However, a declaration made by a betrothed[52] or unmarried woman who is pregnant, that she had had sexual relations with a man forbidden to her under the laws of illegitimacy, *is* believed. Inasmuch as sexual intercourse is forbidden with anyone, even with her betrothed, her pregnancy has destroyed her presumption of innocence. Hence, if she now confesses to having had relations with any man whose degree of prohibition stigmatizes the child (in the case of the betrothed woman: any man other than her betrothed one; in the case of the unmarried woman: a blood-relative, a *nathin,* or a *mamzer*), her confession is accepted by the courts—perhaps not to render her liable to corporal punishment but certainly to besmirch the legitimacy of the child.[53]

The reasoning thus appears to be that once a person's presumption of innocence has been broken, the strict rules of evidence are relaxed; hence even self-incriminating statements are admitted in evidence.

A CONFESSION WHICH DOES NOT AFFECT ONE'S PRESENT STATUS

We have seen that the statements of witnesses who, affirming the signatures on a document as their own, admit that they were bribed to sign it falsely are totally rejected.[54] Moreover, if they declare the document a true one but aver that they had signed it with the knowledge that they were then incompetent to do so (*e.g.,* because of their criminal records), they are not believed, for no man may render himself a *rasha.*[55]

R. Jacob b. Asher goes one step further. Even if they maintain that they have since repented, reformed and been reinstated into the good graces of society, and are therefore now respectable citizens who are qualified to testify—in which case we might be led to believe that they are not rendering themselves *reshaim*—their statements are unacceptable; for the fact remains that their former testimony is being annulled by their self-incriminating statements.[56] They may be held liable, however, for any monetary losses sustained by the "debtor" through their false attestation of the document.[57]

In the case where the confession does not concern the criminal act but rather an item of evidence necessary for conviction, the scholars of early medieval Ashkenaz disagreed among themselves whether such a confession was admissible. Thus, all agreed that were a man to confess that he ate *ḥeleb,* his confession would not be accepted. However, where there were two witnesses who testified that he ate a specified piece of fat and the man himself confessed that it was in fact *ḥeleb,* Rabbi Meir of Rothenberg and Rabbenu Asher would accept his confession, whereas Rabbi Eliezer b. Nathan (*Raban*) would reject it.[58]

CONCLUDING NOTE

A careful study of the sources cited in this chapter reveals the significant observation that even in the small number of instances where Jewish law relaxes its rule against self-incrimination, this relaxation is limited to the disqualification of the confessant to act as a witness. The sources are unanimous in assuming that, with the possible exception of where the confessant had previously been deprived of the presumption of his innocence, under no circumstances could a man be punished, capitally or corporally, on the basis of his own statements, for this would have been construed as a direct violation of the biblical rule of evidence, "At the mouth of two witnesses . . . shall a matter be established."

It is to the everlasting glory of the rabbinic tradition that centuries before enlightened citizenries began to protest against police brutality in the interrogation of suspects and to clamor for its cessation, Jewish law proclaimed unequivocally that confessions extorted by words of inducement or by means of threats, though they appear to be true, may not be used to incriminate, convict or punish anyone.[59] This rule holds true even should such confessions be obtained by the duly constituted officers, appointed to maintain law and order, who know that a crime has been committed but cannot find any witnesses who could testify as to who the criminal is.[60]

A Concluding Word Concerning Some Practical Considerations

A Concluding Word Concerning
Some Practical Considerations

The Mishnah[1] records a remarkable debate among the Rabbis of old:

> A Sanhedrin (Jewish Court) which convicts a man to death once in seven years is called "The Bloody* Sanhedrin." Rabbi Eleazar b. Azariah says, "Once in seventy years." Rabbi Tarphon and Rabbi Aqiba say, "Had we been members of the court, no man would have ever been executed."[2] Rabbi Simeon b. Gamaliel says (about R. Tarphon and R. Aqiba), "They would have also multiplied murderers in Israel."

The strictures of the champions of the stability of society and the security of its members against those who appear to be extreme in their protection of people accused of crimes and their insistence upon meticulous care in prosecution and judgment have often been heard both in the halls of justice as well as in the arena of politics.

The observation of R. Simeon b. Gamaliel has been given a more modern garb in a most eloquent statement by Mr. Justice White. Disagreeing forcefully with the majority opinion in the *Miranda* case, Justice White[3] writes:

* Lit., "destructive."

Equally relevant is an assessment of the rule's consequences measured against community values. The Court's
duty to assess the consequences of its action is not satisfied
by the utterance of the truth that a value of our system of
criminal justice is "to respect the violability of the human
personality" and to require Government to produce the
evidence against the accused by its own independent labors.

More than the human dignity of the accused is involved;
the human personality of others in the society must also be
preserved. Thus the values reflected by the privilege are not
the sole desideratum; society's interest in the general security
is of equal weight. . . .

The most basic function of any Government is to provide
for the security of the individual and of his property. These
ends of society are served by the criminal laws which for the
most part are aimed at the prevention of crime. Without the
reasonable effective performance of the task of preventing
private violence and retaliation, it is idle to talk about human dignity and civilized values.

These are weighty words. The recent Supreme Court decisions strengthening the constitutional guarantee against
coerced self-incrimination and widening its scope have
given rise to earnest discussion and sharp debate among
law-enforcement officers, lawyers and judges, and citizens
throughout America—and abroad.[4]

The wisdom and insights of a hoary tradition have been
herein presented as a refreshing source for reflection and
as a relevant contribution to the discussion. In order that
this source be used intelligently, certain factors must be
mentioned and dealt with, if only in a cursory manner.

(1) The first question that comes to mind is whether
the fact that the Jewish ancients lived a rather uncompli-
cated life in smaller, relatively homogeneous groupings—
both geographically and sociologically—allowed for features in their judicial system that may strike us as starry-

cyed and impractical. Modern historians tend to warn their readers *against* attributing excessive simplicity to the ancients, whether it be to their thoughts or their ways.[5] Moreover, it is important to remember that where a person's presumption of innocence has been shattered, rabbinic law accepts his self-incriminating testimony;[6] and the Rabbis, observing the large, heterogeneous world around them and the corruption of peoples, aptly applied to them the judgment of the Psalmist, namely that their mouths utter falsehoods and their right hands contrive deceit. It is likely that such false mouths and deceitful hands may place in serious jeopardy the kind of presumption of innocence they had in mind.[7]

(2) The Talmud[8] records that the Jewish courts lost authority over capital cases forty years before the destruction of the (Second) Holy Temple in Jerusalem which took place in 70 C.E. Inasmuch as the preponderant majority of the talmudic rabbis lived and did their work after the destruction of the Temple, it is natural to assume that many of the laws of evidence in criminal cases were developed along the lines of theory without the benefit of practical experience.[9] I believe it would be wrong to reject their teachings on these grounds. We must not ignore the general conservatism of the Rabbis who guarded and carefully nurtured the traditions of their ancestors.[10] Nor may we overlook the feverish intensity with which many of them looked forward to the imminent restoration of political independence and its concomitant judicial autonomy.[11] Moreover, it is evident from the pages of this study that they and their medieval successors consistently applied the law against self-incrimination to all cases that did remain within their jurisdiction.

(3) There are, however, two significant factors which indicate that the Rabbis, also, faced the problem of the

clash of values—that of security and stability for the citizenry and that of judicial protection of the accused—and occasionally limited the latter in favor of the former. I refer to the resort to *hora'ath sha'ah* emergency measures and the reliance on *extra-halakhic* law-enforcement; these have been explained and illustrated throughout this study.[12]

(4) It must also be borne in mind that the Rabbis believed sincerely that man could not and was not commanded to solve all problems of law-enforcement. Divine Justice and Divine Retribution were realities in the world-view of the Rabbis.[13]

> R. Joseph said, and so too it was taught in the school of Hezekiah:
> "From the day the Temple was destroyed, although the Sanhedrin was abolished . . . the law of the four modes of execution* was not abolished: (1) He who is worthy of stoning either falls from the roof or is trampled to death by a wild beast; (2) he who merits burning either falls into a fire or is bitten by a serpent; (3) he who is worthy of decapitation either falls into the hands of the Gentile government or is attacked by brigands; and (4) he who is worthy of strangulation either drowns in a river or dies of suffocation."[14]

Again,

> R. Simeon b. Laqish opened his discourse with these two biblical texts: "(1) 'And if a man lie not in wait, but God cause it to come to hand: then I will appoint thee a place whither he may flee' (Exodus 21:13) and (2) 'As saith the proverb of the ancients: Out of the wicked cometh forth

---

* Stoning, burning, decapitation, and strangulation. In the mishnaic penal code (M. Sanhedrin 7 ff.), capital crimes are classified according to the mode of execution they entail.

wickedness but my hand shall not be upon thee' (I Samuel 24:13–14) .

"Of whom does Scripture speak? Of two persons who had slain, one in error and another with intent, there being witnesses in neither case. The Holy One, blessed be He, causes them both to come to the same inn: He who had slain with intent sits under a stepladder, and he who had slain in error comes down the stepladder, falls and kills him (unintentionally, but this time in the presence of witnesses) . Thus, he who had slain with intent is duly slain, while he who had slain in error duly goes into banishment."[15]

Thus, the liberal judicial procedure and heavy protection of the rights of the accused in Jewish law were coupled with a deep religious confidence that the criminal will eventually receive his just deserts and that justice will triumph. The modern reader is quick to perceive in the above quotations a form of resignation and semi-consolation at the loss of Jewish self-government and political freedom. Nevertheless this deep religious faith permeated the people of the time and served as a contributory deterrent to crime. Within such a framework, the law against criminal confession was taken most seriously. It must be regarded as integral to traditional Jewish law. To what degree such law can operate outside that framework is a question which demands serious consideration.[16]

The Jewish Law of Criminal Confession
and the Trial of Jesus

In the Gospel According to Luke (22:66–71), the trial of
Jesus ends as follows:

> And as soon as it was day, the elders of the people and
> the chief priests and the scribes came together, and led him
> into their council, saying, "Art thou the Christ? Tell us."
> And he said unto them, "If I tell you, ye will not believe;
> and if I also ask you, you will not answer me nor let me go.
> Hereafter, shall the Son of Man sit on the right hand of the
> power of God."
>
> Then said they all, "Art thou the Son of God?" And he
> said unto them, "Ye say that I am." And they said, "What
> need we any further witness? For we ourselves have heard of
> his own mouth."

Professor Y. Baer[1] maintains that, whether this passage
is based upon the original version in Mark (14:53–64), or
is an independent version drawing upon older traditions,[2]
it reflects an adaptation of the Roman criminal procedure
against the early Christians as described by Pliny the

Younger in his letter to Emperor Trajan (X, 96). Whereas the characteristic feature of authentically Jewish judicial procedure is the examination of the witnesses, in the Roman law the accused himself undergoes all sorts of questionings and interrogations so that he will confess his guilt.[3] This part of Professor Baer's argument, however, is not very convincing, for in the parallel version in Mark (*ibid.*) and Matthew (26:57–66) there are descriptions of extensive efforts to utilize witnesses against Jesus.

In any event, even taken at face value, the passage and its parallels are irrelevant with regard to the Jewish law of criminal confession. What "we ourselves have heard of his own mouth" was not a confession which served as evidence to bring about conviction; *it constituted the criminal act itself.* Accepting Baer's thesis that we have here a variation on the theme of the Roman trials of the earliest Christian martyrs, Jesus' acknowledgment that he is the "Son of God" is analogous to the *confessio nominis,* the acknowledgment of acceptance of the Christian faith, which in and of itself was fatal,[4] in contradistinction to *confessio facti,* which corresponds to a confession of having committed a criminal act.[5] But even rejecting Baer's thesis,[6] Jesus' declaration itself constituted an act of idolatrous blasphemy for which the penalty was death. This is evident from the parallel passages in Mark and Matthew where not only does the high priest brand his declaration as such, but also rends his clothing—the standard procedure of a Jewish court conducting a trial for blasphemy when it hears the fatal words (from the mouth of the witness).[7]

Modern Jurisdictions and Problems of Self-Incrimination

In September 1964, the United Kingdom National Committee of Comparative Law, with the assistance of the British Institute of International and Comparative Law, organized a colloquium at the University of Birmingham under the direction of Professor T. B. Smith of the University of Edinburgh on "The protection of the public interest and the interest of the accused in the criminal process." This colloquium was attended by a large number of lawyers, practicing and academic, and by judges and magistrates, both from the Common Law countries and from the continent of Europe. The material prepared as the basis of the discussion held on that occasion was subsequently gathered into a volume entitled *The Accused, A Comparative Study,* and published under the editorship of J. A. Coutts, Professor of Jurisprudence at the University of Bristol.

The reader interested in the practices of the various jurisdictions with regard to pleas of guilty and confessions of the accused will find much material in the following articles:

"England: The Trial Procedure" by A. R. N. Cross, pp. 32–34.

"Scotland: Pre-Trial Procedure" by the Hon. Lord Kilbrandon, pp. 60–65.

"Scotland: The Trial Process" by T. B. Smith, pp. 70–74.

"The Position of the Criminal Defendant in the United States of America" by G. O. W. Mueller, pp. 89, 97–99, 101, 108–109.

"Malaysia" by B. L. Chua, p. 157.

"Former British Commonwealth Dependencies" by H. H. Marshall, pp. 170–174.

"The Republic of South Africa" by L. Lazar, pp. 198–199.

Of particular interest is the Introductory Essay by Professor Coutts in which he surveys the entire legal scene and formulates the basic problems raised by a fresh examination of criminal procedural practices throughout the world.

We quote herein his incisive remarks relevant to our study.

The extent of the power of arrest and search (the "stop and frisk" law in New York—and in London), the admissibility of illegally obtained evidence, the status of confessions at the trial, the question whether an accused should have a duty to speak, the problem of how to police the police—these are problems arising in all jurisdictions and affording in practice a variety of solution. Upon the privilege against self-incrimination, for example, opinions clearly differ. In Scotland, for instance, there is a body of opinion which would favour a return to the former Scottish system of permitting the interrogation of the accused before the sheriff. It is argued that there is nothing unfair about requiring an accused to render an explanation of what has happened, failing which an adverse conclusion may be drawn from his silence (as in the French *instruction*). It may be surmised, however, that the majority of English lawyers probably share the opinion of Mr. Milward, the Birmingham stipendiary magistrate, who has said that he would "view with horror" the introduction of a rule placing a duty on the accused to speak. Indeed, one of the dangers of a system such as that of the French *instruction* is remarked on by Monsieur Robert: the legal "guarantees" limiting the interrogation may all too easily disappear in the face of a political crisis, leaving the nature and extent of the questioning to be at the whim of the government. The possibility of this danger is re-emphasized in Mr. Lazar's account of the criminal process in South Africa.

A more specific aspect of this general problem arises in the form of the question whether statements made to the police should be admissible in evidence. In Scotland, statements made to the police by a person in custody have been judicially declared to be inadmissible—a rule to be found in the Indian Penal Code and adopted, for instance, in Malaysian criminal procedure, although that adoption has been qualified so as to allow the admissibility of statements made to a police officer of the rank of inspector or above. The purpose of the rule (which has been adopted in a number of Commonwealth countries) is to bring the accused into the protection of the magistrate before making his confession; the magistrate is regarded as the guardian of the accused, a kind of *cordon sanitaire* to protect him from police pressure. It has, however, been remarked that this is a somewhat unreal safeguard against pressure being applied either before the accused appears before the magistrate or after he has been returned to his gaolers. In the United States of America, the Supreme Court ruled on June 22, 1964, that a confession made to the police is inadmissible if the suspect is not warned of his right to remain silent and of his right to the presence of counsel. It has been objected by Professor Mueller, of New York, that this is too sweeping a decision, since police interrogation, to be effective must, like love-making, be *à deux,* not *à trois.* Professor Nedrud, of the University of Missouri, who has described himself as one "not a policeman, but hired by the police to obtain confessions," has urged, as a professional interrogator, that obtaining a statement is a highly skilled art which should never be left to a magistrate, who in such matters is an amateur and is bound to be ineffective. Mr. Justice Cohen, of Israel, likewise urges that the police must be free to obtain a confession and that they should not be hamstrung by rules such as those obtaining in Scotland or in the Indian Penal Code. He bases this view upon the ground that the confession is the best evidence; but this would not seem to be the opinion of continental lawyers. Mr. Nesterov, of the Soviet Embassy in London, has pointed out that in Soviet criminal procedure, a confession is of no peculiar importance: it is merely one of the factors which go to contribute to the *conviction intime* of the judge. It is accepted that there undoubtedly would be fewer convictions if confessions made to the police were inadmissible, and it is often asserted that it is the knowledge of this fact that drives the police to press for a confession. Indeed, it may well be that in the Anglo-American system too much emphasis is laid on the confession. If that system were prepared to be more readily satisfied beyond reasonable doubt in the absence of a confession it might well be that the police would be less anxious to press for a confession than would at times appear to be the case today.

The problems to which confessions give rise are but a particular aspect of the more general question of how to police the police in order to prevent an illegal excess of zeal on their part. It has been remarked that in the fifty American state jurisdictions, there has been the possibility of an almost infinite number of experiments to find the solution to this problem, but, in order to curb police malpractice, no better solution has been found than the exclusionary rule. To those who believe that a better sanction lies in proscribing such malpractice as a criminal offence, rendering the police officer liable to prosecution, it may be answered that this is already the law in most common law jurisdictions and that it does not appear to afford an adequate sanction. To those who have suggested that a better safeguard might be the requirement that an "outside observer" be present at a police station when a suspect is being questioned, it has been replied by Dr. Winifred Cavanagh, a Birmingham magistrate, that the police might soon learn which observer to invite to sign the order. It may be questioned whether a magistrate could ever perform the role of an "outside observer," since, in the mind of the suspect, he would inevitably be identified with the police. Indeed, it is doubtful whether any system of rules would afford protection against the subtler forms of intimidation—the cane-swinging policeman in the background or the four burly policemen in the back-room, when a nine-year-old suspect is being questioned or Professor Nedrud, who induces an unsavoury type of offender to confess by first gaining his confidence by showing him a photograph of his (the professor's) father and remarking on its likeness to the accused. Indeed, there are those who claim that no system can ever police the police. In England, moreover, the operation of the rules of evidence places the accused who has a police record in a difficulty; he attacks the circumstances surrounding the making of his confession only at the risk of revealing that record to the jury. The ideal solution would be to make the police a mere conduit—a mode of conveyance of the suspect directly before the magistrate; but, whatever the rules might be, it would be quite unrealistic to expect that this would in practice always be so. Many would support the paper solution to the dilemma *quis custodiet custodes ipsos?** evolved in France, namely, that of the *instruction criminelle* by the *juge d'instruction*—a judicialising of the pre-trial stage —coupled with the provision of rigorous, detailed rules cov-

---

* Who is to guard the guardians? In other words, who is to police the police?

ering the *enquete officieuse* while the suspect is "assisting the police with their inquiries."

*　　*　　*　　*　　*

For many years it was hardly questioned in England that public policy required the rule that no one shall be compelled to give evidence which might incriminate him. Recently, the view has been expressed that where a person is reasonably suspected of the commission of a crime the rule against self-incrimination gives him undue protection. Professor Cross, however, has suggested that the adverse inference to be drawn from his refusal to answer questions when once a prima facie case seems to have been established against him provides a sufficient sanction. There would appear to be few common lawyers who would wish to make an accused a compellable witness, particularly in view of the danger that would arise if this were applied in the case of political offences. It may indeed be argued that such a rule would be bad if only for the reason that it would be unworkable (pp. 4–7, 11–12).*

---

* Quoted from J. A. Coutts, ed., *The Accused, A Comparative Study* (London, 1966). Reprinted by permission of Sweet and Maxwell, Ltd.

Inquisitional Police Practices in an Accusatorial System of Justice

From *The New York Times,* July 21, 1966:
SENATORS HEAR AN INTERROGATION
IN STUDY OF CONFESSION RULING
(Special to The New York Times)

Washington, July 20—A Senate subcommittee heard a recording today of police interrogators eliciting a confession from a murder suspect as the panel began an investigation of the impact of the Supreme Court's new limitations on confessions.

The suspect, 18-year-old John F. Biron of Minneapolis, was put through the gamut of psychological influences used by modern police interrogators. The officers never raised their voices, never threatened. After five hours of questioning, edited to an hour in the version played for the Senators, and a night in a cell, Biron confessed.

The recording, which was made secretly by the police for unexplained reasons, was subsequently discovered by Biron's attorneys and led to the reversal of his murder conviction by the Supreme Court of Minnesota.

He was subsequently convicted again on other evidence

and is serving a 7-to-25 year sentence for the third-degree murder of a woman purse-snatching victim in 1962.

As the recording was played by Yale Kamisar, professor of law at the University of Michigan, the various psychological tricks recommended by police manuals were clearly identifiable:

Sympathy: "We know that you didn't intend to kill this woman. She died of exposure."

Divide-and-conquer: "Your friend has cracked. I'm not lying. The best thing you can do is help yourself. Are you the pigeon? The one who gets blamed for everything?"

Flattery: "It takes real guts. You have to be a real man to tell the truth. I think you'll find that I will respect you a lot more, and everybody will, if you're a man and admit it."

Confession is good for the soul: "I think you'll feel a lot better if you tell about it. I am a Catholic, too."

Buddy-buddy: "Right now your best friend is the police officer who's investigating the case."

At the start of the interrogation, Biron said: "I would like to have my sister call a lawyer . . . they're trying to pin a rap on me . . . these cats are trying to boss me."

Professor Kamisar pointed out that the police did not deny or fulfill the request for a lawyer; they just changed the subject and "lost it in the shuffle."

Throughout the questioning, Biron repeatedly denied any connection with the murder, although he admitted snatching one purse on the fatal night. It contained 64 cents.

"But I never put the boot to no old lady," he insisted.

At one point, when Biron asked for a lie detector test, the interrogator responded with what Professor Kamisar called the keep-them-off-balance technique:

"I don't want the machine to explode—those needles would jump right off the chart," the interrogator was said to have remarked.

According to Professor Kamisar, a major flaw in the interrogation was the police promise to try to get Biron a trial in juvenile court, where his mother and sister would be spared the humiliation of a public trial, in exchange for a confession.

Not only would the promise itself render the confession inadmissible, but the police knew an 18-year-old must stand trial in an adult court, he said.

Court Ruling Studied

The subcommittee on constitutional amendments, under the chairmanship of Senator Birch Bayh, Indiana Democrat, is studying the effects of the Supreme Court's recent decision in Miranda v. Arizona. It outlaws all in-custody interrogation by the police outside the presence of the suspect's lawyer, unless the suspect has been first warned of his right to counsel and to remain silent.

Professor Kamisar said this did not stop the police from questioning people in their homes, even without a warning. He added that it would not rule out spontaneous confessions.

Another witness, Dr. Daryl Bem, a psychologist at Carnegie Institute of Technology, said psychological methods could provide false confessions because the less a person is coerced into making false statements, the more likely he is to come to believe them.

Dr. Albert Biderman, a Washington psychologist and author, said that "a skilled inquisitorial system would be able to get almost anybody to confess to almost anything."

The significance of the psychological evidence in general and of the concluding paragraph in particular is outweighed by the historical note (paragraph 4) that, after the confession was rejected, the criminal was convicted on the basis of other (*i.e.*, objective) evidence.

Indeed, the inherent inquisitorial nature of interrogations by police officers intent upon extracting confessions from the mouths of suspects and, paradoxically, the general ability of the police to obtain convictions without resort to confessions on the part of the accused, are the conclusions that were arrived at by a group of scholars who made a careful and exhaustive study of the entire procedure of interrogating suspects. The study is entitled, "Interrogations in New Haven: The Impact of *Miranda*," *Yale Law Journal* 76:8 (1967), pp. 1519–1648. The authors of the study point out that the impact of the *Miranda* decision of the United States Supreme Court on law enforcement has been small because (1) interrogations play but a secondary role mainly since the police rarely arrest suspects without substantial evidence and because (2) a suspect arrested and brought in for questioning is in a crisis-laden situation. Even if the interrogators inform the suspects of their constitutional rights—and this is rarely done fully and fairly—this information cannot eliminate whatever "inherently coercive atmosphere" the police station may have.

The inherently coercive nature of police questioning was further corroborated by a supplementary report entitled, "A Postscript to the *Miranda* Project: Interrogation of Draft Protesters," *Yale Law Journal* 77:2 (1967), pp. 300–320. The report described those arrested and subjected to police questioning, *i.e.,* the draft protesters, as very bright and extremely willful people. Moreover, the police gave the suspects sympathetic and careful explanations of their rights of silence and of counsel. Nevertheless, the conclusion was essentially the same as that of the main report: As long as the situation of interrogation is structured and manipulated by a professional interrogator, persons subject to official questioning inevitably suffer from extreme nervousness and deep anxiety. Warnings and information given to them, as prescribed by the *Miranda* decision, are wholly ineffective even when the suspect is intelligent and the interrogation is polite, noncustodial, and at the home of the suspect himself.

Abbreviations

B.	Babylonian Talmud
beg.	Beginning
bot.	Bottom (of page)
C. Th.	Codex Theodosianus
D.	Digest of Corpus Iuris Civilis
fl.	Flourished
Hil.	Hilkhoth
M.	Mishnah
P.	Palestinian Talmud
R. E.	Realenzyklopädie der Klassischen Altertumswissenschaft, eds. Paully, Wissowa, *et al.*
Resp.	Responsa, Responsum
T.	Tosephta
U.S.	United States (Supreme Court) Reports

Note: Translations are not literal. Renderings from the Hebrew of the Jewish sources have been drawn from the standard English translations where available, but they have been freely revised and even paraphrased according to the dictates of clarity and the need for emphasis.

Notes

CHAPTER I

THE JEWISH LAW OF CONFESSION IN THE LIGHT
OF GENERAL LEGAL HISTORY

1. The description contained in the next four paragraphs is based upon the following: A. Esmein, *A History of Continental Criminal Procedure* (translated J. Simpson), pp. 78–144; H. C. Lea, *The Inquisition of the Middle Ages, Its Organization and Operation;* M. Ploscowe, "The Development of Present-Day Criminal Procedures in Europe and America," *Harvard Law Review* 48 (1935), pp. 433–473; *Watts v. Indiana,* 338 U.S. 49 (Frankfurter); *Jackson v. Denno,* 378 U.S. 368 (White). Z. Frankel, *Der gerichtliche Beweis nach mosaisch-talmudischen Recht,* pp. 71–73, summarizes nineteenth-century German legal literature on this matter. Between the thirteenth and fifteenth centuries, England (accusatorial) and the Continent (inquisitorial) present a fascinating contrast; cf. F. Pollock and F. W. Maitland, *A History of English Law,* Vol. III, pp. 620–623; O. J. Rogge, *Why Men Confess,* pp. 26–29; and, most recently, L. W. Levy, *Origins of the Fifth Amendment,* pp. 3–82.
2. L. Feilchenfeld, *Die Zeugen im Strafprozess des Talmud,* pp. 18–30, contains a survey of many legal systems, ancient and modern, with regard to this question.

3. *Andocides*, 1.71; *Lysias*, 6.24 (Loeb ed.; cf. Introduction, p. 113).
4. Aristotle, *Constitution of Athens*, 52.1.
5. R. J. Bonner and G. Smith, *The Administration of Justice from Homer to Aristotle*, Vol. II, p. 121. Aristotle, *Constitution of Athens* (eds. K. von Fritz and E. Kapp), p. 125, note a.
6. Demosthenes, 23.28–51.
7. *Lycurgus*, 1.117.
8. *Antiphon*, 5.53 ff.
9. Bonner and Smith, *op. cit.*, pp. 126 ff., 223 ff.; J. P. Mahaffy, *Social Life in Greece* (3rd ed.), pp. 240–242.
10. B. B. Rogers, Introduction to *The Wasps of Aristophanes*, pp. XXXVI f. Cf. Bonner and Smith, *op. cit.*, pp. 228–306, and R. J. Bonner, *Lawyers and Litigants in Ancient Athens*.
11. The translation is from C. Pharr, ed., *The Theodosian Code*.
12. C. Mittermeier, *Das deutsche Strafverfahren*, as translated in A. Esmein, *op. cit.*, pp. 21–26; T. Mommsen, *Das Roemisches Strafrecht*, pp. 437–438; and J. L. Strachen-Davidson, *Problems of the Roman Criminal Law*, Vol. II, pp. 112–126, 164–165.
13. L. Mitteis, *Reichsrecht u. Volksrecht;* R. Taubenschlag, *The Law of Greco-Roman Egypt*, Ch. I. "Egyptian, Greek and Roman Law and Their Interrelation."
14. Taubenschlag, p. 413.
15. *Ibid.*, pp. 417–418.
16. S. Lieberman, "Roman Legal Institutions in Early Rabbinics and in the Acta Martyrum," *Jewish Quarterly Review*, 35 (1944), pp. 13 ff.
17. *Ibid.*, pp. 19 ff.
18. A. Esmein, *op. cit.*, pp. 79 ff., and C. H. Lea, *op. cit.*, Ch. 3.
18a. French *Code de Procédure Pénale* (9th ed., 1967–1968), Art. 114; Polish Code (amended text of 1950), Art. 73; Austrian Code of 1960 (see Ludwig F. Tlapek and Eugen Serini, *Die oesterreichische Strafprozessordnung*, 4th ed., 1960), para. 203 and para. 245; German Code of 1877 (see Robert von Hippel, *Der deutsche Strafprozess*, 1941, pp. 276, 417), para. 136 and para. 243; Russian Code of 1960 (see Harold Berman, *Soviet Criminal Law and Procedure, the RSFSR Codes*, pp. 92, 214, 268, 281, 312, and 364–365), Arts. 46, 77, 150, 181 and 280.
18b. Letter to the Editor, *The New York Times*, December 28, 1968. Cf. also Tlapek and Serini, *op. cit.*, p. 211.
18c. Polish Penal Procedure of 1950, Art. 296. I am indebted to Dr.

Rudzinski for this information concerning the European Continental law and, especially, for the documentation thereof which he was kind enough to furnish me in private communications.

19. The literature is vast. An account of the historical antecedents to the Fifth Amendment of the United States Constitution is found in J. H. Wigmore, 8 *Evidence* (McNaughton rev., 1961), paragraph 2250; of the purposes it serves, paragraph 2251; a detailed analysis of its provisions and application, paragraphs 2252–2284. The fullest historical treatment is the work by Levy cited at the end of note 1, *supra*. Students of the history of legal philosophy will find the remarks of Thomas Hobbes of interest; cf. *Leviathan*, Pt. 2, Ch. 21, para. 112. A brief survey of the historical antecedents to the Constitution is contained in E. N. description of subsequent Supreme Court action may be found in Griswold, *The Fifth Amendment Today*, pp. 2–7; and a summary S. H. Hofstadter and S. E. Levitan, "Lest the Constable Blunder: A Remedial Proposal" in *The Record* (of the Association of the Bar of New York), Vol. 20, pp. 630–633. Also very helpful are J. P. Frank, *Cases and Materials on Constitutional Law* (1952), pp. 739–773, 965–967; O. J. Rogge, *The First and the Fifth*, pp. 138–278; and T. I. Emerson *et al.*, *Political and Civil Rights in the United States*, pp. 189–193, 480–493, 1010–1042. For a concise portrayal of the substance of the law, cf. S. H. Hofstadter, "The Fifth Amendment and the Immunity Act of 1954, Aspects of the American Way," *The Record*, Vol. 10, pp. 453–497.

20. J. H. Wigmore, *Code of Evidence* (3rd ed.), pp. 217–222, 414–424. E. M. Morgan, *Basic Problems of Evidence* (1957) pp. 127–159. E. M. Morgan *et al.*, *Cases and Materials on Evidence*, pp. 759–786.

21. Modern Israeli law is rooted in this tradition and is remarkably faithful to it. Thus, Ḥaim H. Cohen, Attorney General of Israel at the time, speaking at an international conference on criminal law administration held in Chicago (1960) reported that in all major crimes "the Israeli practice is to make a tape-recording of the entire police interrogation of the suspect. No confession is received in court in these cases unless the Government produces the recording and uses it to prove that the confession was entirely voluntary." *The New York Times*, Feb. 21, 1960, p. 46. See also R. Gideon and A. Winograd (eds.), *Halakhoth, The*

Israeli Digest, Vol. IV: "Criminal Procedure," edited by M. Kant, pp. 50–52, 118–135; Vol. VII: "Evidence," edited by Y. Gabison, pp. 14–17, 33, 38. Cf. further A. Salant, *Evidence,* Ch. IX: "Confessions in Criminal Trials," and M. Timor, *Rules of Criminal Procedure,* pp. 112–124, 134–135. Also, S. Shohem, "Israel," *The Accused, A Comparative Study* (ed. J. A. Coutts), pp. 184–190; note 13 therein and the statement it purports to document on page 188 are patently erroneous.

22. *Gideon v. Wainwright,* 372 U.S. 335; A. Lewis, *Gideon's Trumpet.*

23. *Escobedo v. Illinois,* 378 U.S. 478; Y. Kamisar, F. Inbau, *et al., Criminal Justice in our Time,* pp. 1–135.

24. *Miranda v. Arizona,* 384 U.S. 436; R. J. Medalie, *From Escobedo to Miranda: The Anatomy of a Supreme Court Decision.*

25. S. Kucherov, *Courts, Lawyers and Trials Under the Last Three Tsars,* pp. 65–69; also discussed by S. Rosenbaum, "HaHokhahoth BeMishpatim Peliliim BeT'kuphath HaMiqra," *HaMishpat,* Vol. I (1927), pp. 284–285. Russian reservations concerning the conclusiveness of pleas of guilty and of confessions persist theoretically even into Soviet criminal procedure; cf. B. S. Nikiforov, "Notes on Criminal Procedure in the U.S.S.R.," *The Accused, A Comparative Study,* (ed. J. A. Coutts), pp. 268–269. As for the inquisitorial technique and the role of confession in the actual practice of Communist Russia, cf. O. J. Rogge, *op. cit.,* pp. 74–142 and 230–247.

26. *Watts v. Indiana,* 338 U.S. 49, p. 54.

26a. Cf. Tosaphoth, Sanhedrin 9a, *s.v. bizman,* where two reasons are given why an accuser-witness may not act as a judge.

27. S. H. Hofstadter and S. R. Levitan, *op. cit., The Record,* Vol. 20, p. 629.

28. E. N. Griswold, *op. cit.,* p. 19.

29. W. O. Douglas, *An Almanac of Liberty,* p. 239; E. A. Roscoe, *The Growth of English Law,* pp. 160–161. See also S. Hook, *Common Sense and the Fifth Amendment,* Chs. 2 and 3.

30. Cf. *infra,* pp. 90–91.

31. Z. Frankel, *op. cit.,* p. 177; S. Rosenbaum, *op. cit.,* p. 289. The Rabbis of the Talmud, a number of whom suffered greatly at the hands of the Romans, were, unfortunately, very familiar with torture as a judicial tool; cf. S. Lieberman, "Roman Legal Insti-

tutions in Early Rabbinics and in ,the Acta Martyrum," *Jewish Quarterly Review,* 35 (1944) , pp. 14 ff.

32. This suggestion was already made at the end of the nineteenth century; cf. Z. Glicksman, "Eduth Adam al Aẓmo," *HaMeliẓ* (1889), No. 257. The same author propounds another possibility: In view of the close kinship ties in ancient Israel, a man could not be allowed to bring disgrace on his family and his clan by mere word of mouth, *i.e.,* by confessing to a criminal act. Cf. passages in B. Shabbath 39a, B. Qiddushin 65a, and B. Kethuboth 41a. As for the biblical roots of these ties, cf. R. de Vaux, *Ancient Israel,* pp. 10–12, 21–23.

33. Cesare Bonesana, Marchese di Beccaria, as quoted by S. Mendelssohn, *The Criminal Jurisprudence of the Ancient Hebrews* (1891), p. 133, note 311. Cf. further the critique of criminal confessions in O. J. Rogge, *op. cit.,* pp. 187–206.

34. On John Selden's knowledge of Jewish law, cf. I. Herzog, "John Selden on Jewish Law," *Journal of Comparative Legislation,* 13 (1931) , pp. 236–245.

35. G. Horowitz, "The Privilege Against Self-Incrimination—How Did It Originate?", *Temple Law Quarterly,* Vol. 31, pp. 121–144. There is confusion, however, in the documentation of the Jewish sources. Note 12 should cite B. Sanhedrin 9b. Note 15 should cite B. Baba Qamma 64b and 75a before the last paragraph and B. Sanhedrin 9b after the last paragraph. Note 67 should cite the older source, T. Baba Meẓia 1:10.

36. *De Synedriis,* Vol. II, p. 545; translation my own.

36a. Levy, *op. cit.,* p. 441, points out that *De Synedriis* was published in 1653, *after* John Lilburne's first treason trial. Thus, "the self-incriminatory oath *ex-officio* had already been abolished and the right against self-incrimination had already been established in the common law."

37. *Twining v. New Jersey,* 211 U.S. 78, 91 (Moody) . Cf. the opening sentence of the excerpts of the supplemental minority statement to the report of The President's Commission on Law Enforcement and Administration of Justice: "We know of no other system of criminal justice which subjects law enforcement to limitations as severe and rigid as those [introduced by the *Miranda* decision]"; quoted in *The New York Times,* Feb. 26, 1967, Section Four. Cf. further 8 Wigmore 2251.

38. S. H. Hofstadter, *op. cit., The Record,* Vol. 10, p. 455. At the end of the article, Hofstadter describes the Jewish law on self-incrimination; pp. 487–490 (compare his remarks to the Horowitz article, *supra,* note 35). Mr. Chief Justice Warren, too, recognizes that there are provisions concerning self-incrimination whose roots go back into ancient times, and he quotes Maimonides as testimony thereof, *Miranda v. Arizona,* 384 U.S. 436, note 27. And, more recently, Mr. Justice Douglas, 87 Supreme Court Reporter 616, p. 619, note 5 (*Garrity v. State of New Jersey*).

CHAPTER II

THE BIBLICAL PERIOD

1. Cf. the standard commentaries; also *The Responsa of Abraham Maimuni* (ed. A. Freimann), Responsum 11.
2. On the technical difficulties in this translation, cf. S. R. Driver, *Notes on the Hebrew Text of the Books of Samuel, ad loc.*
3. I have not included Jonathan's confession to having partaken of food forbidden by Saul (I Samuel 14:43), for the narrative leads us to believe that several people had been witnesses to his act.
4. I. H. Weiss, *Dor Dor We-Dorshaw,* Vol. I, p. 23; H. Tchernowitz, *Toledoth HaHalakhah,* Vol. I, Pt. I, p. 251. An early, and generally successful, refutation of Weiss' thesis as to the biblical and early tannaitic law was written by Z. Glicksman, "Eduth Adam al Azmo," *HaMeliz* (1889), No. 257.
5. Z. Karl, "HaHokhahoth BaMishpat HaIbri We-Hithpathuthan," *HaMishpat HaIbri,* Vol. III (1928), pp. 81–92. It should be pointed out, however, that there is a rabbinic tradition according to which Akhan was put to death after having confessed to violating the Sabbath; *Yalqut Shim'oni, ad loc.*
6. *Ibid.*
7. The literature is vast. For a brief, yet definitive, treatment by a modern scholar, cf. Y. Kaufmann, *Toledoth HaEmunah Ha-Yisraelith,* Vol. I, Bk. II, pp. 499–502. For a concise historic-legal survey, cf. Z. Marqon, "HaGoral," *HaMishpat HaIbri,* Vol. IV, pp. 135–146. As for the Lot in talmudic literature, cf. "Goral," *Encyclopedia Talmudith,* Vol. V, pp. 415–417. For a bibliography

of significant medieval statements, cf. R. Margalioth, "Hagahoth Meqor Ḥesed," *Sepher Ḥassidim,* #579, note 3; *Margalioth HaYam* on Sanhedrin 43b, ##10–11.

8. *E.g.,* Numbers 5:15 ff.; Joshua 14:2; Judges 1:1 ff.
9. R. Moses Zacuta, *Qol Ramaz* on Sanhedrin 6:2 (published in *Qebuẓath Mepharshei HaMishnah*); Y. Kaufmann, (Hebrew Commentary on) Joshua 7:19.
10. Abravanel on Joshua, *ad loc.* Cf. Deuteronomy 7:26 and Joshua 6:18.
11. B. Gemser, "The *Rib*—or Controversy—Pattern in Hebrew Mentality," *Wisdom in Israel and in The Ancient Near East* (eds. M. Noth and D. W. Thomas), pp. 120–137.
12. E. Speiser, "The Stem *PLL* in Hebrew," *Journal of Biblical Literature* 82 (1963), pp. 301–306.
13. *E.g.,* I Kings 8:35 and the book of Psalms, *passim.*
14. Leviticus 7:12–15, 22:29–30; Psalms 100:1. Cf. also the doxological nature of the ancient benediction of thanksgiving, *modim,* in the daily Silent Devotion (M. Rosh HaShanah 4:5), and in the Grace after meals.
15. F. Horst, *Gottes Recht,* pp. 162 ff. Along similar, although not identical lines, H. Grimme, "Der Begriff v. hebraeischen הודה und תודה," *Zeitschrift f.d. alttestamentliche Wissenschaft* 58 (1940–41), p. 236, note 1.
16. R. David Qimḥi, based upon M. Sanhedrin 6:2.
17. Z. W. Falk, *Hebrew Law in Biblical Times: An Introduction* (Hebrew), p. 63.
18. Leviticus 16:21.
19. *E.g.,* the Decalogue expression in Exodus 20:16 and frequently elsewhere.
20. I. H. Weiss, *op. cit.,* p. 23; Glicksman's alternative explanation is forced.
21. Z. W. Falk, *op. cit.,* p. 70. For the present, I am not entering into the question whether this Amalekite stranger was regarded as an Israelite or as a heathen; cf. *infra,* p. 98.
22. Cf. *infra,* pp. 182–183, note 56.
23. C. H. Brichto, *The Problem of "Curse" in the Hebrew Bible,* pp. 44–45 and A. B. Ehrlich, *Mikra Ki-Pheschuto, ad loc.*
24. *Shakh, Ḥoshen Mishpat* 71:7; similarly, the oath in general, B. Baba Meẓia 3b.

CHAPTER III
TANNAITIC TIMES

1. This identification was made by Prof. J. N. Epstein on the basis of the midrashic-type exposition, the terminology, and the names of the *Tannaim* that are found in the entire chapter of T. She-buoth 3. Cf. "Seridim M'd'bei R. Ishmael LeSepher Wayiqra," *Festschrift-Krauss*, pp. 22–28; *Mebo'oth LeSiphruth HaTannaim*, pp. 261, 636–639.

2. Ms. Erfurt, ed. Zuckermandel, p. 450; missing from the standard printed editions.

3. This explication of the text is by Y. Abramsky, *Tosephta Ḥazon Yeḥezqel, ad loc.*

4. I am grateful to Prof. Saul Lieberman for having pointed out to me these two parallel sources.

5. Ed. Friedman, p. 109a; ed. Finkelstein, p. 228.

6. Ed. Zuckermandel, p. 451.

7. This emendation of Friedman (who was preceded in this by the Gaon of Wilna) must be rejected on the basis of the earliest printed editions as well as the parallel versions; S. Lieberman, *Tosepheth Rishonim, ad loc.*

8. S. Lieberman, *ibid.*, following the commentary, *Ḥasdei David*, maintains that פיו, "his mouth," refers to the single witness and is parallel in the *a fortiori* structure to the first פיו, which refers to the defendant. The Gaon of Wilna agrees that this is the *sense* of the passage.

9. This is the reading. Rabbi N. Z. Berlin (*Neẓib*) emends the text "to convict him of a capital crime" to tighten the reasoning and to render this minor premise parallel to the major one.

10. Y. Abramsky, *op. cit.*, on the basis of the Erfurt reading, confirms our rendering of this sentence as a question.

11. *I.e.*, punishment thereof; cf. *infra*, p. 40.

12. It is also convincing evidence that the discussions in B. Baba Meẓia 3a and b and at the beginning of P. Baba Meẓia are limited to monetary matters; *contra* H. Tchernowitz, *Toledoth HaHalakhah*, Vol. I, Part I, p. 253. R. Jose's teachings were generally accepted as authoritative, for he supported his statements with reason (B. Erubin 51a, B. Gittin 67a) or, as others interpret,

his knowledge of the law was incontestable (Z. Frankel, *Darkhei HaMishnah,* p. 177, note 4) .

13. M. Sanhedrin 4:1, 5:4.

14. I have not included T. Sanhedrin 10:5, for the reading which indicates that confession is being discussed is open to serious challenge; cf. ed. Zuckermandel, p. 431, and the traditional commentaries, *ad loc.* By implication, the tannaitic statement recorded in B. Shebuoth 33b and the tannaitic thinking that produced M. Sanhedrin 6:2 may be adduced as indications that the *Tannaim* rejected confessions as items of evidence.

15. This is also clearly implied in M. Baba Qamma 10:7; cf. also B. Gittin 40b and 64a; Maimonides, *Judgments—Litigants* 7. For a summary of the conditions under which this rule is applicable, cf. J. Klein, *Das Gesetz ueber das gerichtliche Beweisverfahren nach mosaisch-talmudischen Recht,* pp. 6–7; and of how it operates, cf. A. Gulak, *Yesodei HaMishpat HaIbri,* Bk. IV, pp. 78 f. The one great exception to this rule is the case where his admission would affect others; *Tur, Ḥoshen Mishpat* 47 on the basis of B. Kethuboth 19a; cf. also B. Baba Bathra 128b.

16. This distinction between *mammon* and *qenas* is basic to talmudic jurisprudence. Cf. the opening discussion in B. Kethuboth, Ch. 4 (42a ff.) with the commentaries. Note the key phrase עמד בדין.

17. B. Baba Qamma 64b, 75a. This rule is utilized by the *Amoraim* to explain R. Aqiba's statement that witnesses (*edim zomemim*) , who had conspired to bring about a monetary loss for their intended victim, are not obligated to pay the money themselves if they confessed to their crime. Although Scripture punishes conspiring witnesses with the same punishment that they had intended to inflict upon the person against whom they testified, inasmuch as their obligation to pay falls into the category of fines, their confession exempts them from payment (B. Makkoth 2b) . Cf. the perceptive remarks of M. A. Amiel, *Darkhei Mosheh,* Bk. II: "Modes of Acquisition" (Hebrew) , pp. 27, 47, 54–55, 112–113.

18. For a list of offenses whose punishment is lashes, cf. Maimonides, *Judges—Sanhedrin,* Ch. 19.

19. B. Baba Qamma 64b. The reasoning may be that inasmuch as the penalty addresses itself to the criminal aspect of the act, it is inappropriate where the perpetrator acknowledges his deed. Moreover, since the confession concerns itself with a criminal

act, the court on general principles of inadmissibility of confessions will not decree any obligation to pay (M. A. Amiel, *op. cit.*, pp. 112–113) . Cf. further Y. A. Warhaftig, *Osher Yeruham,* Sec. 78.

20. Z. Karl, "HaHokhahoth BaMishpat HaIbri We-Hithpat-huthan," *HaMishpat HaIbri,* Vol. III, p. 92.

21. *Qezoth HaHoshen* 34:4. A significant attempt to resolve this difficulty posed by the *Qezoth* is to be found in M. Y. A. Rabinowitz, *Da'ath Mordekhai,* Vol. II, Ch. 10.

22. Deuteronomy 19:15. The translation is that of the Jewish Publication Society of America, 1917 edition. The translation of the Jewish Publication Society of America, 1962 edition, is as follows: "A single witness may not validate against a person any guilt or blame for any offense that may be committed: a case can be valid only on the testimony of two witnesses or more (Lit. 'three') ." Cf. *Siphrei, ad loc.* Maimonides, *Judges—Evidence* 5:1. According to D. Z. Hoffmann in his German *Commentary to Deuteronomy* (Hebrew translation, 1959) *ad loc.,* this verse represents the general rule of evidence; specific legislation for capital cases is laid down in Numbers 35:30 and Deuteronomy 17:6. Similarly, S. R. Driver, *Deuteronomy* (International Critical Commentary) , *ad loc.*

23. Hoffmann, *ibid.,* on the basis of *Targum Jonathan* and Rashi, and citing as proof Genesis 4:13; I Samuel 28:10; I Kings 7:9; and Zechariah 14:19.

24. Although this rule is unanimously accepted, its source is a matter of disagreement among the *Tannaim:* P. Sanhedrin 3:9. The generally accepted opinion, that of R. Aqiba, is that it is Deuteronomy 24:16. Cf. B. Sanhedrin 27:29 and Maimonides, *ibid.,* 13, for the list of disqualified relatives; the list includes *cognati* as well as *agnati.*

25. B. Sanhedrin 28a.

26. B. Baba Bathra 159a. Maimonides, *ibid.,* 13:15. For an attempt at a rational formulation of the reasons for this rule, cf. *Sepher HaHinukh,* Precept 589 (Chavel ed., 586) . See, however, the remarks thereon in *Minhath Hinukh* with regard to B. Sanhedrin 28b. S. Mendelsohn, *The Criminal Jurisprudence of the Ancient Hebrews* (1891) , p. 273, writes:

> The Attic law took no exception to relatives (Smith 626b) , and in some countries the law punished even the nearest

relatives of a criminal for not informing against him. Thus, the law of the Burgundians decreed that, "if the wife or the son of a person guilty of robbery did not reveal the crime, they were to become slaves." "This law," remarks Montesquieu (B. XXVI, c. III) "was contrary to nature: A wife to inform against her husband! a son to accuse his father! to avenge one criminal action, they ordained another still more criminal." In Rome, the evidence of near relatives, though not excluded, did not have much weight. Common law disqualifies a person from acting as a juror if he is related to either party to the suit, within the ninth degree (Blackstone III, 363) ; but it permits the nearest relations, except the lawful husband and wife, to appear as witness against each other (cf. Roscoe 112 sq.) .

In rabbinic law, the requirement of the testimony of two objective, non-related witnesses applies with equal vigor even to those crimes in which the Bible seems to include relatives as aids to the prosecution: *Mesith,* one who entices people to idolatry (Deuteronomy 13:7–12, M. Sanhedrin 7:10) and the Rebellious Son (Deuteronomy 21:18–21; Rashi, Sanhedrin 71b, *s.v. biphnei shenaim*) .

27. "A man is a kinsman to himself, hence no man may incriminate himself"; B. Sanhedrin 9b. Cf. commentaries of Rashi and *Yad Ramah.*

28. Cf. similar conclusions in Y. M. Ginzburg, *Mishpatim LeYisrael,* p. 4, note 47, and M. Y. A. Rabinowitz, *op. cit.,* pp. 37b–38a.

29. I. H. Weiss, *Dor Dor We-Dorshaw,* Vol. I, pp. 23–25; H. Tchernowitz, *op. cit.,* pp. 251–253; Z. Karl, *op. cit.,* pp. 91–92, 95.

30. P. Sanhedrin 6:3. Parallels are found in B. Sanhedrin 43b and *Numbers Rabbah* 23:6. Cf. also *Midrash Tanhuma,* Mass'ei (ed. Buber) , p. 82a.

31. *Midrash Tanhuma,* Wayesheb (ed. Buber) , p. 11; *Yalqut Shim'oni,* Isaiah, p. 482. The influence of this midrashic comparison may be found in the liturgy of Yom Kippur Qatan.

32. 'I'. Sanhedrin 8:3; B. Sanhedrin 37b.

33. Weiss, *op. cit.,* pp. 24–25.

34. Glicksman, cited in note 4 of chapter I, poses a similar question on Rabban Gamaliel's frustration at not being able to effectuate the manumission of his slave, Tabi (B. Baba Qamma 74b) , "Why did he not confess?"

35. M. Sanhedrin 6:2.

36. B. Sanhedrin 44b.

37. A parallel passage, with slight variations, is found in T. San-hedrin 9:5. Rashi's account of the historical background is based upon P. Sanhedrin 6:3 and P. Ḥagigah 2:2. Cf. also O. Baehr, *Das Gesetz ueber Falsche Zeugen nach Bibel u. Talmud,* p. 5, note 9.

38. The parallel passage in the Tosephta does not use the word קולר. The reading there is, literally, "behold, his blood is hang-ing on the neck of the witness."

39. According to the Rabbis, he will certainly not be compelled to confess the crime for which he is being executed if he knows that the verdict is unjust; they, however, silence him and do not allow him to make the statement R. Judah would have him make (H. Albeck, *ad loc.*) .

40. Maharsha, Sanhedrin 43b, *contra* R. Israel Lipschitz, *Tiph'ereth Israel,* and R. Samuel Strashun (*Rashash*) who explain the words of the Mishnah, "he knows not how to confess," as refer-ring to a man who is unaware of any other transgressions that he may have committed. S. Lieberman, *Hellenism in Jewish Palestine,* p. 140, note 11, corroborates the position that the confession-aspect of להתוודות must be substantially deempha-sized. Cf., also, *idem, Tosefta Ki-fshutah, Zeraim,* p. 850, note 79.

41. The principle is formulated succinctly in Maimonides *Madda-' Teshubah* 1:1. Cf. further Z. W. Rabinowitz, *Sha'are Torath Babel,* pp. 143–144.

42. The *baraitha* cited in B. Shabbath 32b, which applies the mish-naic dictum to those who become seriously ill, already under-stood the Mishnah this way.

43. B. Sanhedrin 44b; cf. the commentary of Rashi for the Pales-tinian traditions as to the particulars of the trial and the frame-up. (Rashi's sources are given *supra,* note 37.)

44. M. Aboth 4:22; *Mekhilta,* Mishpatim 3 (ed. Friedman) , p. 79a; B. Berakhoth 16b bottom. The metaphoric assimilation of the term to non-monetary matters, *e.g.,* to a problem in the law of marriage and divorce, is found in late amoraic times; B. Qid-dushin 65b in the name of R. Ashi, one of the last of the *Amoraim.*

45. *E.g.,* B. Hagigah 16b, which appears to be early tannaitic.

46. The civil *Anerkenntnis* as opposed to the criminal *Gestaendnis*.
47. B. Kethuboth 87b and B. Shebuoth 40a.
48. Y. M. Ginzburg, "Ha'ashamah Aẓmith l'phee Mishpat Ha-Torah," *HaTorah We-HaMedinah* 9 (1958), p. 83.
49. In contrast with Numbers 35:30 and Deuteronomy 17:6, which deal specifically with criminal cases, Deuteronomy 19:15 represents the general rule of evidence and is concerned with all cases; cf. *supra,* note 22.

CHAPTER IV
AMORAIC DEVELOPMENT

1. B. Sanhedrin 9b.
2. Leviticus 20:13.
3. Exodus 23:1.
4. *Ibid.*
5. Following Rashi, *ad loc.*
6. The word *rasha* in the Bible generally means "wicked" in the moral sense. There are, however, passages where it is used as a technical legal term for an outlaw, a person convicted of a crime, in contra-distinction to a *ẓaddiq,* a law-abiding citizen; *e.g.,* Deuteronomy 25:1–2. The Rabbis of the Talmud discerned this occasional use of these words as purely legal terms *totally* bereft of moral significance: *viz.* their exegesis of Exodus 23:7, which points to *ẓaddiq,* as meaning "not guilty," "acquitted," though in fact he had committed the crime (*Mekhilta;* B. Sanhedrin 33b; *Targum Onqelos* and Rashi on the verse); cf. also their exegesis of Isaiah 3:10 (B. Qiddushin 40a). Now, inasmuch as the rabbinic principle is that no man may render himself guilty of a crime because a man's confession is inadmissible in evidence, the dictum in later times took on the general meaning, "No man may incriminate himself." Thus רשע which in Raba's statement means simply פסול לעדות took on the general connotation of חייב.
7. The standard commentaries *Qorban HaEdah* and *P'nei Mosheh* explain the Palestinian Talmud on this Mishnah similarly.
8. In his commentary to the Mishnah, *ad loc.* Also Meiri, *ad loc.*
9. Tosaphoth, *ad loc., s.v. lema* (cf. Maharsha).
10. *Infra,* pp. 109 ff.

11. This seems to contradict the contention that self-incriminating statements are "stricken from the record" (*infra*, p. 110) and that "juridically they do not exist" (*infra*, p. 74). This is pointed out by Rabbi Aqiba Eger in his *Novellae to Kethuboth* 18b; cf. however, the explanations of R. Shymon Shkop, Kethuboth 18:5 and 20:1.

12. Since the testimony cannot be split.

13. R. Samuel Strashun (*Rashash*) on Yebamoth 25b, based upon Tosaphoth and Ran to Kethuboth 18b. It should be noted, however, that there are those who maintain that even R. Joseph does not declare the confessing witness a *rasha* and do not disqualify him from even acting as a witness; rather, he has disqualified himself only in this particular case. He will be accepted as a qualified and *bona fide* witness at any other trial (R. Shymon Shkop, *op. cit.,* 18:4 end–5).

14. Following the interpretation of the Tosaphoth, *s.v. b'omer.* The ordinary interpretation is that the witness actually said that he was with them but did not participate in the crime. Had he not actually said so, we would not construe his statement "as if to say . . . ," and R. Judah would not allow the woman to remarry.

15. M. Makkoth 1:7.

16. With the reservation that the Roman *universitas* was almost invariably quantitatively larger than the group of witnesses which usually came to testify in a Jewish court. I am borrowing the Roman term for its conceptual value; the Romans did not use it in connection with criminal procedure (cf. A. Berger, *Encyclopedic Dictionary of Roman Law*).

17. To Maimonides, although *absolute* truth is independent of any human testimony, the testimony of two witnesses serves as the standard model of the ultimate in *operational* truth—this is a dogmatic decree of Sacred Scripture (*Madda—Yesodei HaTorah* 7:7, 8:2).

18. B. Yoma 83a. Maimonides, *Judges—Testimony* 18:3, based on the Mishnah in Makkoth.

19. P. Sanhedrin 3:9.

20. For a definitive listing of persons disqualified from bearing witness under Jewish law, see Maimonides, *Judges—Evidence* 9 ff.

21. Maimonides, *ibid.,* 5:3 based upon M. Makkoth 1:8. That R. Aqiba mentioned in the previous *mishnah* is also the author

of this *mishnah* is clear from the *gemara,* B. Sanhedrin 9a, and
is followed by Rashi, Sanhedrin 41b.

22. B. Makkoth 6a.

23. As for the possibility that kinsmen of the accused might conspire
to deliberately join the witnesses in order to bring about the
eventual rejection of the entire group, cf. the talmudic portion
following and the comment of Tosaphoth thereon (*s.v. l'ass-
hudei*).

24. Nor need we ascribe the disqualification of a defendant or litigant to act as a witness to the general rule disqualifying interested parties; it should be viewed as an ultimate in and of itself
(Y. B. Solte, *Mishnath Yabeẓ, Ḥoshen Mishpat,* sect. 13).

Indeed, the biblical word עֵד, "witness," is itself eloquent
testimony to the sharp distinction between a witness and a
defendant. Verses such as Genesis 43:3, Exodus 19:21, 21:29 and
Jeremiah 11:7 clearly bring out the function of an עֵד as a
"warner." In contrast to the biblical ראה, "spectator" (*e.g.,*
Exodus 22:9; Leviticus 5:1 which may also be interpreted as
contrasting עֵד with ידע on the basis of Jeremiah 29:23; cf. R.
Jose the Galilean in B. Shebuoth 33b), an עֵד actively intervenes
against the accused by warning him (Arabic *wa'ada; contra*
Brown-Driver-Briggs, *s.v.* עֵד), seizing him (Numbers 5:13; Psalms
119:61, cf. Ibn Ezra), testifying *against* him (throughout the
Bible, except Isaiah 43:10 and 44:8 and Proverbs 14:25[?]. In
the Mishnah, a witness who speaks in behalf of the accused
after having given his adverse testimony is not to be heard;
M. Sanhedrin 5:4) and finally executing him (Deuteronomy
17:7). The wide range of meanings of the word עֵד (with the
common connotation of active intervention against the accused)
is not unique; cf. the varied meanings of הוכיח and דין as summarized by B. Gemser, "The *Rib*—or Controversy—Pattern in
Hebrew Mentality," *Wisdom in Israel and in the Ancient Near
East,* p. 124, note 4.

The problematic עֵד in Exodus 22:12 is taken by the Halakhah
(B. Baba Qamma 11a in the name of Abba Shaul; Maimonides,
Torts—Monetary Damages 7:13) as equivalent to עֵד (Genesis
49:27; cf. *Arukh* and *Teshuboth HaGeonim Zikhron LaRishonim* 4 [ed. A. A. Harkavy] Responsum 229) apparently along
the lines of קַו—קָו (Psalms 84:4, Deuteronomy 22:6).

The עֵד as adversary and prosecutor thus precludes the possibility of the defendant's statements in court ever attaining the status of testimony. Cf. N. H. Tur-Sinai's commentary on Job 16:19. The root meaning of עד as meaning "warner" explains the insistence of R. Jose (ben Ḥalaphta) that witnesses who themselves did not administer the warning (התראה) cannot bring about the accused's conviction (M. Makkoth 1:9).

25. *Yad Ramah*, Sanhedrin 9b; Meiri, Sanhedrin (ed. Sopher, p. 27); and especially, a responsum of Rabad quoted by Rosh, Makkoth 7a. This qualitative distinction between the disqualification of the "testimony" of the accused and that of a relative is the dominant view held among the great rabbinic commentators; cf. also *Responsa of Rosh* 60:1; Ramban and Ritba, Makkoth, *ibid.*; also *Responsa of Rashba*, V, 155, and *Responsa of Ritba* (ed. Qappaḥ), Responsum 52; *Nimmuqei Joseph*, Yebamoth 25b; *Responsa of Ribash*, 169, 195. R. Ezekiel Landau, *Noda Bihudah, Eben HaEzer*, 1st ed., 72, gives his stamp of approval to this approach. Rosh, *ibid.*, records a dissenting opinion which makes no such distinction; it would appear that Rashi and Tosaphoth, Sanhedrin 9b, as well as Maimonides (*Judges—Evidence* 12–13) also did not make this distinction. For some recent analyses of the positions of Rashi, Maimonides and Rabad in which attempts are made to describe the extent to which common ground may be ascribed to them, cf. E. Y. Finkel, *Dibrei Eliezer*, Vol. I: Yebamoth, Ch. 17, and Ch. Sachnovitz, *Tosephoth Ḥaim —Sanhedrin*, Ch. 7. Rabbi Finkel interprets the controversy between Raba and R. Joseph as revolving around the proper understanding of the rejection of a team of witnesses when one of the witnesses is discovered to be a relative or is otherwise disqualified. Raba insists that this rule of rejection is operative only when the statements made by the *universitas* had achieved the legal status of "testimony"; R. Joseph maintains that this is not necessary.

26. The talmudic use of a legal term to cover items that are conceptually related to the genre though technically not included is not infrequent. *E.g.*, the use of the terms שליח, שליחות (a duly authorized agent) in M. Baba Meẓia 8:3 to refer to a hired hand or a *cliens* (according to R. Hisda, B. Baba Qamma 104a) or to a father acting on behalf of his minor daughter (B. Gittin 21a).

27. I am aware that these words are a significant departure from Rashi who, in his comments to Sanhedrin 9b, Yebamoth 25b

and Kethuboth 18b, does construe the dictum narrowly: The accused is literally a relative to himself, and, as a *relative*, cannot render himself a *rasha*. In my humble opinion, the talmudic discussion in Kethuboth 18b–19a precludes this interpretation, for the principle that a man may not speak to his own detriment is applied to cases where he would not thereby be rendered a *rasha* and where his qualification to act as a witness is not placed in jeopardy; cf. *infra*, pp. 107 ff. There is a qualitative distinction between a man himself and his "other" kinsmen. Cf. Y. M. Rabinowitz, *Afiqei Yam*, Part I, Ch. 39 for the development of some of the implications of Rashi's position.

CHAPTER V
POST-TALMUDIC EXEGESIS, COMMENTARY AND EXPANSION

1. *Responsa of R. Joseph ibn Migash*, No. 186; Rashi, Yebamoth 25b.
2. Paul, *Digest* 42.2.1.
3. Cf. further, W. Kunkel, *Untersuchungen zur Entwicklung der roemischen Kriminalverfahren*, pp. 102–104, and 113, note 413; and W. Pueschel, *Confessus pro judicato est, passim*. There is full evidence that in Greco-Roman Egypt, this rule prevailed already from the Ptolemaic period; R. Taubenschlag, *The Law of Greco-Roman Egypt in the Light of the Papyri*, pp. 388–389. In English law, cf. 11 *Coke* 30 (King's Bench Reports).
4. Seneca, *Controversiones*, 8.1; Quintilian, *Declamationes*, 314.
5. Sallust, *Catalina*, 52.36.
6. *Römisches Strafrecht*, p. 438, note 2. Cf. further W. Kunkel, "Quaestio," *Realenzyklopädie der Klassischen Altertumswissenschaft*, 24 (1963), pp. 755–756.
7. *Oẓar HaGeonim LeMassekheth Sanhedrin*, p. 81; Rabbenu Yeruḥam, *Sepher Toledoth Adam We-Ḥawwah*, Nathib 18, Pt. 3; and R. Jacob Berab, *Quntres HaSemikhah*, printed in Y. L. Maimon, *Ḥiddush HaSanhedrin Be-Medinathenu HaM'ḥuddesheth*, p. 77, citing a geonic responsum. This corroborates Prof. S. Lieberman's statement to me that the same source cited by R. David ben Zimra, *Judges—Sanhedrin* 18:6, although it is introduced by the word תניא , is geonic. Rashi's application of the rule to non-capital criminal cases (Yebamoth 25b) does not mention the *Geonim*.

8. Cf. *infra*, pp. 114–115.

9. *Oẓar HaGeonim LeMassekheth Sanhedrin, ibid.* and Rabbenu Yeruḥam, *ibid.*

10. *Judges—Sanhedrin* 18:6. *Mordekhai* (*Sanhedrin* 692) writes in a similar vein.

11. Joshua 7.

12. II Samuel 1.

13. Cf. *Encyclopedia Talmudith, s.v.* הוראת שעה, and Rabbi Z. H. Chajes, *Torath HaNebiim,* Ch. III.

14. The existence of an entire body of secular "king's" laws, functioning side by side with the body of Torah law and supplementing it, is recognized by rabbinic law; S. Gandz, *Monumenta Talmudica, II Recht,* pp. 8–10. Maimonides, *Judges—Kings* 3:8–4:10 and cf. remarks of *Or Sameah* on *Torts—Murder* 2:4. Rabbenu Nissim, *Sheneym Asar Derushim,* 11. Rabbi M. Schreiber, *Responsa of Ḥatham Sopher, Orah Ḥaim* 208. E. Waldenberg, *Hilkhoth Medinah,* I, *Sha'ar* III, Chs. 5 and 6. S. Federbush, *Mishpat HaMelukhah BeYisrael,* pp. 70 ff. For its biblical antecedents, cf. Y. Kaufmann, *Toledoth HaEmunah HaYisraelith* II, p. 217 *contra* R. de Vaux, *Ancient Israel,* p. 150 f.

15. For a striking illustration of this, cf. the passage cited *supra,* p. 44.

16. M. Sanhedrin 4:5; cf. Philo, *De Specialibus Legibus,* IV, 60–61; S. Belkin, *Philo and the Oral Law,* p. 180.

17. Cf. also L. Feilchenfeld, *Die Zeugen im Strafprozess des Talmud,* pp. 13 f. Rabbi Ḥaim Joseph David Azulai (*Ḥida*) in his commentary on *Ḥoshen Mishpat* entitled *Birkhei Yoseph* (34:33) considers the interpretation of Maimonides' scriptural decree as being Deuteronomy 19:15–16, as we have indicated (*supra,* pp. 40–41), a forced one. We have been unable, however, to find a more suitable one. The sentence, "This is done only on the evidence of two witnesses," coming after mention of "a scriptural decree," would seem to support our position; cf. *Torath Ha Nebiim,* Ch. III, p. 27, note 2 end. Cf., also, D. M. Shohet, *The Jewish Court in the Middle Ages,* pp. 161 ff., and S. Menḋelsohn, *The Criminal Jurisprudence of the Ancient Hebrews,* pp. 115–119, 133–134. The latter is rich in references to rabbinic sources and replete with quotations that are both apt and telling. A pungent example is the following (p. 115, note 259) :

Common law requires two witnesses in cases of treason only; in almost every other cause one positive witness is sufficent (Blackstone IV, 357). But reason requires two witnesses, since a witness who asserts and an accused who denies counterbalance each other, and it requires the testimony of a third party to make a decision possible (Beccaria Para. 13). Montesquieu (B. XII, C. III) is rightly of the opinion that "those laws which condemn a man to death on the deposition of a single witness are fatal to liberty." By Talmudic criminal law, one witness is not only incompetent to convict a person of an alleged crime, but is also considered a slanderer and liable to the punishment of the slanderer (Cf. *Pesaḥim* 113b).

Cf. Philo, *De Specialibus Legibus,* IV 53–54; E. R. Goodenough, *The Jurisprudence of the Jewish Courts in Egypt,* pp. 188–189.

18. Maimonides, *Judges—Evidence* 12:1.

19. Radbaz, *ad loc.* For a recent (and in my humble opinion, unsatisfactory) attempt to explain Maimonides' resort to scriptural "decree," cf. M. Roth, *Qol Mebasser,* Vol. II, 22:3.

20. Consult the excellent treatment of this aspect of the problem written by N. Lamm, "The Fifth Amendment and its Equivalent in the Halakah," *Judaism* V, 1, pp. 53–59. On the confession generally, cf. O. J. Rogge, *Why Men Confess,* pp. 67–73 (on confessions by innocent people), 187–206 (a negative critique of confessions), and 209–247 (on the compulsion to confess). On the other hand, the work of Theodor Reik, *The Compulsion to Confess* (cf. especially pp. 265–266), is essentially concerned with pieces of unethical behavior, especially those remembered from childhood, which the neurotic imagines to be "crimes." It should not be interpreted as seriously relevant to false criminal confessions to illegal acts.

21. R. Faiwes of Cracow quoted in *Pithḥei Teshubah, Ḥoshen Mishpat* 34:40. Also, *Sema (Sepher Meirath Einaim), Ḥoshen Mishpat* 34:60, in the name of *Mordekhai* (cf., however, *Gib'ath Shaul* by R. Saul of Lomze, Responsum 17, for a better interpretation of Mordekhai's statement).

22. A good example, but not for traditional Jewish law whose penal code never prescribed jail sentences. The biblical jail is either (1) a house of detention, holding the accused until the situation, legal or otherwise, is clarified (Leviticus 24:12; Numbers 15:34; B. Kethuboth 33b on Exodus 21:19) or (2) a form of punish-

ment meted out by royal prerogative (Jeremiah 20:2 f.; 29:26; 32:2–3 ff.). The mishnaic jail (M. Pesaḥim 8:16; M. Moed Qatan 3:1), if Jewish, is not penal; it serves either as a house of detention (*Teshuboth HaGeonim, Sha'arei Teshubah,* Responsum 182) or as a method of coercion for specific performance (Rashi, Pesaḥim 91a; *Responsa of R. Joseph ibn Migash,* No. 122). *Kippah* (M. Sanhedrin 9:5) is not a prison but an (exceptional) form of execution (B. Sanhedrin 81b); L. Kantor, *Beitraege zur Lehre von der Strafrechtlichen Schuld im Talmud (Kippah Strafe).* Prison sentences are apparently post-talmudic; P. Dykon, *Dinei Onashin,* pp. 1318–1322. On all of the foregoing, see M. Elon, "HaMa'assar BaMishpat HaIbri," *Sepher HaYobel LePinchas Rosen,* pp. 171–201.

23. S. Rosenbaum, "HaHokhahoth Bemishpatim Peliliim," *HaMishpat,* I (1927), p. 288. Cf. also J. Bentham, *The Rationale of Judicial Evidence,* Vol. III, Bk. V, Ch. VI, Sect. III and the argument of Dimiter Dhiev in the Petkov case, quoted by O. J. Rogge, *op. cit.,* pp. 203–204.

24. Cf. Maimonides on M. Sanhedrin 6:2 and R. Moses Schreiber, *Responsa on Oraḥ Ḥaim,* No. 208 (paragraph 4).

25. Cf. Maimonides' Introduction to his Code and S. W. Baron, "The Historical Outlook of Maimonides," reprinted in *History of Jewish Historians,* pp. 129 and 161–163. For the biblical antecedents of this rabbinic idea, cf. R. de Vaux, *Ancient Israel,* p. 151.

26. Joshua (5:2–10) introduced many important details into the circumcision ritual (B. Yebamoth 71b); and, from his farewell address (Ch. 24), the Rabbis learn that one should not rebuke others until his life is drawing to a close (*Siphrei,* Deuteronomy 3).

27. E. Waldenberg, *op. cit.,* p. 161. Cf., however, Rabbi A. I. Kook, *Mishpat Kohen,* 144:13 (p. 335).

28. B. Baba Bathra 14b end.

29. Cf. *supra,* note 25.

30. *Supra,* p. 65. *E.g.,* David's reaction to the news of the death of Saul taught the Rabbis many laws of mourning (B. Moed Qatan 22b and 26a). For the talmudic interpretation of the Bathsheba incident, cf. B. Shabbath 56a.

31. In his commentary on Second Samuel, *ad loc.*

32. So, too, Abravanel.

33. I Samuel 24:4–7; 26:8–11.
34. A. B. Ehrlich, *Mikra ki-Pheschuto* on vss. 14–16.
35. Cf. II Samuel 3:39.
36. Attention should be called also to Job 9:20 and 15:6 which, although inconclusive, are relevant to the discussion.
37. Cf. further B. Sanhedrin 49a on Joshua 1:18 and Ramban on Leviticus 27:29; R. Margalioth, *Margalioth HaYam*, Sanhedrin 43b, paragraph 13. Rabbi I. Herzog, *Torath HaOhel*, pp. 55b–56b, presents an interesting juridic analysis of *hora'ath sha'ah* and *din malkhuth;* cf. further Y. M. Ginzburg, "Ha'ashamah Azmith l'phee Mishpat HaTorah," *HaTorah We-HaMedinah* 9 (1958), pp. 86–87. According to Maimonides, executions based upon the extra-halakhic royal prerogative had to be carried out through beheading exclusively. Hence, the stoning and burning of Akhan was not the product of State (royal) law. It may be, then, that Maimonides' mention of emergency law explains Joshua's action, and his mention of royal prerogative explains that of David. I am grateful to Rabbi Yaakov Hopfer for this novel suggestion.
38. As quoted by R. Joseph Qaro in *Beth Yoseph, Ḥoshen Mishpat,* 388. Cf. *Responsa of Rashba*, Vol. III, No. 393.
39. *Supra,* p. 51, limiting *rasha* only as it is used in Exodus 23:1, *i.e.,* with regard to acting as a witness. Thus רשע = לעדות פסול. All the other authorities take it as meaning "condemned," "declared guilty"; thus רשע = חייב.
40. *Judges—Evidence* 12:1, cited fully *infra,* p. 73.
41. *Judges—Sanhedrin* 18:6, cited fully *supra,* p. 62.
42. The disqualification of relatives, *supra,* p. 63.
43. M. Nedarim 11:12.
44. In accordance with the amoraic interpretation of the Mishnah, B. Nedarim 91a.
45. On the basis of Leviticus 21:7.
46. B. Kethuboth 10a.
47. All the foregoing, *Sepher HaRashbash*, Responsa 521, 532 and 544.
48. *Shittah Mequbbezeth, ad loc.*
49. B. Sanhedrin 46a. This talmudic passage is referred to as "the *hora'ath sha'ah* clause." For a comprehensive legal commentary on this passage, cf. Y. M. Ginzburg, *Mishpatim LeYisrael*, pp. 1–70.
50. Cf. *supra,* pp. 65–67.

51. *Responsa of the Rosh,* 11:5. Extra-halakhic measures and punishments were frequently invoked in the Middle Ages in accordance with the needs of the times. S. Assaf, *HaOnashin Aharei Ḥathimath HaTalmud; Oẓar HaGeonim—Sanhedrin,* p. 357. This will be discussed in detail in the next section.

52. Similarly *Responsa of Ribash,* 281 and *Kenesseth HaGedolah, Eben HaEzer* (section *Tur*), 115:17 and *Mishpat Ẓedek,* I, Responsum 59 (who stipulates, however, that the brazen confession must have been uttered when the man was sober and fully aware of the import of his words).

53. *Judges—Sanhedrin* 18:6.

54. *Supra,* p. 62.

55. R. Joseph Azulai in his *Birkhei Yoseph, Ḥoshen Mishpat* 34:33, takes up the cudgels against R. Solomon and musters all the authoritative contradictions to and refutations of his thesis.

56. *Judges—Sanhedrin* 18:6.

57. Suicide is a grave sin, B. Baba Qamma 91b; Maimonides, *Torts—Wounding* 2:2–3 (cf. thereon M. Guttmann, "Zur Quellenkritik des Mishnah Thora," *Monatsschrift f. Geschichte u. Wissenschaft d. Judenthums,* 79 [1935], pp. 151–152).

58. B. Baba Qamma, *loc. cit.;* Maimonides, *ibid.,* 5:1; *Responsa of R. Joseph ibn Migash,* No. 186.

59. *Viz.,* the manifold dietary laws.

60. *Supra,* p. 39.

61. Exodus 22:24.

62. Leviticus 20.

63. Maimonides, *Judges—Evidence* 12:1. For a thoroughgoing discussion of various aspects of these rules, cf. *Qeẓoth HaḤoshen* 28:8.

64. R. Shymon Shkop, *Novellae to Kethuboth* 18:5. These words should in no wise be construed as impinging on the doctrine of freedom of will. What we are discussing are rules of court procedure and standards of evidence; man of course remains morally free both in action and in speech. This must be kept in the mind as one reads, for example, the opening remarks of Mr. Justice White in the *Miranda* case (384 U.S. 436).

65. R. Aqiba Eger, *Novellae to Kethuboth* 18b.

66. Cf. Job 9:20 and 15:6.

67. R. Shymon Shkop, *ibid.* For a fuller understanding of the Radbaz' position, we call attention to the *halakhic* requirement

that, in order to convict the accused of a capital crime, it was necessary that witnesses testify not only that he committed the crime with full knowledge and intent but also that התיר עצמו למיתה, "he gave himself up to death," *i.e.*, he made a kind of suicidal statement such as, "I am committing this act with the purpose of rendering myself subject to the death penalty" (B. Sanhedrin 40b). Doesn't this halakhic requirement constitute a refutation of Radbaz' interpretation inasmuch as the accused is being convicted on the basis of a statement he has made, on the basis of his own utterance?! In reply we maintain: This halakhic requirement of התיר עצמו למיתה has been variously identified as (a) an independent requirement of the Jewish criminal code necessary for conviction in a capital case (Tosaphoth, Sanhedrin 41a, *s.v. b'ishah,* first opinion) and as (b) an additional element in the general legal requirement of *hathra'ah,* "prior warning" *(ibid.,* second opinion, and Maimonides, *Judges— Sanhedrin* 12:2). But whichever form this identification takes, it is clear that the act of murder objectively and duly attested to is the decisive factor that convicts the murderer; his suicidal statement can be nothing more than a necessary condition for conviction. (Rashi's statement, Sanhedrin 41a, *s.v. ha-meth* must be understood this way.) On התיר עצמו למיתה , cf. M. A. Amiel, *Darkhei Mosheh,* Bk. II: "Modes of Acquisition" (Hebrew), p. 19.

68. A. N. Enker and S. H. Elsen, "Counsel for the Suspect," 49 *Minnesota Law Review* (1964), p. 67. Note 67 there provides ample evidence of the influence of Radbaz. It is of interest to note that this article is cited by Mr. Chief Justice Warren in *Miranda v. Arizona,* 384 U.S. 436, note 2.

69. *Kenesseth HaGedolah, Ḥoshen Mishpat* (section *Tur*) 34:62–63; *Pithei Teshubah, ibid.,* citing the case from a responsum of *Shemen Rokaḥ,* I, No. 61. Among the authorities who reject the decision of the court are Maharam Lublin (Responsum 81) and Rama (R. Moses Isserles). For further details on this question, cf. *Ḥina WaḤisda,* Pt. 2, p. 27b (col. 1).

70. Cf. *infra,* pp. 114–116.

71. *Infra,* p. 127.

72. Cited by *Qeẓoth HaḤoshen,* 34:4. For the further development of the idea expressed herein in his name, cf. *Oholei Aharon,* Ch. 14.

73. *Ḥoshen Mishpat* 40:1. A brief analysis of the juridical nature of confession in money matters may be found in S. Rosenbaum, *op. cit.*, pp. 282–283. For all the ramifications of the question as to what extent such a confession could effectuate acquisition, cf. *Encyclopedia Talmudith*, "Oditha"; and M. Elias, "HaHoda'ah," *HaMishpat HaIbri*, I, pp. 184–185. The Roman parallel may be found in the form of acquisition known as *in iure cessio;* cf. Sohm-Mitteis-Wenger, *Institutionen* (1924), pp. 55–56; Wenger-Fisk, *Institutes of the Roman Law of Civil Procedure* (1940), pp. 170 ff.

74. *Shakh, Ḥoshen Mishpat* 37 beg.

75. *Supra,* pp. 56–58.

76. *Qeẓoth HaHoshen* 34:4 and 241:1. For the further development of this idea, cf. *Oholei Aharon*, Ch. 13.

77. Leviticus 7:22–25. Cf. also 3:14–17.

78. *Ibid.,* 4:27–28. The same holds true for all sins the deliberate violation of which is punishable by *kareth,* extirpation. For a list of such violations, see Maimonides, *Offerings—Errors* 1:4.

79. M. Kerithoth 3:1. Maimonides, *Offerings—Errors* 3:1.

80. Maimonides, *Judges—Sanhedrin* 19:1 (item 8).

81. Tosaphoth, Yebamoth 25b, *s.v. w'en.*

82. Tosaphoth, Baba Meẓia 3b, *s.v. mah.*

83. *Ar'a DeRabbanan* 17. This approach is clearly implied also in the words of Rabbenu Asher, *Shittah Mequbbeẓeth*, Kethuboth, at the end of 19a, and *Kenesseth HaGedolah, Oraḥ Ḥaim*, 163:21. Incidentally, it is worthwhile to note that a man—and not witnesses, as many and as trustworthy as they may be—is the ultimate authority in deciding his status before his Maker. Indeed, if two witnesses say that he ate the forbidden food and he says that he did not, we have seen that he is not obligated to bring the sin-offering. If, on the other hand, two witnesses say that he did not eat it but he insists that he did, then he must bring the sin-offering, although by doing so he is, according to these two witnesses, committing the sin of bringing an unsanctified and unnecessary offering to the Temple (Tosaphoth, Baba Meẓia 3b, *s.v. mah*). When a man's own soul is involved, says the Talmud, he is more trustworthy than one hundred witnesses (B. Kerithoth 12a).

84. Of course these variations in the interpretation of the credibility of a man acknowledging his own indebtedness imply correspond-

ing differences in the interpretation of the role of the court that hears the case: According to the interpretation of Mahari ibn Leb, the court is analogous to a notary public who merely certifies the fact that a "gift" is being granted; according to the interpretation of R. Aryeh Leib HaCohen, however, the court is performing its classic task of sifting and accepting items in evidence (M. A. Amiel, *Darkhei Mosheh,* pp. 3–4). According to the interpretation of R. Jacob Algasi, we may regard the court as an ecclesiastical tribunal facilitating a sinner in his act of repentance.

CHAPTER VI
MEDIEVAL RABBINIC CRIMINAL PROCEDURE

1. Quoted in full, *supra,* p. 70. Cf. also Maimonides, *Judges— Sanhedrin* 24:4–10. For an application of the *hora'ath sha'ah* principle to the rule against self-incrimination, in a period earlier than the one under discussion in this section, cf. *infra,* pp. 114–115.

2. *HaOnashin Aharei Hathimath HaTalmud.* The three examples of medieval departures from the Talmud mentioned in the previous paragraph are documented on pp. 12–15. The problem of basic changes in the collection of debts and related questions has been recently dealt with in an exhaustive manner in M. Elon, *Freedom of the Debtor's Person in Jewish Law* (Hebrew); cf. summarizing remarks on pp. 255–264. For a description of the vast powers wielded by the Spanish-Jewish judicial authorities and the questions raised by many of their innovations, cf. A. Neuman, *The Jews in Spain,* Vol. I, pp. 46–47, 138–146, and Y. Baer, *A History of the Jews in Christian Spain,* Vol. II, pp. 64–71.

3. Cf. *Siphrei,* Deuteronomy 25:12.

4. Cf. *supra,* p. 169, note 22.

5. Assaph, pp. 15–31. On pp. 31–44 the author describes excommunication, banishment, public humiliation, deprivation of one's right to vote, and confiscation of property.

6. Actually listed as a series of responsa, nos. 234–239. The relevant sections are quoted by Assaph, pp. 83–84.

7. Cf. Baer, Vol. III, pp. 73 ff; A. M. Hershman, *Rabbi Isaac ben Sheshet Perfet and His Times.*

8. The preceding three paragraphs are based upon Neuman, Vol. I, pp. 19–33.

9. *Zikhron Yehudah,* Responsum 63; main excerpt also in Assaph, p. 79.

10. Neuman, Vol. I, pp. 130 and 132; documentation omitted.

11. Assaph, *ibid.,* p. 19 f. Neuman, *ibid.,* pp. 130–138. D. Kaufmann "Jewish Informers in the Middle Ages," *Jewish Quarterly Review* (Old Series), Vol. VIII (1896), pp. 217 ff. English digest in I. Agus, *Rabbi Meir of Rothenberg,* Vol. II, pp. 672–676. Legal precedent for death of the informer may be found in B. Baba Qamma 117a, B. Berakhoth 58a, B. Abodah Zarah 26b, Maimonides, *Torts—Assault* 8:10–11, *Knowledge—Idolatry* 10:1. In tracing the medieval development, S. Albeck, "The Principles of Government in the Jewish Communities of Spain until the 13th Century" (Hebrew) in *Zion* XXV (1960), pp. 106–114, is careful to point out that although the *hora'ath sha'ah* principle of B. Sanhedrin 46a is most often cited, there is no doubt that it was combined with the self-defense clause as the basis for prosecution and punishment of informers (B. Berakhoth 58a; B. Sanhedrin 72a ff.).

12. Neuman, Vol. I, pp. 35–36. As for the historical antecedents and the juridical basis of the *qahal* in its judicial capacity, cf. Albeck, *op. cit.,* pp. 85 ff.

13. Neuman, Vol. I, p. 61.

14. Assaph, p. 83, note 1; Baer, Vol. II, p. 81.

15. It was sometimes difficult to draw the line between legitimate use of the non-Jewish law-enforcement agencies and informing; cf. Baer, Vol. I, pp. 285–286.

16. Cf. *supra,* note 6.

17. Cf. *e.g.,* Baer, Vol. II, p. 33. The term used is הרמנא דמלכא. Cf. *Responsa of Rabbenu Asher* 17:8 and the remarks of I. Agus, *Rabbi Meir of Rothenberg,* Vol. I, p. 71, note 85.

18. Italics by the editor, Assaph.

19. Valencia; Hershman, *op. cit.,* p. 229.

20. *Berurim,* a term of the widest application, sometimes more general than and sometimes identical with *muqdamim* (Neuman, Vol. I, pp. 35–36).

21. On the general attitude of the rabbinic authorities of the time to lawyers, cf. Neuman, Vol. I, pp. 118–120; in medieval Ger-

many, cf. L. Finkelstein, *Jewish Self-Government in the Middle Ages,* p. 72.

22. Assaph, pp. 85–86.
23. Responsum 239. For a summary of the case and its background, cf. Hershman, pp. 137–140.
24. *E.g.,* F. Baer, *Die Juden im Christlichen Spanien,* Vol. I: *Urkunden u. Registen,* Nos. 317, 356, 398.
25. Legal, not philosophical, standards are meant; J. L. Teicher, "Laws of Reason and Laws of Religion: A Conflict in Toledo Jewry in the Fourteenth Century," *Essays and Studies Presented to Stanley Arthur Cook* (London, 1950), pp. 88–94.
26. *Zikhron Yehudah,* Responsum 58; Assaph, pp. 77–78.
27. *Ibid.,* p. 53a.
28. *Ibid.,* Responsum 58, using the word *pesquisa,* inquisition. Cf. Baer, Vol. II, "Appendix: The Inquisition of the Catholic Church and the Criminal Jurisdiction of the Jewish Communities," pp. 444–456, on the differences between *inquisitio* and *pesquisa,* on the Aragonian ban on *inquisitio,* and on the differences between talmudic law and Jewish-Spanish practice. On p. 453, the Baer translation of the relevant excerpt from Responsum 58 indicates that the prohibition of ferreting out people who could invalidate the witnesses, an act of *pesquisa,* is forbidden by the *laws of the land;* although this has no basis in the original (Hebrew) text of the responsum, it seems to be historically correct.

CHAPTER VII

RANGE OF APPLICABILITY

1. *Supra,* p. 53.
2. Cf. Maimonides' *Introduction to the Mishnah* (ed. *Rambam La'am*), pp. 37–42.
3. *E.g.,* certain types of gamblers; "He who raises his hand to strike his fellow is rabbinically disqualified." Cf. *Shulḥan Arukh, Ḥoshen Mishpat* 34 *passim.*
4. *Kenesseth HaGedolah* 34 (sect. *Tur*), 58 citing Responsum 13 of R. Solomon b. Isaac HaLevi (sect. *Eben HaEzer*), who, however, does not make the statement explicitly. Also by implication, R. Simeon B. Ẓemaḥ Duran, *Tashbaẓ,* Vol. II, Responsum

55. Proof of the soundness of this application of the law against self-incrimination has been adduced from the Talmud itself (B. Sanhedrin 9b, quoted fully *supra*, p. 50) and Maimonides (*Civil Laws—Pleading* 2:3), for were there to have been a rabbinic law disqualification, the rulings mentioned in these sources would have been rendered inoperative (*Ḥina WaḤisda*, p. 30a, and *Ar'a DeRabbanan* 17).

5. Thus, the passage from B. Sanhedrin 25a (*infra*, p. 109) which deals with a rabbinic disqualification to act as a witness (Tosaphoth, R. Aaron HaLevi, and *Nimmuqei Yoseph*) also is based on the assumption that even in such matters our principle applies. Rabad also agrees; *Responsa of Rabad*, ed. Y. Qappaḥ, No. 20. Cf. *Birkhei Yoseph, Ḥoshen Mishpat* 34:34 for a survey of the *Rishonim*, the early medieval commentators, on this question, and *Ar'a DeRabbanan* 17 who establishes the point on the basis of B. Kethuboth 18a. There are, however, those who disagree. Thus, R. Moses Benveniste, *P'nei Mosheh*, Vol. II, Responsum 105, finds it necessary to refute the contention of one R. Aaron Sasoon that the law against self-incrimination does not apply to rabbinic enactments. R. Ḥaim Abulafia, in his Hebrew treatise, "No Man May Incriminate Himself," pt. 1 (p. 8b, published at the end of *Ashdoth HaPisgah* by R. Joseph Naḥmuli), surveys the pros and cons on this question, and, basing himself on many earlier interpreters (Naḥmanides, R. Solomon ibn Adreth, R. Aaron HaLevi and R. Joshua Falk), concludes that only one authority has declared that the law against self-incrimination does *not* apply to rabbinic enactments, namely Rashi (R. Joel Sirkes, *Bah, Ḥoshen Mishpat* 46:34 maintains that even Rashi agrees); and, inasmuch as all the other authorities are arrayed against him, Rashi's view is rejected. (This deliberate rejection of Rashi's view is significant. In *Halakhah,* as long as there exists a controversy among the authorities, the plaintiff, with the *onus probandi* placed squarely upon his shoulders, cannot collect; for, where one of the witnesses who testifies in behalf of the creditor-plaintiff is a self-confessed violator of a rabbinic enactment, the defendant can argue, "Prove to us that the definitive law is not in accordance with Rashi's interpretation." When a view of an authority is *deliberately* rejected, however, this counter-argument falls away.) No less an authority than Rabbi Jonathan Eybeschitz demurs,

however, and finds great merit in Rashi's position *("Kizzur Kelalei Miggo,"* para. 105 end, in *Urim WeThummim* 82). Rabbi Ezekiel Landau maintains that the question has not been resolved *(Noda Bihudah, Eben HaEzer,* 2nd ed., Responsum 156).

6. R. Abraham B. David of Posquieres *(Rabad)*, cited by R. Nissim Gerondi *(Ran)*, Kethuboth 72a; R. Israel Jacob Algasi, *Qehillath Ya'aqob,* 17; R. Hezekiah Medini, *Mikhtab LeḤezekiah,* Mishnah Sukkah 2:9; R. Solomon, *Ḥina WaḤisda,* Kethuboth 18 (p. 29b).

7. *Ar'a DeRabbanan* 17, citing a responsum of R. Solomon b. Isaac HaLevi; similarly R. Israel Lipschitz, *Tiph'ereth Yisrael,* Yebamoth Ch. 5, *Boaz* para. 2. It was on the basis of a similar line of reasoning that the New Jersey Supreme Court recently ruled that the United States constitutional safeguards barring involuntary confessions applied to juvenile as well as adult defendants. "Assuming a juvenile is not entitled to all the requirements of a criminal trial," the court asserted, "we firmly believe that he is at least entitled to a fact-finding process which measures up to the essentials of due process and fair treatment." *The New York Times,* Nov. 22, 1966, p. 43.

8. B. Sanhedrin 56a (bot.) ff.; Maimonides, *Judges—Kings* 9:1.

9. B. Sanhedrin 57b; cf. Maimonides, *Judges—Kings* 9:14.

10. A. Schmiedl, "A Comparison of Roman to Talmudic Law" (Hebrew), *HaShaḥar,* X, pp. 52–54, correlates these Noahide rules with the actual court procedure practiced in the Roman world.

11. P. Qiddushin 1:1. Prof. Saul Lieberman, too, believes this to be the correct reading. Cf. further *Midrash Bereshit Rabba* (J. Theodor and Ch. Albeck, eds.), notes to 34:14.

12. Ed. Chavel, 28. Cf. remarks in *Minhath Ḥinukh, ad loc.* The author of the *Sepher HaḤinukh* reaffirms his position in Precept 192.

13. Cf. *supra,* p. 58.

14. The last two paragraphs are based upon R. Joseph Babad, *Minhath Ḥinukh, ad locum.*

15. A. Sopher, ed., *Meiri's Beth HaBeḥirah on Sanhedrin,* p. 224, note 8. Cf. further M. Roth, *Qol Mebasser,* Vol. II, 22:3.

16. II Samuel 1.

17. Maimonides, *Civil Laws—Pleading* 2:1, 3. Indeed, the *only* way one may be disqualified from taking an oath in court is by the testimony of two witnesses; cf. *Tashbaz*, Pt. I, Responsum 55.

18. R. Don Vidal of Toulouse, *Maggid Mishneh, ad loc.*, R. Solomon ibn Adreth (*Rashba*) and R. Yom Tob b. Abraham Ishbili (*Ritba*), Shebuoth 46b. R. Nissim Gerondi (*Ran*), however, disagrees; he maintains that disqualification to take an oath is a monetary liability, in which case self-incrimination does obtain.

19. R. Sabbetai Cohen, *Shakh*, and R. Jacob b. Moses of Lisa, *Nethiboth HaMishpat, Hoshen Mishpat* 92:5.

20. R. Meir Todros HaLevi (*Ramah*) cited in *Tur Hoshen Mishpat* 92; R. Isaac Alfasi cited in *Bah* (*ibid.*); and R. Jacob b. Asher, *Tur, Hoshen Mishpat* (*ibid.*).

21. M. Shebuoth 7:1 gives examples of such oaths.

22. *Supra*, pp. 38–39.

23. B. Baba Qamma 64b. According to R. Avigdor b. Elijah (quoted with approval by *Mordekhai*, Baba Qamma, para. 180 end) this rule applies only to fines ordained by the Bible; rabbinically ordained fines must be paid upon one's admission of guilt.

24. Exodus 22:3.

25. *Civil Laws—Pleading* 1:17.

26. For other examples of how this distinction applies, cf. *Tur Hoshen Mishpat* 46 in the name of R. Asher b. Yehiel (*Rosh*) and R. Zebi Ashkenazi, *Hakham Zebi*, Responsum 150.

27. B. Baba Qamma 75a.

28. Cf. *supra*, pp. 79–80, where, however, the act of repentance *requires* payment, for it concerns *mammon*.

29. Cf. *supra*, p. 63.

30. This suggestion was made by R. Moses Steinberg of New York, formerly of Brod, Galicia, in a talmudic discourse, *Shabbath Shubah*, 5727.

31. In contrast to the interpretation presented throughout.

32. Maimonides, *Torts—Theft* 3:8.

33. Rashi and Tosaphoth, Makkoth 5a (*s.v. d'bedina*), and Zebahim 71a (*s.v. al*), and Baba Qamma 41b (*s.v. al*). Rashi's comment to Qiddushin 50a (*s.v. lo abid inish*) can be understood better if one bears in mind his general approach to the question as it has been herein delineated (although the author of *Ar'a DeRabbanan* interprets it in line with Tosaphoth, *Baba Mezia* 3b,

s.v. mah; cf. *supra,* pp. 79–80) . See further Yiẓhaq Arieli, *Einaim LaMishpat: Makkoth,* pp. 33–34.

34. *Responsa of Rashba,* Vol. II (entitled *Sepher Toledoth Adam*) , no. 231. Similarly, Meiri, Nedarim 90b. For an explanation of the apparent contradiction between this ruling and the talmudic passage in B. Kethuboth 18b, cf. *Novellae* of R. Aqiba Eger, *ad loc.*

35. Katz, D., and Glasner, Y., eds., *Pisqei Din* etc. (Cases of the District Rabbinical Courts of Israel) , Vol. I, pp. 145–159.

36. This distinction is also implied in the statements of Ribam, cited in the *Glosses to Asheri,* Baba Qamma 102b, and of Radbaz, cited in *Birkhei Yoseph, Ḥoshen Mishpat* 34:33 and also alluded to in para. 34.

37. For detailed treatments of *Oditha,* cf. *Qeẓoth HaḤoshen,* 194, note 4, and *Encyclopedia Talmudith.*

38. Cf., however, *Qeẓoth HaḤoshen* 34:4 (end) who finds difficulty in ascertaining the basis for this rule.

39. This extension, however, is not unanimous. Cf. *infra,* note 47.

40. *Kenesseth HaGedolah, Ḥoshen Mishpat* 34:68, in the name of R. Moses Mintz.

41. *Noda Bihudah, Eben HaEzer,* 2nd ed., Responsum 71.

42. *Beth Yoseph, Ḥoshen Mishpat* 46 citing a responsum of Rashba; also in chapter 49.

43. *Mordekhai,* Baba Meẓia, para. 338 end.

44. *Mordekhai,* Baba Qamma, para. 180 end, in the name of R. Avigdor b. Elijah.

45. R. Joseph Saul Nathanson, *Shoel U-Meshib,* 1st ed., part 3, Responsum 62 (concerning minutiae in the writing of a Torah scroll) ; and 5th ed., entitled *Dibrei Shaul WeYoseph Da'ath* 83 based upon *Shittah Mequbbeẓeth,* Kethuboth 18b–19a (concerning the ritual washing of the hands in preparation for the priestly benediction) .

46. *Shittah Mequbbeẓeth,* Kethuboth 19a, in the name of Ramban and Rashba interpreting R. Ḥisda. Also Qeẓoth HaḤoshen 35:4, in the name of Rashi.

47. *Shittah Mequbbeẓeth, ibid.,* interpreting Raba. *Sheb Shematetha* 7:5; cf. further *Zera Abraham,* 6:5, and *Imrei Yeruḥam,* Ch. 96. Indeed, there are some who reject *any* extension of the law against self-incrimination beyond the five categories enumerated

on p. 107; cf. *Responsa of Ritba,* ed. Qappah, p. 109, note 90:6, and *Pilpula Hariphta,* p. 5a.

48. B. Sanhedrin 25a; review the passage from B. Sanhedrin 9b, quoted above on p. 50.

49. Borrowing as well as lending money on interest is forbidden by Jewish law; *Oẓar HaGeonim . . . Sanhedrin,* p. 199.

50. Exodus 23:1. This is not an exact quotation but rather the general implication of the text.

51. P. Yebamoth 2:11.

52. R. Aqiba Eger, *Novellae to Kethuboth,* 18b.

53. R. Meir Simḥah of Dvinsk, *Or Sameaḥ, Hilkhoth Eduth* 12:2 based on the works of earlier commentators. The author is careful to point out that the identity of the party to the crime, *i.e.,* the witness himself, is *not* an integral part of the testimony, and the judges are obligated *not* to pay attention to his self-incriminating statements. "Why should we be concerned with that which has been concealed from the eyes of man?" he asks, inasmuch as there have not been found the necessary two eyewitnesses. It does not mean, however, that the self-incriminating statement of our witness is to be regarded as false. Such an interpretation must certainly be rejected; for were it true, we—to be consistent— would be obligated to brand the independent witness as a liar, for he too testifies to our witness' complicity. It is obvious that the independent witness is not considered a liar, for the Talmud indicates that his testimony is utilized to convict the defendant. It is thus clear that the self-incriminating section of our witness' testimony is not construed to be false; it is simply stricken from the record. This interpretation is corroborated by Meiri, Sanhedrin 9b (ed. Sopher, pp. 26–27) and is to be preferred to that of R. Baruch Epstein, *Torah Temimah,* Exodus 23:1, comment 6, and R. Ya'aqob Konefsky, *Qehilloth Ya'aqob,* Vol. IX, Ch. 7 who would resort to the "splitting of the testimony" of the second witness in order to avoid contradictions between the depositions of both witnesses.

54. *Judges—Evidence* 12:2.

55. Cf. Z. Chaffee, *The Blessings of Liberty,* pp. 213–214 and C. D. Williams, "Problems of the Fifth Amendment," 24 *Fordham Law Review* 19.

56. A citizen's duty to step forward and to testify concerning a crime he has witnessed is clear. A society dedicated to the pursuit of

justice cannot compromise on this point. "This contribution is not to be regarded as a gratuity or a courtesy, or an ill-requited favor. It is a duty not to be grudged or evaded. Whoever is impelled to evade or resent it should retire from the society of organized and civilized communities, and become a hermit. He is not a desirable member of society. He who will live by society must let society live by him, when it requires to. . . . From the point of view of society's *right* to our testimony, it is to be remembered that the demand comes not from any one person or set of persons, but from the community as a whole—from justice as an institution and from law and order as indispensable elements of civilized life." J. H. Wigmore, 8 *Evidence* (McNaughton rev. 1961) para. 2191, pp. 72–73. Leviticus 5:1 indicates that an *alah* was promulgated to bring forth reluctant witnesses. This *alah* has been shown to be a kind of "public summons backed by a contingent curse which served as a powerful stimulus to the ancient Hebrew to come forth and testify." H. C. Brichto, *The Problem of "Curse" in the Hebrew Bible,* pp. 42–44; also J. L. Saalschutz, *Das Mosaische Recht* (2nd ed.), Vol. I, pp. 609–611; *contra* M. Noth, *Leviticus, ad loc.* who apparently overlooked Proverbs 29:24. For the significant medieval development which brought about enforcement by human authority, cf. A. Neuman, *The Jews in Spain,* Vol. I, pp. 121–122. For a comparative treatment, cf. B. Cohen "Testimonial Compulsion in Jewish Law," IURA 9 (1958), pp. 1–21 (reprinted in *Jewish and Roman Law,* pp. 734–754). The line of demarcation between the duty to testify and the prohibition to inform does not concern us in this study; see, however, S. Hook, *Common Sense and the Fifth Amendment,* pp. 68–72.

57. Leviticus 5:1; B. Baba Qamma 55b; Maimonides, *Judges— Evidence* 17:7.

58. This English formulation of Rashi's comment is from the Soncino edition of the Talmud.

59. B. Kethuboth 18b.

60. *Beth Yoseph, Ḥoshen Mishpat* 46, in the name of earlier authorities.

61. This does not contradict the doctrine expounded by R. Jacob Algasi (*supra,* pp. 79–80) : the courts will act on an individual's act of repentance in money matters alone.

62. *Pseudo-Ran* to Sanhedrin 10a. See further Tosaphoth and *Yad Ramah* to Sanhedrin 9b as well as Meiri, Sanhedrin (ed. Sopher), p. 26 f.; *Shittah Mequbbezeth*, Kethuboth 18b; Tosaphoth, Yebamoth 25b; Maimonides, *Judges—Evidence* 3:6; R. Aqiba Eger, *Novellae* to Kethuboth 18b; and *Tosaphoth Rabbi Aqiba Eger* to M. Yebamoth 2:9.

CHAPTER VIII

CONFESSION ACCOMPANIED BY CORROBORATING FACTORS

1. R. Eliezer b. Nathan (*Raban*) cited in *Mordekhai*, Baba Bathra, para. 528. R. Ḥaim Benveniste, *Kenesseth HaGedolah, Ḥoshen Mishpat* (sect. *Tur*) 34:57, derives a similar opinion from a Responsum (no. 837) of Rashba. Rabbi Solomon Ardit, the author of *Ḥina WaHisda,* on Kethuboth 18 (p. 28b–29a), is careful to point out that the rule must be limited to those cases where the single witness testifies *before* the confession. Where, however, the confession has already been made, the corroborating testimony of one witness will not render the confessant a *rasha*. This limitation is derived from B. Sanhedrin 25a, quoted *supra,* p. 109. Cf. further *Zera Abraham,* 6:2.
2. Cf. for example, *Yad Ramah* on Sanhedrin 9b.
3. *Supra,* pp. 75–77; cf. also the remarks following on pp. 115 ff.
4. *Supra,* p. 77.
5. Cf. M. Nedarim 11:12, quoted on p. 69.
6. *Infra,* note on p. 121.
7. This decision was rendered by Rav Yehudai Gaon (d. 763). It is quoted in S. Assaph, *HaOnashin* etc., p. 45, and in *Ozar HaGeonim . . . Sanhedrin.*
8. The full procedure of a *rasha's* rehabilitation is summarized by Maimonides, *Judges—Evidence* 12:4–10.
9. This interpretation of R. ibn Migash's ruling is expounded by R. Moses Benveniste; see below, note 13.
10. The statements of R. Joseph ibn Migash, Naḥmanides and R. Aaron HaLevi are recorded in *Shittah Mequbbezeth*, Kethuboth 18b.
11. *Supra,* pp. 62–65, 75–77.
12. *Supra,* pp. 72 ff.
13. *Glosses to Asheri,* Baba Qamma 102b. This may be the source

to which R. Samuel of Modena (*Maharshdam*, Responsum 183, *Ḥoshen Mishpat*) alludes in his statement, ". . . someone has already declared that to absolve oneself of a monetary liability, one may make a self-incriminating statement. However, there is someone else who has stated that one cannot render himself a *rasha* by such a statement." Among the later medieval authorities (*Aharonim*) holding views similar to those of Ribam is R. Moses Benveniste, *P'nei Mosheh*, Vol. II, Responsum 105.

14. *Glosses to Asheri, ibid.* Also R. Moses Coucy, *Sepher Miẓwoth Gadol (Semag)*, Prohibition no. 193, in the name of Rabbenu Jacob.

15. Following the principle described above, pp. 79–80.

16. R. Moses Benveniste, *P'nei Mosheh*, II, Responsum 105. The distinction, also made on p. 100, is based upon the fundamental rule הראיה עליו מחבירו המוציא, "The burden of proof is on the plaintiff."

17. *Supra*, pp. 79–80. Cf. also Tosaphoth, Makkoth 2a *s.v. m'eedim* and Maharsha, *ad loc.*

18. Numbers 6:22 ff.

19. *Responsa of R. Levi ibn Ḥabib*, No. 117, based upon the Tosaphoth in Baba Meẓia 3b and in Qiddushin 50a. The content of this responsum may also be found in *Kenesseth HaGedolah, Ḥoshen Mishpat* (sect. *Tur*) 34:67.

20. *Ḥina WaḤisda*, Kethuboth 18 (p. 29a).

21. *Responsa Shebuth Ya'aqob*, 44.

22. B. Yebamoth 112a.

23. In accordance with the principle quoted *supra*, pp. 103 ff.

24. B. Gittin 54b; R. Joseph Saul Nathanson, *Shoel U-meshib*, 1st ed., Part III, Responsum 62. Rabbi Nathanson, however, proceeds to distinguish between an ignorant and a scholarly scribe: In the case of the former, inasmuch as he does not realize the full import of his confession, we accept his words even to the point of disqualifying the Torah scroll; in the case of the latter, no man may render himself a *rasha*, hence it would appear that the scroll is to be considered valid. (I am afraid that I fail to appreciate the distinction inasmuch as we are dealing with a scribe whose intention is to repent of his evil ways. If, even as an act of repentance, his confession cannot affect others adversely, of what added significance is his general state of ignorance?)

R. Yair Bakhrakh, *Sheeloth U-theshuboth Hawwoth Yair*, Responsum 72, apparently disagrees and accepts a self-incriminating statement (made as an act of repentance) even to the detriment of others. R. Moses Schreiber, *Sheeloth U-theshuboth Hatham Sopher, Yoreh Deah*, Responsum 4, expresses his astonishment at such an approach and challenges R. Yair to prove his thesis (Responsum 231 of R. Yair may not be adduced to clarify his position, for it involves too many extraneous factors). The digest of responsa literature, known as *Pith'hei Teshubah (Yoreh Deah* 1:6) by R. Abraham Eisenstadt, reports that R. Saul of Lomze, *Sheeloth U-theshuboth Gib'ath Shaul*, Responsum 17, also does not allow a man to incriminate himself and thereby adversely affect others even if he does so in the process of repentance. R. Schreiber's own position is to distinguish between cases on the basis of the rules of evidence that govern them: In cases (criminal, civil and matrimonial), which require the evidence of two eyewitnesses, a man's confession made even as an act of repentance (*e.g.*, on his deathbed, "for no man speaks frivolously at the time of death," B. Baba Bathra 175a) carries no weight; in cases (ritual) however, wherein one witness suffices, a man's confession under circumstances that convince us of his sincerity can affect others adversely. Hence, he would oppose the decision of R. Joseph Saul Nathanson, even in the case of a scholarly scribe. (Cf. R. Hezekiah Medini, *S'dei Hemed*, I, para. 34). Cf. further, *Pilpula Hariphta*, p. 4b.

25. *Kenesseth HaGedolah, ibid.* 64.
26. R. David ben Zimra, *Responsa*, Pt. I, No. 19.
27. Rabbenu Yeruham b. Meshullam, *Sepher Toledoth Adam WeHawwah*, Nathib 18, Pt. 3; *Hina WaHisda, ibid.* (p. 29b). Also, *Kenesseth HaGedolah, Yoreh Deah* 157 (Notes to *Beth Yoseph*, 56), who, however, writes, "Raba's statement that a man may not incriminate himself does not refer to cases involving *kareth*, extirpation, which is a punishment not administered by the human, but rather by the heavenly court, but to capital cases. Thus did the *Geonim* write in a responsum." This ruling, which invokes the *Geonim* as its authority, is not in conflict with the whole series of rulings cited *supra*, pp. 107 ff. and with their main authority, R. Solomon ibn Adreth (*Rashba*), p. 181, note 46. The *Geonim* merely state that, in contrast to

capital cases, a man who asks for lashes as penance for an act involving *kareth* may be given lashes. In any event, he will in no wise be rendered a *rasha* thereby. (*Oẓar HaGeonim . . . Sanhedrin*, p. 81; R. Jacob Berab, *Quntres HaSemikhah*, printed in Y. L. Maimon, *Ḥiddush HaSanhedrin Bemedinathenu HaMeḥuddesheth*, pp. 77–78. The author of *Ar'a DeRabbanan*, 17, was apparently unaware of this interpretation of the *Geonim* given by R. Jacob Berab.)

28. The opinion of R. Levi ibn Ḥabib is cited in Y. M. Ginzburg, "Ha'ashamah Aẓmith l'phee Mishpat HaTorah," *HaTorah We-HaMedinah* 9 (1958), p. 86.

29. M. Qiddushin 3:10.

30. Rashi, Qiddushin 65a; cf. also B. Kethuboth 23b.

31. *Qeẓoth HaḤoshen*, 241 beg.

32. R. Isaac b. Moses Belmonte, *Sha'ar HaMelekh, Hilkhoth Ishuth*, 9:15. Cf. also *supra*, pp. 69–70.

33. *Shibath Ẓion*, Responsum 23.

34. B. Qiddushin 65b.

35. *Supra*, pp. 118 f. The scholars mentioned there in note 24 would reject any attempt to distinguish these cases from the talmudic source cited in note 22.

36. *Responsa of Ḥakham Ẓebi*, Nos. 3 and 150.

37. M. Nedarim 11:12; Maimonides, *Nashim—Ishuth* 24:17. The *mishnah* in Nedarim then proceeds to explain that the obligation of the husband to divorce his self-confessed unfaithful wife was subsequently suspended to prevent a woman who desired to marry another man from purposely making such a declaration in order to obtain a divorce against her husband's will. If, however, there are circumstances which lead us to believe that we have here a *bona fide* confession, she would be believed; cf. *Sheeloth U-theshuboth Ḥatham Sopher, Yoreh Deah*, Responsum 4.

38. Maimonides, *Judges—Evidence* 5:3; 11:7.

39. R. Joseph Saul Nathanson, *Dibrei Shaul WeYoseph Da'ath, Shoel U-meshib*, 5th ed., Responsum 48. Cf. *supra*, note 24, where R. Moses Schreiber utilizes this distinction to the point of affecting even others adversely.

40. *Responsa Mass'ath Binyamin*, 51.

41. *Responsa Maharam Lublin*, 81.

42. Similarly, a man's self-disqualifying confession is not accepted in court although it is corroborated by the charges of his wife and by circumstantial evidence; R. Meir b. Shem Tob Melamed, *Mishpat Zedeq*, I, Responsum 59.

43. Cf. *supra*, p. 79.

44. *Ibid.*, pp. 79–80.

45. *Hina WaHisda*, Kethuboth 18 (p. 28a), based on earlier authorities.

46. B. Baba Qamma 30b; Tosaphoth, *s.v. wahakhamim*.

47. *Hina WaHisda, ibid.*, based upon his defense of R. Judah Rosanes, *Mishneh LeMelekh, Hilkhoth Malweh WeLoweh*, 4:6. Cf. also *Birkhei Yoseph, Hoshen Mishpat* 34:32, and *Pilpula Hariphta*, p. 5a.

48. *Ar'a DeRabbanan*, 17 end, based upon Maimonides, *Offerings— Errors* 2:1 and 6:4.

49. *Ibid.*, basing his opinion upon Maimonides, *Torts—Murder* 6:10. Rabbi Algasi, the author of *Ar'a DeRabbanan*, goes much further and limits the law against self-incrimination to nothing less than the open admission of the willful violation of the law. It seems to me that the position taken by R. Joshua Solomon Ardit, the author of *Hina WaHisda*, and presented on the previous pages, is a faithful extension of the approach of R. Solomon Adreth (*Rashba*) which we have described *supra* on pp. 107 ff. and p. 181, note 46.

50. Cf. previous note.

51. R. Solomon Luria, *Yam Shel Shelomoh*, Baba Qamma 8:23, and Responsa of *Hakham Zebi*, 3 (Ed. Lemberg, 1900, p. 5, col. 1) based upon Maimonides, *Holiness—Forbidden Intercourse* 15:14. Cf. *Mishneh LeMelekh, Hilkhoth Malweh WeLoweh*, 4:6 (quoting *Kenesseth HaGedolah's* citation of *Shiltei HaGibborim*); and the debate between *Qehillath Ya'aqob*, 17 (negative), and *Hina WaHisda*, Kethuboth 18 (p. 28b, affirmative) as to whether the author of *Mishneh LeMelekh* agrees with the thesis of R. Zebi Ashkenazi or not. R. Judah Rosanes, the author of *Mishneh LeMelekh*, speculates that perhaps the law against self-incrimination is limited to those confessions which cover the entirety of the crime, intent and act. Where, however, there is objective testimony that the defendant committed the act, and the confession is on the forethought and intention, perhaps it is acceptable.

Later authorities appear unanimous in rejecting this distinction; cf. R. Ḥaim Abulafia, "No Man May Incriminate Himself," Pt. 5.

52. "Betrothed" is used in the technical sense of ארוסה, *i.e.,* after קידושין but before נישואין.

53. The last clause is not stated explicitly in the responsum but it emerges clearly from the halakhic development and conclusions contained therein. Moreover, it would also appear that by confession she will have disqualified herself from taking an oath in court.

54. B. Kethuboth 18b, quoted *supra,* p. 111.

55. *Ibid.* This case is clearly different from the one cited *supra,* p. 115, in that the statement of the witnesses here is neither tangential nor (to them) irrelevant.

56. *Tur, Ḥoshen Mishpat* 46. Moreover, this case must be distinguished from those on pp. 78–80 in that the *present* statement of the witnesses cannot be construed as an act of repentance; they have long since mended their ways.

57. *Ibid.,* in the name of Rabbenu Asher. Cf. also *supra,* p. 101 and pp. 104–107.

58. Cf. Y. Konefsky, *Qehilloth Ya'aqob,* Vol. IX, Ch. 7, for sources and discussion.

59. *Ḥina WaḤisda,* Kethuboth 18 (p. 29a).

60. *Ibid.,* citing *Qol Elijah, Ḥoshen Mishpat,* I, Responsum 34.

A CONCLUDING WORD CONCERNING SOME
PRACTICAL CONSIDERATIONS

1. M. Makkoth 1:10. Cf. Z. Frankel, *Darkhei HaMishnah,* pp. 191–192.

2. For a summary of the methods they would have employed to acquit the accused, cf. R. Obadiah of Bertinoro, *ad loc.*

3. *Miranda v. Arizona,* 384 U.S. 436, pp. 537 and 539.

4. For one striking example, cf. O. J. Rogge's review of "Criminal Interrogation and Confessions" by F. E. Inbau and J. E. Reid, *Harvard Law Review,* 76 (1963), pp. 1516 ff.

5. On this, both R. W. Livingstone (*The Greek Genius*) and H. J. Muller (*The Uses of the Past*) are agreed.

6. *Supra,* pp. 77–78 and 126 f.

7. Psalms 144:8; B. Baba Bathra 45a. For the many ramifications of the matter, cf. *Encyclopedia Talmudith,* Vol. V., pp. 337 ff.

8. P. Sanhedrin 1:1; 7:2; B. Shabbath 15a; B. Sanhedrin 41a; Z. Frankel, *op. cit.,* p. 47; H. Mantel, *Studies in the History of the Sanhedrin,* pp. 291–294, 316. G. Alon, *History of the Jews in Palestine During the Times of the Mishnah and Talmud,* pp. 129–131, indicates that the Jewish courts apparently did continue in practice to deal with such cases—at least until the destruction of the Temple in 70 C.E.

9. Cf. B. Cohen, "Evidence in Jewish Law," *Recueils de la Société Jean Boden,* 16 (1965), p. 111; P. Dykan, *Criminal Law,* p. 618.

10. M. Eduyoth 1:3; B. Sukkah 28a; note the examples listed by S. Mendelsohn, "Capital Punishment," *Jewish Encyclopedia,* Vol. III, p. 558a, of traditions which were preserved by the Rabbis and whose antiquity is attested to by Josephus. Cf. Y. Baer, "Some Aspects of Judaism as Presented in the Synoptic Gospels" (Hebrew), *Zion,* XXXI (1966), pp. 144–145, and B. Rabinowitz-T'omim, "Mishp'tei Nephashoth B'din HaSanhedrin U-B'din HaMalkhuth," *HaTorah We-HaMedinah,* 4 (1952), pp. 49 ff.

11. The same R. Aqiba who expressed his determination to abolish capital punishment was prepared to accept Bar Kokhba as heralding political restoration; P. Ta'anith 4:5 and B. Sanhedrin 97b.

12. Cf. M. Sanhedrin 9:5 and P. Dykan, *op. cit.,* pp. 1251–1252. For recent halakhic studies of *hora'ath sha'ah,* i.e., the definition and delineation of the power of the courts to invoke it, cf. Y. M. Charlop, *Beth Zebul,* Vol. 6, Ch. 11, and Y. M. Ginzburg, *Mishpatim LeYisrael,* pp. 1–70.

13. The idea, of course, is biblical; cf. I Kings 8:32 and elsewhere.

14. B. Sanhedrin 37b. Cf. Meiri, Sanhedrin, Ch. IV end (ed. Sopher, p. 170).

15. B. Makkoth 10b.

16. Significantly, there is a passage in the Talmud (B. Abodah Zarah 8b) which characterizes the Sanhedrin's loss of jurisdiction over capital cases as voluntary on the part of the Jewish authorities who were brought to their decision by the marked increase in the incidence of murder throughout the land.

APPENDIX I

THE JEWISH LAW OF CRIMINAL CONFESSION AND
THE TRIAL OF JESUS

1. "Some Aspects of Judaism as Presented in the Synoptic Gospels," (Hebrew) *Zion,* XXXI (1966), pp. 137–145.
2. *Ibid.,* p. 138, note 48.
3. Cf. *supra,* p. 10.
4. Tertullian, *Apologeticus* 2.3. Cf. Mommsen, *Römisches Strafrecht,* p. 438, note 4, and Baer, p. 141.
5. Cicero, *Pro Milone* 6.15. Cf. Mommsen, *ibid.,* p. 437, note 5.
6. R. W. Husband, *The Prosecution of Jesus,* pp. 149 ff., 281, propounds the thesis that the "trial" was nothing more than a preliminary hearing of an investigative nature.
7. M. Sanhedrin 7:5. Jesus' declaration, of course, does not fit into the Jewish concept of blasphemy as known from all the Jewish sources; Baer utilizes this fact to bolster his own thesis (p. 141, end of note 53). Cf. H. L. Strack and P. Billerbeck, *Kommentar zum neuen Testament,* Vol. I, pp. 1022–1023; H. Mantel, *Studies in the History of the Sanhedrin,* pp. 273 ff.

Bibliography

A. BIBLICAL TEXTS, TRANSLATIONS, COMMENTARIES AND STUDIES

Miqra'oth Gedoloth, standard editions containing *Targum Onqelos, Targum Jonathan,* and the commentaries of Rashi, Ibn Ezra, Naḥmanides and Gersonides.

The Bible . . . the Old and New Testaments in the King James Version (known as the Authorized Version). New York, 1937.

The Holy Scriptures (Jewish Publication Society of America). Philadelphia, 1917.

The Torah: The Five Books of Moses (Jewish Publication Society of America). Philadelphia, 1962.

Abravanel, I. *Commentary on the Former Prophets* (Hebrew). Jerusalem, 1956.

Brichto, C. H. *The Problem of "Curse" in the Hebrew Bible.* Philadelphia, 1963.

Brown-Driver-Briggs. *A Hebrew and English Lexicon of the Old Testament.* Oxford, 1906.

Driver, S. R. *Deuteronomy* (International Critical Commentary). 3rd ed. Edinburgh, 1901.

———— *Notes on the Hebrew Text of the Book of Samuel.* 2nd ed. Oxford, 1960.

Ehrlich, A. B. *Mikra ki-Pheschuto.* 3 vols. Berlin, 1900.

Epstein, B. *Torah Temimah.* 5 vols. Wilno, 1904.

Falk, Z. W. *Hebrew Law in Biblical Times: An Introduction* (Hebrew). Jerusalem, 1964.

Greenberg, M. "Crimes and Punishments," *Interpreter's Diction-ary of the Bible,* Vol. I, pp. 733–744. New York, 1962.

———— "Some Postulates of Biblical Criminal Law," *Fest-schrift—Y. Kaufmann* (ed. M. Haran), pp. 5–28. Jerusalem, 1960.

Grimme, H. "Der Begriff v. hebraischen הודה und תודה," *Zeit-schrift f.d. alttestamentliche Wissenschaft,* 58 (1940/41).

Horst, R. *Gottes Recht.* Munich, 1961.

Kaufmann, Y. *Commentary on Joshua* (Hebrew). Jerusalem, 1959.

———— *Commentary on Judges* (Hebrew). Jerusalem, 1964.

———— *Toledoth HaEmunah HaYisraelith.* 8 vols. Tel Aviv, 1956.

Noth, M. *Leviticus.* Philadelphia, 1962.

Saalschutz, J. S. *Das Mosaische Recht.* 2nd ed. 2 vols. Berlin, 1853.

Segal, M. Z. *Siphrei Shemuel.* Jerusalem, 1956.

Speiser, E. "The Stem Pll in Hebrew," *Journal of Biblical Liter-ature,* 82 (1963), pp. 301–306.

Tur-Sinai, N. H. *Sepher Iyob.* Tel Aviv, 1954.

de Vaux, R. *Ancient Israel, Its Life and Institutions* (trans. J. McHugh). New York, 1961.

B. TANNAITIC LITERATURE, COMMENTARIES AND STUDIES

Mishnayoth, standard editions with the commentaries of Oba-diah Bertinoro, *Tosaphoth Yom Tob* by Yom Tob Lipman Heller, *Tosaphoth* by Aqiba Eger and *Tiph'ereth Yisrael* by Israel Lipschitz. English Translation: *The Mishnah* by H. Danby. Oxford, 1933.

Mekhilta (ed. M. Friedmann). Vienna, 1870.

(ed. I. H. Weiss). Vienna, 1865.

(ed. H. S. Horovitz and I. A. Rabin). 2nd ed. Jeru-salem, 1960.

Siphrei (ed. M. Friedmann). Vienna, 1964.

(ed. L. Finkelstein). Berlin, 1940.

(ed. N. Z. Y. Berlin). 3 vols. Jerusalem, 1959.

Midrasch Tannaim zum Deuteronomium (ed. D. Hoffmann). Berlin, 1909.

Tosephta (ed. M. S. Zuckermandel). Reprinted: Jerusalem, 1963.

Abramsky, Y. *Tosephta Ḥazon Yeḥezqel: Shebuoth and Makkoth.* Jerusalem, 1960.

Albeck, H. *Introduction and Commentary to the Mishnah* (Hebrew) . 7 vols. Jerusalem, 1958–1959.

Epstein, J. N. *Mabo LeNusaḥ HaMishnah*. 2 vols. Jerusalem, 1948.

———— *Mebo'oth LeSiphruth HaTannaim*. Jerusalem-Tel Aviv, 1957.

———— "Seridim M'd'bei R. Ishmael LeSepher Wayyiqra," *Festschrift—Krauss* (Hebrew) . Jerusalem, 1937.

Frankel, Z. *Darkhei HaMishnah*. Tel Aviv, 1959.

Lieberman, S. *Tosepheth Rishonim*. 4 vols. Jerusalem, 1937–1939.

————*Tosefta Ki-fshutah, Zeraim*. 3 vols. New York, 1955.

Maimonides, M. *Introduction to the Commentary on the Mishnah* (Hebrew) (ed. M. D. Rabinowitz) . Jerusalem, 1961.

Zacuto, M. "Qol Ramaz," *Qebuẓath Mepharshei HaMishnah*. Jerusalem, 1960.

C. TALMUD AND MIDRASH, COMMENTARIES AND RELATED WORKS

Babylonian Talmud, standard editions containing the commentaries of Rashi and Tosaphoth, *Ḥiddushei Halakhah—Maharsha* by Samuel Edels, and *Ḥiddushei Rashash* by Samuel Strashun; the *Code of the Rosh* by Asher b. Yeḥiel with accompanying *Glosses* and *Halakhoth,* the Code of Isaac Alfasi with the commentary of Nissim Gerondi *(Ran)* and *Nimmuqei Yoseph* by Joseph Ḥabiba; the *Code of Mordekhai;* and the Tosephta. English Translation: *The Talmud* (ed. I. Epstein) . Soncino Press.

Palestinian Talmud, standard editions containing the commentaries of *Qorban HaEdah* by David Frankel of Dessau and *P'nai Mosheh* by Moses Margulies.

Midrash Bereshit Rabba (eds. J. Theodor and Ch. Albeck) . 2nd printing: Jerusalem, 1956.

Midrash Rabbah, standard editions.

Midrash Tanḥuma (ed. S. Buber) . 2 vols. Reprint: New York, 1946.

Yalqut Shim'oni, standard edition.

Abulafia, Meir b. Todros HaLevi. *Yad Ramah, Sanhedrin*. Reprinted: New York, 1953.

ibn Adreth, Solomon. *Ḥiddushei HaRashba*. 2 vols. Reprinted: New York, 1952.

Ashkenazi, B. *Shittah Mequbbeẓeth—Kethuboth*. 2 vols. Reprinted: New York, 1955.

Gerondi, Nissim b. Reuben. *Ḥiddushei HaRan* (with *Pseudo-Ran* to Sanhedrin). Reprinted: New York, 1952.

————— *Sheneym Assar Derushim*. Reprinted: New York, 1953.

Ishbili, Yom Tob b. Abraham. *Ḥiddushei HaRitba* (ed. Z. H. Bleiweis). 5 vols. Reprinted: New York, no date.

Meiri, Menaḥem b. Solomon. *Beth HaBehirah—Sanhedrin* (ed. A. Sopher). Frankfurt am Main, no date. *Nedarim*. Halberstadt, 1850 (Reprinted: Jerusalem, 1961).

Naḥmanides, M. *Ḥiddushei HaRamban* (ed. I. Z. Melzer). 2 vols. Jerusalem, 1928.

Yeruḥam b. Meshullam. *Sepher Toledoth Adam WeḤawwah*. 2 vols. Venice, 1553.

Abulafia, Ḥ. "No Man May Incriminate Himself" (Hebrew), *Ashdoth HaPisgah* by Joseph Naḥmuli. Salonika, 1790.

Algasi, J. *Ar'a DeRabbanan*. Constantinople, 1745.

————— *Qehillath Ya'aqob*. Salonika, 1779.

Ardit, S. *Ḥina WaḤisda*, Smyrna, 1864.

Arieli, Y. *Einaim LaMishpat: Makkoth*. Tel-Aviv, 1967.

Aryeh Leib HaKohen. *Sheb Shematetha*. Reprinted: New York, 1955.

Berab, J. "Quntres HaSemikhah," printed in *Ḥiddush HaSanhedrin BeMedinathenu HaMehuddesheth* by Y. L. Maimon. Jerusalem, 1951.

B. N. Z'eb. *Pilpula Ḥariphta*. Pietrikov, 1903. Bound with: B. Z. Rosenbloom. *Lequtei Geonim*. Pietrikov, 1905.

Chajes, Z. H. "Torath HaNebiim," *Kol Siphrei Maharaẓ Chajes*. 2 vols. Jerusalem, 1958.

Charlop, Y. M. *Beth Zebul*. Vol. 6. Jerusalem, 1966.

Eger, A. *Novellae to the Talmud* (Hebrew). Brooklyn, 1949.

Elijah Aaron b. Mordecai Uriah. *Oholei Aharon*. Graebo, 1909.

Encyclopedia Talmudith (ed. S. J. Zevin). 12 vols. Jerusalem, 1951–1967. "Adam Qarob Eẓel Aẓmo," "Oditha," "Urim We-Thummim," "Ein Adam Messim Aẓmo Rasha," "Beth Din," "Ba'al Din," "Dina DeMalkhutha Dina," "Dinei Memonoth," "Dinei Nephashoth," "Dinei Qenasoth," "Derishah WaḤaqirah," "Hoda'ath Ba'al Din," "Hora'ath Sha'ah," "Halakhah," "Halakhah LeMosheh Mi-Sinai," "Hathra'ah."

Finkel, E. Y. *Dibrei Eliezer*. Jerusalem, 1964.

[Konefsky], S. Y. H. *Qiriath Melekh*. 2nd ed. Bnai Brak, 1964.

Konefsky, Y. *Qehilloth Ya'aqob*. Vol. 9. Jerusalem, 1954.

Kohut, A. *Aruch Completum*. 8 vols. Vienna, 1926. Supplementary Vol. 9 (ed. S. Krauss). Vienna, 1937.

Lampronti, I. "Ein Adam Messim Aẓmo Rasha," *Paḥad Yiẓḥaq* (ed. Meqiẓei Nirdamim). Lyck, 1846.

Luftbear, A. *Zera Abraham*. Warsaw, 1920.
Luria, Solomon. *Yam Shel Shelomoh*. 3 vols. Reprinted: New York, 1953.
Margalioth, R. "Hagahoth Meqor Ḥesed," *Sepher Ḥassidim*. Jerusalem, 1957.
———— *Margalioth HaYam*. 2 vols. Jerusalem, 1958.
Medini, H. "Ein Adam Messim Aẓmo Rasha," *Sedei Ḥemed*. Warsaw, 1903.
———— *Mikhtab LeḤezekiah*. 2 vols. Smyrna, 1868.
Rabinowitz, M. Y. A. *Da'ath Mordekhai*. Vol. II. Jerusalem, 1959.
Rabinowitz, Y. M. *Afiqei Yam*. Reprinted: New York, no date.
Rabinowitz, Z. W. *Sha'are Torath Babel*. Jerusalem, 1961.
Sachnovitz, Ch. *Tosephoth Ḥaim—Sanhedrin*. Jerusalem, 1966.
Shkop, S. *Ḥiddushei Rabbi Simeon Yehuda HaKohen—Yebamoth, Kethuboth*. New York, 1956.
Solte, Y. B. *Mishnath Yabeẓ, Ḥoshen Mishpat*. Jerusalem, 1963.
Wahrhaftig, Y. A. *Imrei Yeruḥam*. Jerusalem, 1951.
———— *Osher Yeruham*. Jerusalem, 1962.

D. CODES AND RELATED WORKS

Alfasi, Isaac. *Code*. See: *Babylonian Talmud*.
Maimonides, M. *Yad HaḤazaqah,* standard editions containing the commentaries: *Maggid Mishneh* by Vidal of Toulouse, *Kesseph Mishneh* by Joseph Qaro, the *Commentary of Radbaz* by David ben Zimra, and *Mishneh LeMelekh* by Judah Rosanes. Transl., Yale Judaica Series. Also: *Rambam La'Am* Edition. Jerusalem, 1957–1959.
Asher b. Yeḥiel (*Rosh*) . *Code*. See: *Babylonian Talmud*.
Mordekhai. See: *Babylonian Talmud*.
Belmonte, Isaac b. Moses. *Sha'ar HaMelekh*. Lvov, 1859.
Meir Simḥah of Dvinsk. *Or Sameaḥ*. 2 vols. Reprinted: New York, 1963.
Coucy, M. *Sepher Miẓwoth Gadol (Semag)* . Muncacz, 1905.
Sepher HaḤinukh (ed. C. B. Chavel) . Jerusalem, 1952.
Babad, J. *Minhath Ḥinukh HaShalem*. 2 vols. New York, 1952.
Jacob b. Asher. *Arba'ah Turim,* standard editions with the commentaries: *Beth Yosef* by Joseph Qaro and *Baith Ḥadash (Bah)* by Joel Sirkes.
Qaro, Joseph. *Shulḥan Arukh,* standard editions with the commentaries: *Sepher Meirath Einaim* by Joshua Falk; *Siphthei Kohen* by Sabbatai Cohen; *Qeẓoth HaḤoshen* by Aryeh Leib HaKohen; *Nethiboth HaMishpat* by Jacob b. Moses of Lisa; *Pithḥei Teshubah* by Abraham Eisenstadt.

Azulai, H. J. D. *Birkhei Yoseph*. Salonika, 1810.
Beneviste, H. *Kenesseth HaGedolah*. Constantinople, 1716.
Eybeschitz, J. *Urim WeThummim*. Dubno, 1806.

E. RESPONSA LITERATURE

Abraham b. David of Posquières. *Responsa of Rabad*. (ed. Y. Qappaḥ). Jerusalem, 1964.
ibn Adreth, S. *Responsa of Rashba*. Vol. II: *Sepher Toledoth Adam*. Lemberg, 1811. Vol. III, Bnai Brak, 1959.
Agus, I. *Rabbi Meir of Rothenberg*. 2 vols. Philadelphia, 1947.
Asher b. Yeḥiel. *Responsa of Rosh*. Venice, 1607.
Ashkenazi, Ẓ. *Responsa of Ḥakham Ẓebi*. Lemberg, 1900.
Bakhrakh, Yair. *Responsa Ḥawwoth Yair*. Lemberg, 1896.
Barfat (or Perfet), Isaac b. Shesheth. *Responsa of Ribash*. Lemberg, 1805.
Benjamin Aaron b. Abraham Slonik. *Responsa Mass'ath Binyamin*. Metz, 1776.
Benveniste, M. *P'nei Mosheh*. 3 vols. Constantinople, 1669–1719.
David b. Zimra. *Responsa of Radbaz*. Warsaw, 1882.
Duran, Simeon b. Ẓemaḥ. *Tashbaẓ*. Amsterdam, 1738.
Duran, Solomon b. Simeon. *Sepher HaRashbash*. Livorno, 1742.
Eleazar b. Aryeh Leib of Pielz. *Responsa Shemen Rokaḥ*. Nawidwahr, 1788.
ibn Ḥabib, Levi. *Responsa of Ralbaḥ (Maharalbah)*. Lemberg. Reprinted: New York, 1962.
Indices to the Responsa of Jewish Law: The Responsa of R. Asher b. Yeḥiel (ed. M. Elon). Jerusalem, 1965.
Ishbili, Yom Tob b. Abraham. *Responsa of Ritba* (ed. Y. Qappaḥ). Jerusalem, 1959.
Judah b. Asher. *Zikhron Yehudah*. Berlin, 1846.
Kook, A. I. *Mishpat Kohen*. Jerusalem, 1937.
Landau, E. *Noda Bihudah*. 2 vols. Reprinted: Paris, 1947.
Landau S. *Shibath Ẓion*. Prague, 1827.
Meir b. Gedaliah Lublin. *Responsa Maharam Lublin*. Metz, 1764.
Melamed, Meir b. Shem Tob. *Mishpat Ẓedeq*. 3 vols. Salonika, 1791.
ibn Migash, Joseph. *Responsa*. Warsaw, 1870.
de Modena, S. *Responsa of Maharshdam*. Lemberg, 1862.
Nathanson, J. S. *Shoel U-Meshib*. 6 vols. (Vol. V.: *Dibrei Shaul WeYoseph Da'ath*). Lemberg, 1865–1879.
Oẓar HaGeonim LeMassekheth Sanhedrin (ed. H. Z. Taubes). Jerusalem, 1966.

Pisqei Din . . . (Cases of the District Rabbinical Courts of Israel). Vol. I. (eds. D. Katz and Y. Glasner). Jerusalem, 1954.

Reischer, J. *Shebuth Ya'aqob.* Lemberg, 1860.

Roth, M. *Qol Mebasser.* 2 vols. Jerusalem, 1962.

Schreiber, M. *Responsa of Hatham Sopher.* Pressburg-Vienna, 1877–1883.

Teshuboth HaGeonim Zikhron LaRishonim (ed. A. A. Harkavy). Berlin, 1885.

F. MODERN STUDIES IN JEWISH HISTORY, LITERATURE AND LAW

Albeck, S. "The Principles of Government in the Jewish Community of Spain until the 13th Century" (Hebrew), *Zion*, 25 (1960), pp. 85 ff.

Alon, G. *The History of the Jews in Palestine During the Times of the Mishnah and Talmud* (Hebrew). Hakibbutz Ha-M'uhad, 1953.

Amiel, M. A. *Darkhei Mosheh,* Book VI: "Modes of Acquisition" (Hebrew). Antwerp, 1928.

Assaph, S. *HaOnashin Aharei Hathimath HaTalmud.* Jerusalem, 1922.

Baer, Y. *A History of the Jews in Christian Spain.* 2 vols. Philadelphia, 1966.

———— *Die Juden in Christlichen Spanien.* Vol. I: *I Urkunden u. Regesten.* Berlin, 1929.

———— "Some Aspects of Judaism as Presented in the Synoptic Gospels" (Hebrew), *Zion,* 31 (1966), pp. 117–152.

Bahr, O. *Das Gesetz über falsche Zeuge nach Bibel u. Talmud.* Berlin, 1882.

Baron, S. W. *History and Jewish Historians.* Philadelphia, 1964.

Belkin, S. *Philo and the Oral Law.* Cambridge, Mass., 1940.

Cohen, B. "Evidence in Jewish Law," *Recueils de la Société Jean Bodin,* 16 (1965), pp. 103–115.

Cohen, B. "Testimonial Compulsion in Jewish Law," *Iura,* 9 (1958), pp. 1–21. Reprinted: *Jewish and Roman Law,* Vol. II, pp. 734–754. New York, 1966.

Cohn, H. H. "[The Privilege Against Self-Incrimination Under Foreign Law. E.] Israel," *The Journal of Criminal Law, Criminology and Police Science,* 51 (1960–1961), pp. 175–178.

Cohn, M. "Geständnis," *Jüdisches Lexicon* (eds. G. Herlitz and B. Kirschner). Berlin, 1927.

Dembitz, L. N. "Accusatory and Inquisitorial Procedure," "Acquittal in Talmudic Law," "Crime," "Criminal Procedure,"

"Evidence," *Jewish Encyclopedia* (I. Singer, ed.). New York, 1901.

Dykan (Dikshtein), P. *Criminal Law* (Hebrew). 6 vols. Tel Aviv, 1955.

———— "HaHathra'ah BaMishpat HaIbri," *Sinai*, 60 (1960), pp. 51–62.

Elias, M. "HaHoda'ah," *HaMishpat HaIbri*, 1 (1926), pp. 184–185.

Elon, M. *Freedom of the Debtor's Person in Jewish Law* (Hebrew). Jerusalem, 1964.

———— "HaMa'assar BaMishpat HaIbri," *Sepher HaYobel LePhinchas Rosen*, pp. 171–201.

Federbush, S. *Mishpat HaMelukhah Be-Yisrael*. Jerusalem, 1952.

Feilchenfeld, L. *Die Zeugen im Strafprozess des Talmud*. Berlin, 1933.

Finkelstein, L. *Jewish Self-Government in the Middle Ages*. 2nd Printing: New York, 1964.

Frankel, Z. *Der gerichtliche Beweis nach mosaisch-talmudischen Recht*. Berlin, 1846.

Gandz, S. *Monumenta Talmudica: II. Recht*. Vienna and Leipzig, 1913.

Gemser, B. "The *Rib*—Or Controversy—Pattern in Hebrew Mentality," *Wisdom in Israel and the Ancient Near East*. (eds. M. Noth and D. W. Thomas), pp. 120–137. Leiden, 1955.

Ginzburg, Y. M. "Ha'ashamah Aẓmith l'phee Mishpat Ha-Torah," *HaTorah We-HaMedinah*, 9 (1958).

———— *Mishpatim LeYisrael*. Jerusalem, 1956.

Glicksman, Z. "Eduth Adam al Aẓmo," *HaMeliẓ* (1889), No. 257.

Goodenough, E. R. *The Jurisprudence of the Jewish Courts in Egypt*. New Haven, 1929.

Gulak, A. *Yesodei HaMishpat HaIbri*. 2 vols. Warsaw, 1913.

Guttmann, M. "Zur Quellenkritik des Mischnah Thora," *Monatsschrift f. Geschichte u. Wissenschaft d. Judenthums*, 79 (1935), pp. 151–152.

Hershman, A. M. *Rabbi Isaac b. Sheshet Perfet and His Times*. 1st ed.: New York, 1943. 2nd ed., revised and translated into Hebrew: Jerusalem, 1956.

Herzog, I. "John Selden and Jewish Law," *Journal of Comparative Legislation*, 13 (1931), pp. 236–245.

———— *Torath HaOhel*, Part I. Jerusalem, 1948.

Horowitz, G. "The Privilege Against Self-Incrimination—How Did It Originate?" *Temple Law Quarterly*, 31 (1958), pp. 121–144.

Husband, R. W. *The Prosecution of Jesus: Its Date, History and Legality.* Princeton, 1916.

Kantor, L. *Beiträge z. Lehre ü. der Strafrechtlichen Schuld im Talmud (Kippah Strafe)*. Giessen, 1926.

Karl, Z. "Hahokhahoth BaMishpat HaIbri We-Hithpat-ḥuthan," *HaMishpat HaIbri*, 3 (1927), 89.

Kaufmann, D. "Jewish Informers in the Middle Ages," *Jewish Quarterly Review* (Old Series), 3 (1896), pp. 217 ff.

Klein, J. *Das Gesetz über d. gerichtliche Beweisverfahren nach mosaich-talmudichen Recht.* Halle, 1885.

Lamm, N. "The Fifth Amendment and Its Equivalent in the Halakah," *Judaism,* 5 (1956), p. 53 ff.

Lauterbach, J. Z. "Sanhedrin," *Jewish Encyclopedia* (I. Singer, ed.). New York, 1901.

Lieberman, S. *Greek in Jewish Palestine.* New York, 1942.

————— *Hellenism in Jewish Palestine.* New York, 1950.

————— "Roman Legal Institutions in Early Rabbinics and in the Acta Martyrum," *Jewish Quarterly Review* (New Series), 35 (1944), pp. 1 ff.

Mandelbaum, S. "The Privilege Against Self-Incrimination in Anglo-American and Jewish Law," *The American Journal of Comparative Law,* 5 (1956), pp. 115–119.

Mantel, H. *Studies in the History of the Sanhedrin.* Cambridge, Mass., 1965.

Marqon, Z. "HaGoral," *HaMishpat HaIbri,* 4 (1929), 135.

Mendelsohn, S. "Capital Punishment," "Hatra'ah," *Jewish Encyclopedia* (I. Singer, ed.). New York, 1901.

————— *The Criminal Jurisprudence of the Ancient Hebrews.* Baltimore, 1891.

Neuman, A. *The Jews in Spain.* 2 vols. Philadelphia, 1948.

Philo. *De Specialibus Legibus,* Book IV (Loeb Edition; trans. F. H. Colson). Cambridge, Mass., 1954.

Rabinowitz-T'omim, B. "Mishp'tei Nephashoth B'din HaSanhedrin U'B'din HaMalkhuth," *HaTorah We-HaMedinah,* 4 (1952), 45–81.

Rosenbaum, S. "HaHokhahoth BeMishpatim Peliliim Be-T'quphath HaMiqra," *HaMishpat,* 1 (1927), pp. 281 ff.

Schmiedl, A. "A Comparison of Roman to Talmudic Law" (Hebrew), *HaShaḥar,* 10, pp. 50 ff.

Selden, J. *De Synedriis Veterum Ebraeorum.* London, 1653.

Shohet, D. M. *The Jewish Courts in the Middle Ages.* New York, 1931.

Stern, S. T. "Hossaphah Ḥamishith BaḤaqiqath Arẓoth Ha-Berith," *HaDarom,* Nissan 5717, pp. 38–45.

Strack, H. L. and Billerbeck, P. *Kommentar z. Neuen Testament aus Talmud u. Midrasch.* 4 vols. in 5. Munich, 1922–1928.

Tchernowitz, H. *Toledoth HaHalakhah.* 2 vols. New York, 1935–1936.

Teicher, J. L. "Laws of Reason and Laws of Religion: A Conflict in Toledo Jewry in the 14th Century," *Essays and Studies Presented to Stanley Arthur Cook,* pp. 83–94. London, 1950.

Waldenberg, E. *Hilkhoth Medinah.* 3 vols. Jerusalem, 1952–1955.

Weiss, I. H. *Dor Dor We-Dorshaw.* 5 vols. Berlin, 1924.

G. ROMAN LAW: SOURCES AND STUDIES

Ancient Roman Statutes (eds. A. C. Johnson *et al.*) Austin, 1961.

Codex Theodosianus cum Constitutionibus Sirmondianis . . . (eds. T. Mommsen and P. M. Meyer). 3 vols. Berlin, 1905.

Corpus Iuris Civilis. Vol. I: Institutiones (ed. P. Krueger). Digesta (ed. T. Mommsen and P. Krueger). 15th stereotype edition: Berlin, 1928.

Fontes Iuris Romani Anteiustiniani. Vol. I: Leges (ed. S. Riccobono). Florence, 1941.

The Theodosian Code (ed. C. Pharr). Princeton, 1952.

Kunkel, W. "Quaestio," *Realenzyklopädie der Klassischen Altertumswissenschaft,* 24 (1963).

————— *Untersuchungen zur Entwicklung des römischen Kriminalverfahrens.* Munich, 1962.

Mitteis, L. *Reichsrecht und Volksrecht.* Leipzig, 1891.

Mittermeier, C. "Das Deutsche Strafverfahren," *A History of Continental Criminal Procedure* (transl. J. Simpson) by A. Esmein. Boston, 1913.

Mommsen, T. *Römisches Strafrecht.* Leipzig, 1899.

Puschel, W. *Confessus pro judicato est.* Heidelberg, 1924.

Sohm, R. *Institutionen, Geschichte u. System d. römischen Privatrechts* (eds. L. Mitteis and L. Wenger). 17th ed.: Leipzig, 1924.

Strachan-Davidson, J. L. *Problems of the Roman Criminal Law.* 2 vols. Oxford, 1912.

Taubenschlag, R. *The Law of Greco-Roman Egypt in the Light of the Papyri, 332 B.C.–640 A.D.* New York, 1944.

Wenger, L. *Institutes of the Roman Law of Civil Procedure* (transl. O. H. Fisk). New York, 1940.

H. CITATIONS FROM LATIN LITERATURE

1. *Non-Juridical*

Sallust	*Catalina* 52.36
Seneca	*Controversiones* 8.1
Quintilian	*Declamationes* 314
Cicero	*Pro Ligario* 1.2
	Pro Milone 6.15
Tertullian	*Apologeticus* 2.3

2. *Juridical*

Twelve Tables	3.1
Paul, *Digest*	42.2.1
Codex Theodosianus	9.40.1; 11.36.1
Codex Iustinianus	9.47.16

I. CITATIONS FROM GREEK LITERATURE

Aristotle *Constitution of Athens* (eds. K. von Fritz and E. Kopp). New York, 1950. 52.1
Demosthenes (Loeb, ed. J. H. Venice). London, 1935. 23, 28–51
Lycurgus (ed. F. Durrback). Paris, 1932. 1.117
Antiphon (ed. T. Thalheim). Leipzig, 1914. 5.53 ff.
Andocides (ed. G. Dabmeyda). Paris, 1930. 1.71.
Lysias (Loeb, ed. W. R. M. Lamb). London, 1930. 6.24
Rogers, B. B. *The Wasps of Aristophanes.* London, 1915.

J. ANGLO-AMERICAN LEGAL CITATIONS

Brown v. Walker (1895), 161 U.S. 591
11 *Coke* 30 (King's Bench Reports)
Escobedo v. Illinois (1963), 378 U.S. 478
Garrity v. State of New Jersey (1967), 87 Supreme Court Reporter 616
Gideon v. Wainwright (1962), 372 U.S. 335
Jackson v. Denno (1963), 378 U.S. 368
Miranda v. Arizona (1966), 384 U.S. 436
Palko v. Connecticut (1937), 302 U.S. 325
Twining v. New Jersey (1908), 211 U.S. 78
Watts v. Indiana (1948), 338 U.S. 49

K. WORKS RELATED TO ANGLO-AMERICAN LAW

Bentham, J. *The Rationale of Judicial Evidence.* London, 1827.
Chaffee, Z. *The Blessings of Liberty.* Philadelphia, 1956.

Douglas, W. O. *An Almanac of Liberty*. Garden City, N.Y., 1954.

Emerson, T. I., Haber, D. and Dorsen, N. *Political and Civil Rights in the United States*. 2 vols. Boston, 1967.

Enker, A. N. and Elsen, S. H. "Counsel for the Suspect," 49 *Minnesota Law Review* (1964).

Frank, J. P. *Cases and Materials in Constitutional Law*. Chicago, 1952.

Griswold, E. N. *The Fifth Amendment Today*. Cambridge, Mass. 1955.

Hofstadter, S. H. "The Fifth Amendment and the Immunity Act of 1954, Aspects of the American Way," *The Record* (of the Association of the Bar of New York), 10 (1955), pp. 453–497.

——— and Levitan, S. R. "Lest the Constable Blunder: A Remedial Proposal," *The Record* (of the Association of the Bar of New York), 20 (1965), pp. 629–644.

Holdsworth, W. S. *A History of English Law*. 3rd ed. 7 vols. London, 1923.

Hook, S. *Common Sense and the Fifth Amendment*. Chicago, 1957.

Kamisar, Y., Inbau F. *et al. Criminal Justice in our Time*. Charlottesville, 1965.

Levy, L. W. *Origins of the Fifth Amendment: The Right Against Self-Incrimination*. New York, 1968.

Lewis, A. *Gideon's Trumpet*. New York, 1964.

Medalie, R. J. *From Escobedo to Miranda: The Anatomy of a Supreme Court Decision*. Washington, 1966.

Morgan, E. M. *Basic Problems of Evidence*. Philadelphia, 1957.

——— *et al. Cases and Materials on Evidence*. 4th ed.: New York, 1957.

Ploscowe, M. "The Development of the Present-Day Criminal Procedures in Europe and America," 48 *Harvard Law Review* (1935), pp. 433–473.

Pollock, R. and Maitland, F. W. *The History of English Law*. 1st ed. 2 vols. Cambridge, 1895.

Rogge, O. J. *The First and the Fifth*. New York, 1960.

——— Review of "Criminal Interrogation and Confessions," 76 *Harvard Law Review* 7.

Roscoe, E. S. *The Growth of English Law*. London, 1911.

Wigmore, J. H. *Code of Evidence*. 3rd ed.: Boston, 1942.

——— 8 *Evidence* (McNaughton rev., 1961).

Williams, D. C. "Problems of the Fifth Amendment," 24 *Fordham Law Review* 19.

Yale Law Journal 76:8 (1967), "Interrogations in New Haven: The Impact of *Miranda*."

———— 77:2 (1967), "A Postscript to the *Miranda* Project: Interrogation of Draft Protestors."

L. MISCELLANY

The Accused, A Comparative Study (ed. J. A. Coutts). London, 1966.

Berman, Harold J., ed. *Soviet Criminal Law and Procedure, The RSFSR Codes*. Cambridge, Mass., 1966.

Bonner, R. J. *Lawyers and Litigants in Ancient Athens*. Chicago, 1927.

———— and Smith, G. *The Administration of Justice from Homer to Aristotle*. 2 vols. Chicago, 1930.

Esmein, A. *A History of Continental Criminal Procedure* (transl. J. Simpson). Boston, 1913.

French *Code de Procédure Pénale*. 9th ed. Paris, 1967–1968.

Halakhoth, The Israeli Digest (eds. R. Gideon and A. Winograd). Vol. IV: "Criminal Procedure" (ed. M. Kant). Vol. VII: "Evidence" (ed. Y. Gabison). (Hebrew). Tel Aviv, no date.

Hippel, Robert von. *Der deutsche Strafprozess*. Marburg, 1941.

Hobbes, Thomas. *Leviathan*. Oxford, 1958.

Kuckerov, S. *Courts, Lawyers and Trials Under the Last Three Tsars*. New York, 1953.

Lea, H. C. *A History of the Inquisition of the Middle Ages*. 3 vols. New York, 1888–1911.

———— *The Inquisition of the Middle Ages, Its Organization and Operation*. 1 vol. ed. New York, 1963.

Livingstone, R. W. *The Greek Genius*. London, 1939.

Muller, H. J. *The Uses of the Past*. New York, 1957.

"The Privilege Against Self-Incrimination: An International Symposium," *The Journal of Criminal Law, Criminology and Police Science*, 51 (1960–61), pp. 129–188.

Reik, T. *The Compulsion to Confess*. New York, 1959.

Rogge, O. J. *Why Men Confess*. New York, 1959.

Salant, E. *Evidence* (Hebrew). Tel Aviv, 1963.

Schacht, J. *Introduction to Islamic Law*. Oxford, 1964.

Timor, M. *Rules of Criminal Procedure* (Hebrew). Tel Aviv, 1965.

Tlapek, Ludwig F. and Serini, Eugen, eds. *Die oesterreichische Strafprozessordnung*. 4th ed. Vienna, 1960.

Index

Aaron HaLevi, Rabbi (*R'ah*), 116
Abbayei, 41
Abravanel, Don Isaac, 29
Accusatorial system of court procedure, 3–4, 5
of classical Roman law, 7–9
and voluntary confession, 14
Accused, *see* Defendant
Accused, The, A Comparative Study (ed. J. A. Coutts), 140–41
Introductory Essay by Professor Coutts, quoted, 141–45
Accuser: in accusatorial trial, 3–4
in inquisitorial trial, 4–5
Acta Martyrum, 10
Adversary system of court procedure, 4–5
Aggadah, 42, 43
Aharonim, 100
Algasi, Rabbi Jacob, 79, 80–81
Amoraim, 41, 59, 65, 69
controversy among, over rendering oneself a *rasha* by self-incrimination, 50–58, 109–12

Anglo-American tradition of law, and rights of defendant, 14–16, 21
Aqiba, Rabbi, 34, 36, 57, 133
Aryeh Leib HaKohen, Rabbi, 79, 81
Asher, Rabbenu (*Rosh*), 70–71, 71*n.*–72*n.*, 91, 128
Ashkenazi, Rabbi Zebi, 77, 121, 127
Assaph, Rabbi Simhah, 82, 89
Atonement, confession in ritual of, 30, 47, 119
Austrian rules of criminal procedure, 13

Baer, Y., 138–39
Benjamin Aaron b. Abraham Slonik, Rabbi, 124
Bible (Hebrew) references: Deuteronomy, 33, 35, 36, 42, 44, 48, 51, 56, 57, 63, 77
Exodus, 35, 39, 51, 52–53, 136
Ezekiel, 72
Joshua, 25, 26, 29, 42, 46
Judges, 31

Index by Jerome H. Kanner, Ph.D., L.H.D.

I Kings, 33
II Kings, 116n.
Leviticus, 25, 34, 35, 40, 55
Numbers, 40, 66n., 120
I Samuel, 30, 112, 136–37
II Samuel, 26–28, 41
Biblical law: and acceptance of criminal confessions, 28, 30, 32–33, 41–49, 65–67
rabbinic law, as distinguished from, 53n., 95
and the Torah, 53n., 95
and rabbinic exegesis of Scripture, 53n., 95
and application of rule against self-incrimination, 95–96
Biblical period, episodes of confession to criminal acts in, 25–33, 61
Joshua, and Akhan ben Karmi, 25–26, 28–30, 32, 41–43, 45, 62, 65–66
David, and the Amalekite stranger, 26–27, 28, 30, 32–33, 41, 62, 66–67, 98
David, and Rekhab and Ba'anah, 27–28, 32–33, 41, 67
Micah, and theft of his mother's pieces of silver, 31–32
acceptance of confession as act of emergency, 65–67
and extra-biblical system of "law of the king," 67–68
Book of Agadatha of School of Rab, 97
British Institute of International and Comparative Law, 140
Brown v. Walker, 14n.

Canon Law of Medieval Church, inquisitorial system of court procedure of, 11
Capital crime, and single witness as corroborating testimony to confession, 114
Cardozo, Justice Benjamin Nathan, 16n.
Cato, 60
Cicero, 8

Codex Iustinianus, 8
Codex Theodosianus, 8, 9
Coercion of accused in legal procedures, 4, 14, 15, 21, 74–75, 80, 129
Coke, Sir Edward, 20
Colloquium on public interest and interest of accused in the criminal process, 140
Common Law, 15, 21
"Concerning the Courts of the Ancient Hebrews" (Selden), 20
Confession of defendant: in ancient Greek law, 6–7, 46
in classical Roman law, 8–9, 60
under criminal law of Greco-Roman Egypt, 10
under Roman criminal law in Palestine, 10
securing of, under Canon Law of Medieval Church, 11
and differences between inquisitorial and accusatorial procedures, 12
and European Continental law, 12–14
probative value of, as evidence, 13, 15–16
coerced confession, Anglo-American formulation against, 14, 21
under Russian law in 19th century, 16–17
and Jewish talmudic law, 17–18, 21, 59, 61, 63
acceptability of, in biblical period, 32–33
tannaitic law dealing with, 34–41
amoraic rules on admissibility of, in evidence, 50–58
post-Talmudic exegesis, commentary and expansion, 59–81
and Sanhedrin, 62
biblical acceptance of, as act of emergency, 65–67
and medieval rabbinic criminal procedure, 82–92
see also Confessions, and corrob-

orating factors, in Jewish law;
Self-incrimination.

Confessions, and corroborating
factors, in Jewish law, 113–29

corroborating testimony of one
witness, 114–15

factors pointing to authenticity
of confession, 115–22

when confessant is ignorant of
having really confessed, 115–17,
122

and desire to bolster monetary
claims, 117, 122

for purpose of repentance, 117–
19, 122

to effectuate personal atonement,
119

and votive power to render oneself as "piece of forbidden
food," 119–21, 122

destruction or weakening of
defendant's presumption of
innocence, 122–27, 129, 135

confession that does not affect
one's present status, 127–28

Confrontation between accuser and
accused: in accusatorial trial,
3–4

absence of, in inquisitorial trial,
5

absence of, under Roman criminal law in Palestine, 10

Constantine, 8

Counsel, right of suspect to, 15

Court procedure in prosecution of
crimes, accusatorial vs. inquisitorial systems, 3–6

Coutts, J. A., 140, 141

David ben Zimra, Rabbi (Radbaz),
72–77, 81, 117

David, and confessions of Amalekite
stranger and of Rekhab and
Ba'anah, see Biblical period

Defendant: in accusatorial trial, 3–4

in inquisitorial trial, 4–5

right of, to remain silent, 12–13,
15

rights of, and Anglo-American

tradition of law, 14–15

see also Confession of defendant

Divine Justice and Divine Retribution, as realities to the ancient
Rabbis in law-enforcement,
136–37

Douglas, W. O., 12n.

Eleazar b. Azariah, Rabbi, 133

Eliezer b. Jacob, Rabbi, 70

Eliezer b. Nathan, Rabbi (Raban),
128

Emergency principle (hora'ath
sha'ah) in acceptance of confession, 62, 65–67, 70–71, 82, 86,
91, 98, 136

Escobedo v. Illinois, 15

European Continental criminal
procedures, 12–14

Evidence: in accusatorial trial, 3

in inquisitorial trial, 5

probative value of confession as,
13, 15–16

see also Testimony

Extra-halakhic measures taken for
protecting public morals, 114,
136

Fifth Amendment of U.S. Constitution, 12n., 14

Frankel, Rabbi David, 97

Frankfurter, Justice Felix, 17

French Code of Penal Procedure, 12

Gemara, 44, 52, 57, 111

Gentiles under talmudic law, 96–99

and self-incrimination, 97–99

Geonim, and talmudic law on self-
incriminating testimony, 61, 88

German rules of criminal procedure, 13

Gersonides, Rabbi Levi, 66–67, 98

Gideon v. Wainwright, 15

Gospel references: Luke, 138

Mark, 138, 139

Matthew, 139

Greco-Roman Egypt, criminal law
of, 10

Greek law, ancient, confession of defendant as evidence in, 6–7, 46
Guilt, one's admission of, equal to one hundred witnesses, *see* Liability, one's acknowledgment of

Halakhah, 74, 82, 86, 98, 100
Hezekiah, School of, 136
Hinukh, 97, 98
Horowitz, George, 19

Ignorance of prohibitions of Jewish law, and confessant's presumption of innocence, 126–27
Inquisitorial system of court procedure, 3, 4–5, 11
of Canon Law of Medieval Church, 11
repudiation of, by all modern legal systems, 12
trilemma of, over self-incrimination of accused, 13
in Spanish-Jewish practices in Middle Ages, 92
"Interrogations in New Haven: The Impact of *Miranda*" (study in *Yale Law Journal*), 149
Isaac b. Meir, Rabbi (*Ribam*), 117
Isaac b. Shesheth Barfat, Rabbi (*Ribash*), 83, 86, 89, 92
see also Ribash, responsum of
Ishmael, Rabbi, School of, 34
Islamic thought, possible influence of, on Maimonides, 62*n.*–63*n.*

Jacob b. Asher, Rabbi, 128
Jesus, trial of, and Jewish law of criminal confession, 138–39
Jewish law, 17–21
difference between Anglo-American law and, 18, 21
difference between Canon Law and, 18
and the biblical period, 25–33
and tannaitic times, 34–49

and the *Amoraim*, 50–58
post-Talmudic exegesis, commentary and expansion, 59–81
and the geonic period, 61
medieval rabbinic criminal procedure, 82–92
range of applicability of rule against self-incrimination, 95–112
conflicting principles in, over self-incrimination, in criminal and civil law, 103–7
and confessions accompanied by corroborating factors, 113–29
historical background of development of traditions of, 134-37
authority of Jewish courts after destruction of Second Holy Temple in Jerusalem, 135
See also Biblical law; Rabbinic law
Jose, Rabbi, 35, 36
Joseph ben David ibn Leb, Rabbi (Mahari ibn Leb), 78, 79, 81
Joseph ibn Migash, Rabbi, 116
Joseph, Rabbi, 50–54, 109–11, 136
Joshua, and confession of Akhan, *see* Biblical period
Judaeo-Christian tradition as root of Western law, 18
Judah, Rabbi, 46, 52, 53, 54, 55
Judah ben Asher, Rabbi, 84, 90, 92
Judah ben Pazi, Rabbi, 97
Judge: in accusatorial trial, 3–4, 5
in inquisitorial trial, 4, 5
in trial under Canon Law of Medieval Church, 11

Kinsman: not acceptable as witness, 40–41, 56, 57, 63, 98
a man regarded as kinsman to himself, 56, 57, 58, 63, 78–79

Landau, Rabbi Samuel, 120
Legal history, Jewish law of confession in light of, 3–21
accusatorial vs. inquisitorial systems, 3–6
ancient Greek law, 6–7

classical Roman law, 7–9
non-classical Roman law, 9–11
Canon Law of Medieval Church, 11
European Continental law, 12–14
Anglo-American tradition, 14–16, 21
Russian law in 19th century, 16–17
Jewish talmudic law, 17–21
Levi ibn Ḥabib, Rabbi, 119
Liability, one's acknowledgment of, same as one hundred witnesses, 36, 38, 39, 40, 47, 48, 59, 81, 103
Luria, Rabbi Solomon, 77, 127

Mahari ibn Leb, 78, 79, 81
Maimonides (Rambam), 20, 54, 62–68, 72, 75–77, 81, 99, 101, 105, 116, 122, 126
Code of Maimonides, 62, 97, 105, 110, 122
Manasseh, Rabbi, 53, 54
McCarthy, Joseph R., era of, 14
Meir b. Gedaliah Lublin, Rabbi, 124
Meir, Rabbi, of Rothenberg, 128
Micah, and confession of stealing his mother's silver, see Biblical period
Midrash, 43
Midrash to Leviticus, 34
Miranda v. Arizona, 15, 149
Mr. Justice White's disagreement with majority opinion in, 133–34
Mishnah, 37, 44, 46, 52, 53, 54, 55, 57, 69, 80, 111, 119, 121, 133
Mishnah references: Kethuboth, 38, 39
Sanhedrin, 37
Mommsen, Theodor, 60
Money lending or borrowing on interest, Jewish law on, 126
Moses ben Maimon, Rabbi, see Maimonides (Rambam)
Moses Naḥmanides, Rabbi (Ramban), 116

Naḥman, Rabbi, 69, 70
Nissim b. Reuben, Rabbi (Ran), 112
"Noahide" commandments for the Gentile, under Talmudic law, 97

Oath, subjection to, in Jewish legal procedure, 99–100
Oral Tradition, 33
Ordeal, trial by, under Canon Law of Medieval Church, 11
Ostow, Mortimer, 64n.

Palestine, Roman criminal law in, during first centuries C.E., 10–11
Palestinian Midrashim, 10
Palestinian Talmud, 10, 97
Palko v. Connecticut, 16n.
Pentateuch, legal corpora of, 32
Plea of guilty by defendant, 14, 15
Pliny the Younger, 138–39
Police inquisitional practices, 15n., 19, 146–49
enlightened citizenries' protest against police brutality, 129
"Senators Hear an Interrogation in Study of Confession Ruling," Washington Special to The New York Times, quoted, 146–48
Polish code of criminal procedure, 12, 13–14
"Postscript to the Miranda Project: Interrogation of Draft Protesters" (report in Yale Law Journal), 149
Post-Talmudic exegesis, commentary and expansion, 59–81
Geonic period, 61, 88
Maimonides (Rambam), 62–68
Rabbi Solomon b. Simeon Duran (Rashbash), 68–72
Rabbi David ben Zimra (Radbaz), 72–77, 81, 117
late Middle Ages, 77–81
Presumption of innocence of confessant, and rule against self-

incrimination, 77–78, 122–27, 129, 135
Prosecutor: in accusatorial trial, 3–4
in inquisitorial trial, 4–5
Punishments After the Redaction of the Talmud (Assaph) , 82–83

Qaro, Rabbi Joseph, 112
Qorban HaEdah (Frankel) , 97

Rab, 102
School of Rab, 97
Raba, 41, 50–56, 58, 68, 109–12
Rabbinic law: as distinguished from biblical law, 53*n.*, 95
and invoking emergency measures when public mores are at stake, 70–71, 82, 86, 91, 98, 136
on disqualification of witnesses on grounds of criminality and sinfulness, 73
on criminal confessions, differences between interpretations of Maimonides and Radbaz, 75–77
criminal procedure in medieval times, 82–92
modes of punishment introduced in medieval times, 83
and application of rule against self-incrimination, 95–96
application of, in Rabbinical Court in modern Israel, 104–7
Rami b. Hama, 111
Rasha, rendering oneself as, by self-incrimination, 50–58, 68, 71, 80, 96, 103, 114, 116, 122, 128
Rashi, 39, 102
Reischer, Rabbi Jacob, 118
Relative as witness, *see* Kinsman
Repentance, confession for purpose of, 47, 117–19, 122
Ribash, responsum of, on accepting confessions, 83, 87–89, 92
Rishonim, 119
Roman law, classical: accusatorial criminal procedure of, 7–9

confession of accused as evidence in, 8–9, 60
Roman law, non-classical: legal systems of city-states, 9
for the provinces, 10
criminal law of Greco-Roman Egypt, 10
Roman criminal law in Palestine, 10–11
criminal procedure against early Christians, 138–39
Rudzinski, Aleksander Witold, 13
Russian rules of criminal procedure in 19th century, 16–17

Sabbetai Cohen, Rabbi, 78–79
Samuel, 102
Sanhedrin, 37, 46, 62, 67, 68, 82, 133, 136*n.*
"The Bloody Sanhedrin," 133
Schacht, Joseph, 62*n.,* 63*n.*
Selden, John, 19, 20
Self-incrimination: and modern European Continental Law, 12–14
Anglo-American formulation against, in Fifth Amendment, 12*n.,* 14
Jewish law in criminal cases, 17–18, 19, 21, 35, 59, 60, 61
Jewish law in civil cases, 18, 35, 37–38, 39, 48, 59, 60, 100–103, 135
and claim for uniqueness of Anglo-American law against, 21
rendering oneself a *rasha* by, 50–58, 68, 71, 80, 96, 103, 114, 116, 122, 128
"splitting the testimony" in, 54–55, 103–4, 110, 111, 112
post-Talmudic exegesis, commentary and expansion, 59–81
and divine decree on, 62, 68
and masochistic desire for punishment, 63–64
and ulterior motives for using, for disqualification as witness, 64–65, 76, 77

range of applicability of rule against, in Jewish law, 95–112
in biblical and in rabbinic law, 95–96
by male and female defendants, in Jewish law, 96
and law of the non-Jew, 96–99
and subjection to oath, in Jewish legal procedure, 99–100
in pecuniary cases involving penalties and compensation, in Jewish law, 100–3
conflicting principles in Jewish law in criminal and civil law, 103–7
application of Jewish law against, in minor infractions, 107–9
and immunity of witnesses under Jewish law, 109–12
in testimony concerning others, in American legal procedure, 110–11
and recent U.S. Supreme Court decisions, 134, 146, 149
problems of, and modern jurisdictions, 140–45
see also Confession of defendant; Confessions, and corroborating factors, in Jewish law
Sepher HaḤinukh, 97, 98
Simeon b. Gamaliel, Rabbi, 133
Simeon b. Laqish, Rabbi, 136
Simeon ben Shetaḥ, Rabbi, 44
Siphrci, 35, 49, 71
Smith, T. B., 140
Solomon b. Adreth, Rabbi (Rashba), 67
Solomon b. Simeon Duran, Rabbi (Rashbash), 68–72
Spain of 14th century: laws of, 82
Jewish residents of, 83–84
and the informer (malsin) in Jewish community, 84–86
rabbinic criminal procedure in, 84–92
Supreme Court, U.S., decisions of, on limitations on confessions, 134, 146, 149

Talmud, 10, 39, 40, 47, 48, 50, 52, 55, 56, 59, 60, 68, 71, 91, 92, 97, 102, 106, 109, 110, 125, 135
Talmud references: B. Baba Bathra, 106
B. Baba Meẓia, 106
B. Ḥullin, 72n.
B. Kethuboth, 105
B. Makkoth, 105
B. Qiddushin, 39
B. Sanhedrin, 68, 82, 109
B. Yebamoth, 52, 54
Talmudic criminal procedure: and modern European Continental law, 13
and rejection of confession of accused, 17–18, 19, 21, 35, 59, 60
changes in medieval times, 82
differences between talmudic traditional and Spanish-Jewish practices of 14th century, 92
talmudic tradition as norm in all other Jewish communities in Middle Ages, 92
Tannaitic literature, law of confession as found in, 34–41, 44, 54, 56, 59, 71
in capital cases, 34–37, 39
in monetary cases, 35–36, 37–38, 39
scriptural authority for rules, 39–41
theory of a change in tannaitic law, 41–49
Tannaitic times, dates of, 34n.
Tarphon, Rabbi, 133
Testimony: of two witnesses to same fact needed in judicial trials, 33, 37, 40, 41, 49, 54, 56, 62, 63, 77, 96, 98, 129
"splitting the testimony" in self-incriminating statement, 54–55, 103–4, 110, 111, 112
universitas principle in Jewish law, 56–57, 58
corroborating testimony of one witness, 114–15
Torah, 50, 52, 53n., 57, 62n., 67, 69–70, 79, 91, 95, 96, 111, 112, 120

Torture of accused in legal procedures, 4, 14
  as judicial tool in ancient Greece, 7
  under classical Roman law, 8
  under Roman criminal law in Palestine, 10
  under Canon Law of Medieval Church, 11
  absence of, in Jewish law, 19, 21, 91
Tosaphoth, 102

Tosephta, 46, 47, 71
Tosephta references: Baba Meẓia, 38
  Sanhedrin, 36, 37
  Shebuoth, 34, 35, 49
Twelve Tables of Roman law, 60

United Kingdom National Committee of Comparative Law, 140

White, Justice Byron R., 133–34
Witnesses, see Testimony